COWLES FOUNDATION
FOR RESEARCH IN ECONOMICS
AT YALE UNIVERSITY

MONOGRAPH 23

COWLES FOUNDATION

For Research in Economics at Yale University

The Cowles Foundation for Research in Economics at Yale University, established as an activity of the Department of Economics in 1955, has as its purpose the conduct and encouragement of research in economics, finance, commerce, industry, and technology, including problems of the organization of these activities. The Cowles Foundation seeks to foster the development of logical, mathematical, and statistical methods of analysis for application in economics and related social sciences. The professional research staff are, as a rule, faculty members with appointments and teaching responsibilities in the Department of Economics and other departments.

The Cowles Foundation continues the work of the Cowles Commission for Research in Economics founded in 1932 by Alfred Cowles at Colorado Springs, Colorado. The Commission moved to Chicago in 1939 and was affiliated with the University of Chicago until 1955. In 1955 the professional research staff of the Commission accepted appointments at Yale and, along with other members of the Yale Department of Economics, formed the research staff of the newly established Cowles Foundation.

A list of Cowles Foundation Monographs appears at the end of this volume.

Efficient Estimation
with A Priori Information,

Thomas J. Rothenberg

New Haven and London, Yale University Press, 1973

Published with assistance from the foundation
established in memory of Philip Hamilton McMillan
of the Class of 1894, Yale College.

Set in Times Roman type
and printed in the United States of America by
The Murray Printing Co., Forge Village, Massachusetts.

Published in Great Britain, Europe, and Africa by
Yale University Press, Ltd., London.
Distributed in Canada by McGill-Queen's University Press, Montreal;
in Latin America by Kaiman & Polon, Inc., New York City;
in Australasia and Southeast Asia by John Wiley & Sons
Australasia Pty. Ltd., Sydney; in India by UBS Publishers' Distributors
Pvt., Ltd., Delhi; in Japan by John Weatherhill, Inc., Tokyo

Contents

347556

Preface

Over the years econometricians have developed special statistical methods for handling the problems that arise in analyzing economic data. These special problems and methods are the topic of numerous textbooks and are studied by nearly every economics graduate student. Although econometric techniques do have features which distinguish them from the techniques used in other fields of application, there is a danger that these special features are being overemphasized. By concentrating on the uniqueness of econometric methods one tends to lose sight of the fact that these methods are based on a general theory of inference. Often it is possible to gain a better understanding of econometric problems, not by emphasizing their peculiar characteristics, but rather by seeing how they fit into the broader structure of statistical theory.

This book presents an attempt at unifying certain aspects of econometric theory by embedding them in a more general statistical framework. The unifying feature is the use of a priori information and the basic tool is the traditional Cramér-Rao inequality. I believe that many confusing aspects of the simultaneous equations problem can be cleared up by viewing that problem in a broader context. Certain results on identification and efficiency turn out to be quite elementary when viewed at a general level but are not at all elementary when studied in the particular. Furthermore, the limitations of our econometric theory are made clearer when seen in the general framework of traditional statistical theory.

The present monograph can usefully be viewed as an extension of the research reported in Cowles Foundation Monographs 10 and 14. These earlier studies, many of them written by leading statisticians, represent a systematic application of the methods of mathematical statistics to econometric problems. The present book uses the same basic approach and many of the same techniques. By generalizing and extending these earlier studies it has been possible to develop a unified theory of estimation which contains many of their results as special cases.

The use of considerable mathematics is unavoidable in a book dealing with econometric theory. The reader should be familiar with the material contained in an introductory course in mathematical statistics and should be comfortable with matrix notation. Nevertheless, this is not a treatise in mathematical statistics. My purpose has been to help bridge the gap between the textbook presentation of econometric methods and the mainstream of modern statistical theory. Many of the more difficult results are stated without proof; and most of the tedious algebra has been placed in appendixes or omitted entirely.

The theory of efficient estimation is only a part of theoretical econometrics; and theoretical econometrics is but a small part of the broad subject of empirical economics. There has been in recent years an unfortunate tendency to overemphasize formal econometric theory at the expense of the commonsense application of econometrics to real social problems. In addition to the gap between econometric theory and traditional statistical theory, there is an even greater gap between econometric theory and good econometric practice. The reader will understand that this book's concentration on the former problem in no way diminishes its author's concern over the latter.

The research for this monograph has extended over an embarrassingly long period of time. The first five chapters are a major revision of my doctoral thesis submitted to the Economics Department at M.I.T. in 1966. Chapter 6 presents the results of research that I began in 1963 while a staff member of the Econometrics Institute of the Netherlands School of Economics (Rotterdam). Various other parts of the book were written while I was associated with the Transportation Center at Northwestern University, the Cowles Foundation at Yale University, and the Center for Operations Research and Econometrics at Louvain (Belgium). I am grateful to these institutions, as well as the University of California, Berkeley, for providing me with financial support, secretarial and research facilities, and, most of all, stimulating colleagues. Additional support from the Ford Foundation, the National Science Foundation, and a U.S. Government Fulbright Fellowship is gratefully acknowledged.

It is impossible to acknowledge all the help I have received in the many years of this research. However, my debt to Ralph Beals, Jacques Drèze, Frank Fisher, and H. Theil is enormous. I am also grateful to Walter Fisher, Edmond Malinvaud, and Roy Radner, who read earlier versions of the manuscript and made valuable comments. My thanks also to Donald Dillaman, Ronald Lanstein, Itzhak Venezia, and Greg Woirol for programming and research assistance.

Berkeley, California   T.J.R.
December 1972

CHAPTER 1

Estimation and Information

1. A PRIORI INFORMATION

Econometrics is concerned with the use of sample data to learn about unknown economic parameters. In many applications, however, the econometrician possesses, in addition to the sample, other information about the parameters. For example, he may know from theoretical arguments that the marginal propensity to consume lies between zero and one or that a demand function is homogeneous of degree zero in all prices and income. Or he may know from past experience that the demand for salt is price inelastic. If this information is correct, it is surely useful to incorporate it into statistical estimation procedures. Such additional information may be valuable in increasing the precision of estimates particularly when samples are small.

Perhaps the most important example of the use of prior information in econometric estimation is in the simultaneous equations model. In this model identifying restrictions, which usually take the form of excluding certain variables from an equation, are imposed on the structural parameters. These restrictions are thought to reflect valid information about the true economic structure and are used in the recommended estimation procedures. If no such information is available, the structural parameters are unidentified and cannot be estimated at all. Furthermore, the reduced-form parameters are then estimated imprecisely due to the collinearity typically found among predetermined variables. Hence, the existence of a priori information is basic to statistical inference for simultaneous equation systems.

These examples suggest that a wide class of econometric problems involve inference in models where there are a priori constraints on the parameters. Although these problems have received considerable attention in recent years, there seems to exist no general treatment of the subject. The known results appear as isolated theorems and are scattered throughout the literature. The present monograph develops a unified theory of estimation in the presence of prior information. The analysis incorporates both the Bayesian and the classical approaches to statistical inference. In addition, the problem of estimating the parameters of simultaneous equation systems is shown to be a special case of the general theory. In this study we shall concentrate on two basic questions. First, how valuable is a priori information in increasing the precision of parameter estimation? Second, what are efficient methods of incorporating this information into estimation procedures? The first question is basic to the practical use of outside information. If the loss from ignoring information is small, there is no need to develop complicated methods of estimation which incorporate it. If, however, the loss is large, then it is worth obtaining and using such information in our statistical research. In this latter case, the second question becomes important. If we wish to incorporate non-sample information into our estimates, it is desirable to have convenient and flexible means to do so.

Our concern here will be solely with the problem of optimal point estimation. The theory of hypothesis testing and confidence intervals is not discussed explicitly, although optimal point estimates often form the basis for optimal tests and optimal confidence regions. There are three reasons for concentrating on point estimation. First, most econometric application seems to be concerned with finding good point estimates of economic parameters, rather than with the formal testing of theories. Second, the theory of estimation can be presented at a general, yet useful, level without getting involved in the distribution-theoretical problems which arise in the theory of hypothesis testing. Finally, in many statistical decision problems, finding the optimal decision is equivalent to finding an optimal parameter estimate. Hence, by concentrating on the problem of point estimation we shall be able to explore the parallel between the classical and the decision-theoretic approaches to inference.

Although we shall analyze only the problem of finding good estimates using prior information, it should be emphasized that there also exists in classical statistics the alternative problem of testing whether a body of prior information is correct. For any given sample these are generally mutually exclusive problems. Either one uses prior information to improve sample estimates or one uses the sample to test the validity of the information. If one is unsure of the information, then it is dangerous to use it; if one is sure of the information, then there is no need to test it. In practice, of course, econometricians sometimes combine these alternative problems in a two-stage procedure which first tests a parameter restriction and, if it is accepted, then uses the restriction in estimation.

Little is known about the properties of such two-stage procedures. Indeed, it appears that these properties necessarily depend on the value of the unknown parameter and cannot therefore be easily studied within the classical framework of statistical inference.[1]

The testing of prior information is a separate problem from using the information in estimation, but there is a definite relationship between their mathematical structures. Using an analogy with mathematical programming, one may say (somewhat heuristically) that deriving the optimal way of using correct prior information is the *dual* to the problem of finding an optimal test of that information (treated as a null hypothesis). We shall not pursue this relationship, however, and shall study only the former problem. Thus, throughout this examination of the value of using prior information it will always be assumed that the information is correct.

In practice, however, prior information is not known with certainty. We are never absolutely sure that our theoretical constraints are valid. What then is the purpose of analyzing the value of using prior information when the possibility of error is excluded? There is a simple classical answer to this question. If the value of correct information is found to be small, then it is clearly unwise to use doubtful information. If the value of correct information is large, then it may pay to use even dubious information. The study of valid prior knowledge is a necessary and useful beginning to the study of imperfect knowledge. Furthermore, if one is willing to accept the Bayesian approach to inference, even uncertain prior information can be incorporated into statistical procedures.

2. ALTERNATIVE APPROACHES

Prior information about parameter values may arise in various ways. Sometimes theoretical reasoning or introspection suggests constraints on the parameter space. Other times the results of past samples are thought to give information about the parameters. In all these cases there exists a priori information in the sense that the information does not arise from the particular body of data currently being analyzed. To be more precise about the meaning of a priori information and the ways it can be incorporated into statistical procedures, it will be necessary first to describe more carefully the type of statistical problem we have in mind.

The basis of any statistical problem is a sample of observations. We shall consider the sample to have arisen from n independent repetitions of an

---

1. See, for example, BANCROFT (1944).

experiment. If each outcome of the experiment can be described by a number, then the sample is described by an n-dimensional random variable Y_n. The joint probability function for Y_n is assumed to have a known mathematical form but depends on a number of unknown parameters. Specifically, the probability law for Y_n is assumed to be represented by a density function belonging to the family of densities

$$f_n(y, \theta)$$

where y represents the vector of n observations on the random variable Y_n and θ is a vector of m unknown parameters. (The restriction to density functions is solely for convenience; all of the results can be extended to more general classes of probability distributions.) The statistician is assumed to know the function f_n and also the set A of possible values for θ. The problem is to choose a vector of m functions of the sample Y_n to be used as an estimator of the true parameter θ^0.

The knowledge of f_n and A constitutes important information about the random experiment. In this sense every estimation problem involves a priori information. However, our interest is not in this necessary information that describes the stochastic process, but rather in *extra* information that narrows down our ignorance about the unknown parameter. That is, we consider a basic estimation problem (characterized by a family of density functions f_n and a parameter space A) and study the value of additional information in improving the precision of estimating θ^0. Henceforth the phrase "a priori information" will mean this additional information; the basic knowledge of the pair (f_n, A) will always be understood as given.

In order to measure the value of additional information we must have some criterion for evaluating estimation procedures. Unfortunately, there seems to be no criterion that is completely satisfactory. Currently there are two alternative approaches to the statistical estimation problem that are widely used. On the one hand there is the "classical" mode of analysis which is based on a frequency interpretation of probability and typically makes use of the concept of unbiasedness. This approach is found in most of the leading econometrics textbooks and is accepted by most practicing econometricians. On the other hand there is the Bayesian mode of analysis which is rooted in decision theory and based on a subjective notion of probability. This latter approach has become widely used in recent years and seems particularly suited for certain economic decision problems. We shall analyze the value of a priori information using both approaches. Detailed descriptions of both are given in later sections. Here we shall indicate only their general features.

In classical statistics the original "givens" of the estimation problem are characterized by the pair (f_n, A). The function f_n is sometimes called the likelihood function and the set A is called the parameter space. Prior information takes the form of modifying the pair; for example, knowledge that a parameter must be positive reduces the parameter space A. Estimating procedures are evaluated on the basis of their sampling distributions (or at least on the basis of approximations to these distributions). Typically a "best" estimator is defined to be one that has smallest variance out of the class of all unbiased estimators. Thus, under the classical theory, we study the following situation: A sample is available from a process characterized by the likelihood function f_n and the parameter space A. Based on that sample a best estimate is calculated. If additional information were available, the process would be characterized by a different likelihood function and parameter space. In general a different estimator would be best. If the new estimator is more tightly distributed around the true parameter than was the old estimator, we may say that the a priori information has value. Furthermore, by specifying some measure of dispersion, we can determine quantitatively the amount of gain.

Given the principle of unbiasedness, the classical estimator depends only on f_n and A. The Bayesian approach, however, dispenses with the unbiasedness assumption and replaces it with a prior probability distribution on θ. That is, in Bayesian statistics every process is characterized by the triple (f_n, A, P) where P is a multivariate probability function defined over the parameter space A. The density f_n is then interpreted as representing the conditional distribution of Y_n given θ. Additional prior information typically is expressed by modifying the prior probability distribution P. The Bayesian estimate is obtained by first calculating the conditional distribution of θ given the observed value of Y_n. The mean (or some other measure of central tendency) of this posterior distribution is taken as the estimate. Thus, the Bayesian approach to our problem can be stated as follows: A sample is available from a process characterized by the triple (f_n, A, P). Based on that sample a best estimate is calculated. If additional information were available, the process would be characterized by a different triple (presumably one with a less dispersed prior distribution) and a different estimate would be best. Again, the value of the a priori information can be measured by the decrease in dispersion of the resulting estimator.

Since the Bayesian and classical approaches to statistical inference are rather different, two modes of analysis are called for. In the first five chapters of this book the classical approach is used. Alternative ways of incorporating prior information into the classical analysis are explored (chapters 2 and 3) and the results obtained are applied to the simultaneous equations model (chapters 4 and 5). In chapters 6 and 7 the Bayesian mode of analysis is employed and compared with the classical one.

3. CLASSICAL ESTIMATION THEORY

The next few chapters will extend some of the important classical results on efficient estimation so that they apply when a priori information is available. It is useful to begin by summarizing these well-known classical results. Since we are primarily interested in developing methods for practical application, we shall not be concerned with fine mathematical detail. For a comprehensive treatment of classical estimation theory the reader may consult CRAMÉR (1946), DUGUÉ (1958), or WILKS (1962).

The classical estimation problem is to find a function of the sample vector Y_n to use as an estimate of the unknown parameter vector θ^0. The model presented in section 2 can be formalized as follows. Let the parameter space A be a subset of m-dimensional Euclidean space E^m. Consider the function

$$(3.1) \qquad\qquad f_n(y, \theta)$$

which maps $E^n \times E^m$ into the real line. We assume that (3.1) is a proper density function in E^n for every θ in A. In particular, f_n is nonnegative and the equation

$$(3.2) \qquad\qquad \int f_n(y, \theta)\, dy = 1$$

holds for all θ in A. The integral is to be interpreted as a multivariate Riemann integral over E^n. We further assume that the sample vector Y_n is distributed according to the density

$$f_n(y, \theta^0)$$

where θ^0 lies in A.

The likelihood function $f_n(y, \theta)$ and the parameter space A characterize a given estimation problem. The classical analysis usually is conducted under the following assumptions:

1) The set A of possible values for θ is a full m-dimensional set in E^m. That is, A is either an open set or an open set augmented by some of its boundary points.

2) The set S of y values for which (3.1) is strictly positive does not depend on θ. We shall refer to S as the sample space of Y_n.

3) The density (3.1) arises from independent sampling and hence factors into *n* terms.

4) The likelihood (3.1) is a smooth function of θ. In particular, for all θ in a convex set containing *A* and for almost every *y* in *S*, the functions $f_n(y, \theta)$ and $\log f_n(y, \theta)$ possess partial derivatives with respect to θ up to the third order. Furthermore, twice differentiation under the integral in (3.2) is possible.

5) For any two vectors θ and θ' in *A*, the functions $f_n(y, \theta)$ and $f_n(y, \theta')$ differ for some value of *y*. That is, distinct values of θ give rise to distinct probability functions for the sample and, hence, every θ in *A* is identifiable.

6) The likelihood function is sufficiently well behaved to insure the asymptotic normality of the maximum-likelihood estimator. These conditions are discussed in CRAMÉR (1946), pp. 500–01, and LE CAM (1953) and will not be listed here; they are needed only for the asymptotic results given below.

The above regularity conditions are used in the derivation of the classical theorems of estimation. It may be noted in passing that most of the familiar distributions satisfy the above assumptions. (Discrete distributions can be included if the integrals are replaced by sums.) The most notable exceptions are the rectangular distribution and truncated distributions with the point of truncation depending on θ; these distributions violate assumption 2). Although it is possible to prove some of the classical theorems using weaker regularity conditions, no attempt to do so will be made here.

EFFICIENT ESTIMATORS

The traditional theory of estimation, as developed by Fisher, Cramér, Rao, and others, is concerned with finding efficient, or at least asymptotically efficient, estimators of the unknown parameter vector θ on the basis of the sample Y_n.[2] An estimator $t(Y_n)$ is a vector of functions which does not depend on the unknown θ. An estimator *t* is unbiased if it is integrable and

$$(3.3) \qquad \mathscr{E}t \equiv \int_S t(y) f_n(y, \theta) \, dy = \theta$$

for every θ in *A*.[3] An unbiased estimator *t* is efficient if it is square

2. When there is no chance of confusion we shall drop the distinction between the arbitrary element θ and the true value θ^0. Thus we shall speak of estimating θ rather than estimating θ^0.

3. The symbol $\mathscr{E}$ represents the expectation operator. By $\mathscr{E}t$ we mean the column vector whose *i*th element is $\mathscr{E}t_i$.

integrable with covariance matrix

$$V_t = [v_{ij}] = [\mathscr{E}(t_i - \theta_i)(t_j - \theta_j)]$$

at least as small as that of any other unbiased estimator. That is, t is efficient if, for every θ in A,

(3.4) $$V_s - V_t$$

is positive semidefinite for all unbiased estimators s.

The use of the covariance matrix V to compare estimators can be motivated in the following way. A best estimator is one which is as close as possible to the true parameter. If θ is a scalar, the traditional measure of distance has been the squared error $(t - \theta)^2$. The natural multiparameter measure is the quadratic loss function

$$(t - \theta)'Q(t - \theta)$$

where Q is a positive semidefinite matrix that determines the relative weight given to each component of the estimation error vector and to interactions between pairs of components. Since the distance between an estimator and the true parameter is a random variable, the usual estimation criterion is to minimize *expected* distance. If we restrict ourselves to unbiased estimators, this results in ranking according to the measure

$$\mathscr{E}(t - \theta)'Q(t - \theta) = \mathscr{E}(t - \mathscr{E}t)'Q(t - \mathscr{E}t) = \operatorname{tr} QV_t$$

where $\operatorname{tr} QV_t$ represents the sum of the diagonal elements of QV_t.

A best unbiased estimator could be defined as one which minimizes $\operatorname{tr} QV_t$. More precisely, an unbiased estimator $t(y)$ is best if, for every θ in A,

(3.5) $$\operatorname{tr} QV_s \geq \operatorname{tr} QV_t$$

for all unbiased estimators s. It would appear that a best unbiased estimator for the vector θ must depend on the matrix Q of the quadratic loss function. However, that is not the case. If $V_s - V_t$ is positive semidefinite, then (3.5) will be satisfied for any positive semidefinite matrix Q. Thus the classical estimation criterion may be characterized as follows:

An unbiased estimator $t(Y_n)$ is efficient if, for all θ in A, the difference in the covariance matrices

$$V_s - V_t$$

is positive semidefinite for all unbiased estimators $s(Y_n)$. An efficient estimator minimizes expected loss for any nonnegative quadratic loss (or distance) function.

ASYMPTOTIC EFFICIENCY

Since it is often impossible to find an efficient estimator, it is useful to have an approximate concept. Consider a sequence of samples Y_1, Y_2, ..., Y_n (where the index refers to the sample size) and the corresponding sequence of density functions f_1, f_2, ..., f_n, where each of the f_i depends on the same parameter vector θ. A sequence of estimators $t_1(Y_1)$, $t_2(Y_2)$, ..., $t_n(Y_n)$ (where t_n represents the estimator based on a sample of size n) is *consistent* if, as n approaches infinity,

$$\lim \text{Prob}\{|t_n - \theta| > \varepsilon\} = 0$$

for any positive number ε. In such a case we say that the estimator sequence converges in probability to θ and write

$$\text{plim } t_n = \theta.$$

A consistent estimator t_n (or more precisely, a consistent estimator sequence) is said to have an asymptotic covariance matrix V_t if, for all θ in A, the sequence of random variables $\sqrt{n}(t_n - \theta)$ converges in distribution to a normal random variable with mean zero and covariance matrix V_t.[4] A consistent estimator t_n is said to be asymptotically efficient if its asymptotic covariance matrix is smaller than that of any other estimator. That is, $V_s - V_t$ is positive semidefinite for all consistent, asymptotically normal estimators s_n.

The concept of asymptotic efficiency is not as simple as the concept of efficiency for fixed sample size n. For example, it is not necessarily true that the asymptotic covariance matrix of an estimator is the limit of n times the finite-sample covariance matrix. Indeed, it is possible for an estimator to be asymptotically efficient but to possess no finite moments at all. This results from the fact that classical asymptotic theory deals with approximating distribution functions, not with approximating moments. It is quite possible (in fact it is very common) for two distribution functions to be "close" to each other while their moments are far apart. For example, the Student distribution with 30 degrees of freedom is well approximated by a normal distribution, but none of its higher order moments are finite whereas all the moments of the normal density are finite.

---

4. A sequence of random variables X_1, X_2, X_3, ... is said to converge in distribution to the random variable Z if the corresponding sequence of distribution functions for the X_n converge pointwise to the distribution function for Z at all continuity points of that distribution function. It should be noted that some authors use the term "asymptotic covariance matrix" to refer to V_t/n rather than V_t. The convention used here is somewhat more convenient notationally.

A second problem with the concept of asymptotic efficiency is that it is meaningful only if we restrict the class of estimators being considered. Otherwise one can demonstrate that there are no asymptotically efficient estimators! This results from the fact that it is possible to construct estimator sequences which, for a few points in the parameter space A, have arbitrarily small asymptotic variances. Since these estimators are highly irregular and the set of parameter points for which they are "super-efficient" has measure zero, they are of no practical concern. However, they do point up the fact that asymptotic estimation theory is very tricky and requires considerably more advanced mathematical tools than does the small-sample theory.[5]

TWO FUNDAMENTAL INEQUALITIES

The basis theorems of efficient estimation are usually stated in terms of the *information matrix*. If Y_n is a sample of size n and $f_n(y, \theta)$ is its density function, the information matrix is defined as

$$(3.6) \qquad R_n = -\mathscr{E}\left[\frac{\partial^2 \log f_n(Y_n, \theta)}{\partial \theta_i\, \partial \theta_j}\right] = \mathscr{E}\left[\frac{\partial \log f_n}{\partial \theta_i} \cdot \frac{\partial \log f_n}{\partial \theta_j}\right]$$

where the last equality is verified by differentiating equation (3.2). The asymptotic information matrix associated with a sequence of samples $Y_1, Y_2, \ldots$, and a sequence of densities $f_1, f_2, \ldots$, is defined as

$$(3.7) \qquad R = \lim_{n \to \infty} \frac{1}{n} R_n.$$

It will be assumed that, for every possible parameter value, R and each R_n exist and are positive definite. We shall return to this assumption in chapter 2 when the identification problem is discussed.

Two major results of classical estimation theory may now be stated:

CRAMÉR-RAO INEQUALITY. *The matrix R_n^{-1} is a lower bound for the covariance matrix of any unbiased estimator of θ. There exists an unbiased estimator whose covariance matrix attains this bound if and only if there exists a vector function $t(y)$ not depending on θ such that the logarithmic derivative of the likelihood function takes the form*

$$(3.8) \qquad \frac{\partial \log f_n}{\partial \theta} = R_n(t - \theta);$$

the vector t is the minimum variance bound (MVB) estimator.

---

5. For more detailed discussions of the pitfalls in asymptotic estimation theory, see LE CAM (1953), RAO (1965), and WOLFOWITZ (1965).

ASYMPTOTIC CRAMÉR-RAO INEQUALITY. *The matrix R^{-1} is essentially a lower bound for the asymptotic covariance matrix of any consistent estimator of θ. Furthermore, this lower bound is attained by the maximum-likelihood estimator.*

These two results have a long history and are associated with such statisticians as H. Cramér, D. Dugué, R. A. Fisher, M. Fréchet, and C. R. Rao. They are the starting point for our study of efficient estimation with prior information. Indeed, the remaining chapters of this book deal almost entirely with generalizations and applications of the two inequalities when a priori information is available.

Before proceeding, however, some comments concerning these classical theorems are in order. The inverted information matrix is a lower bound in the sense that $V_s - R_n^{-1}$ is positive semidefinite for all unbiased estimators s. It would be a greatest lower bound if there were an estimator t that had R_n^{-1} as its covariance matrix. Unfortunately, equation (3.8) is quite restrictive and for only a few density functions will such an estimator exist. In fact it can be shown that the bound will be attainable only if there exists a set of m sufficient statistics. This will be the case only if f_n is a member of the exponential class of densities. Moreover, if the bound is attainable for one set of parameters θ, it will in general not be attainable for any new set of parameters obtained by nonlinear transformation. (For example in the one-parameter case, if the lower bound is attainable for an estimator of θ, the bound is *not* attainable for an estimator of θ^2.)

Since the bound R_n^{-1} is not usually a greatest lower bound, it may reasonably be asked whether the bound is worth much attention. The answer to the question lies in the fact that, for large n, the bound is approximately attained. That is to say, when n is large there exists an estimator whose distribution can be well approximated by a normal density having covariance matrix R_n^{-1}. The asymptotic Cramér-Rao inequality is a statement of this approximation. Although R_n^{-1} may not be attainable for finite n, R^{-1} is always attainable in infinite samples. The word "essentially" in the statement of the second theorem allows for certain pathological cases where covariance matrices, for a few values of θ, are smaller than R_n^{-1}. These cases can be eliminated by stating regularity conditions on the class of estimators considered or by redefining efficiency by changing the phrase "for all θ" to the phrase "for all θ except for a set of measure zero." A precise statement of the asymptotic inequality where careful account is taken of the conditions needed for its validity can be found in LE CAM (1953) and in WOLFOWITZ (1965). Our concern is the generalization of the classical theorems for nonpathological cases and hence all of the results that follow should be understood to require the same qualifications as discussed here. The proof of the asymptotic theorem is difficult and will not be presented here. The reader may consult KENDALL AND STUART (1967) for a sketch of the proof and for further references. The proof of the finite-sample theorem is not difficult. Indeed the result is a direct consequence of the unbiasedness assumption. If $t(Y_n)$ is an unbiased estimator then

$$(3.9) \qquad \int_S (t_i - \theta_i) f_n(y, \theta)\, dy = 0 \qquad (i = 1, \ldots, m)$$

for all θ in A. Let θ^0 be the true parameter vector and $\theta^0 + \xi$ some other vector in A. Then, for all i,

$$\int (t_i - \theta_i^0)[f_n(y, \theta^0 + \xi) - f_n(y, \theta^0)]\, dy = \xi_i,$$

and for any nonstochastic vector $c = (c_1, \ldots, c_m)'$

$$(3.10) \quad \int \sum_i c_i(t_i - \theta_i^0) f_n(y, \theta^0) \frac{f_n(y, \theta^0 + \xi) - f_n(y, \theta^0)}{f_n(y, \theta^0)}\, dy = \sum_i c_i \xi_i.$$

If θ^0 is an interior point of A, then $\theta^0 + \xi$ will also lie in A for any ξ with sufficiently small length. Hence (3.10) is valid if we set $\xi = \lambda x$ and take the limit as the scalar λ goes to zero. Given our regularity assumptions we obtain

$$(3.11) \quad \int \sum_i c_i(t_i - \theta_i^0)\sqrt{f_n} \cdot \sum_j \frac{\partial \log f_n}{\partial \theta_j} x_j \sqrt{f_n}\, dy = \sum_i c_i x_i.$$

Application of the Cauchy-Schwartz inequality for integrals yields the result

$$(3.12) \qquad c'Vc \geq \max_x \frac{(c'x)^2}{x'R_n x}$$

where V is the covariance matrix of t and R_n is the information matrix, both evaluated at θ^0. It can be verified that the maximum occurs for x proportional to $R_n^{-1}c$. Thus we obtain

$$(3.13) \qquad c'Vc \geq c'R_n^{-1}c$$

for all c. Furthermore, equality will obtain in (3.12) if and only if, for all c and all y,

$$(3.14) \qquad c'(t - \theta) = Kc'R_n^{-1} \frac{\partial \log f_n}{\cdot \partial \theta}$$

where K is some scalar. This proves the small-sample theorem for θ^0 an interior point of A. By our continuity assumptions, however, the matrices V and R_n are continuous in θ. Hence the result must also hold on the boundary.

4. Some Mathematical Results

In the following chapters repeated use is made of some elementary properties of matrices. Some of the more important of these properties are summarized here. Consider a real symmetric matrix A of order n and the quadratic form

$$(4.1) \qquad x'Ax = \sum_i \sum_j x_i x_j a_{ij}$$

where x is an arbitrary real column vector. If the quadratic form is non-negative for all nonzero x, then A is said to be positive semidefinite. If the quadratic form is strictly positive for all nonzero x, then A is said to be positive definite. The following are well-known facts about positive semidefinite matrices:[6]

1) A positive semidefinite matrix with rank r has r positive characteristic roots and $n - r$ zero roots. A positive definite matrix necessarily has full rank and n positive roots.

2) If P is any matrix with rank r, then $P'P$ is positive semidefinite with the same rank. Conversely, any positive semidefinite matrix A can be written as $A = P'P$ where P and A have the same rank.

3) If A is positive definite, then A^{-1} exists and is also positive definite.

4) If A is positive semidefinite, then $P'AP$ is also positive semidefinite for any P where multiplication is defined. If A has full rank, then the rank of $P'AP$ equals the rank of P.

5) If A is positive definite and B is positive semidefinite, then $(A + B)^{-1}$ exists and is positive definite. Furthermore, the difference $A^{-1} - (A + B)^{-1}$ is positive semidefinite with the same rank as B.

6) If B is symmetric and idempotent (that is $B = B' = B^2$), then B is positive semidefinite with rank equal to the trace of B. (The trace of a

---

6. See, for example, Graybill (1961), pp. 1–17.

square matrix B is defined as the sum of the diagonal elements and is written tr B. The trace is always equal to the sum of the characteristic roots.)

THE GENERALIZED INVERSE OF A SYMMETRIC MATRIX

Consider an $n \times n$ symmetric matrix A having rank ρ. By a generalized inverse for A, we mean any symmetric matrix A^+ with the properties

$$AA^+A = A \quad \text{and} \quad A^+AA^+ = A^+.$$

If $\rho = n$, then the ordinary inverse A^{-1} exists and is the unique generalized inverse of A. If $\rho < n$, there will be many generalized inverses. One of them can be constructed as follows. Since A is symmetric, it can be written as $Q'DQ$ where Q is an orthogonal matrix whose columns are the characteristic vectors of A and D is a diagonal matrix consisting of the characteristic roots. If D^+ is defined as the diagonal matrix formed by replacing the nonzero elements of D by their reciprocals, then $A^+ = Q'D^+Q$ is a generalized inverse.

Generalized inverses arise in the study of solutions to systems of linear equations. As is well known, if the matrix of a linear equation system is nonsingular, the unique solution can be written in terms of the inverse of that matrix. If the matrix is singular, the set of solutions can be expressed in terms of the generalized inverse. Our definition, which holds only for symmetric matrices, is but a special case of the broader concept of a generalized inverse of an arbitrary matrix. For details, the book by RAO (1965), pp. 24–26, may be consulted.

THE KRONECKER PRODUCT OF TWO MATRICES

Let X be an $n \times m$ matrix and let vec X be the nm-dimensional column vector formed from the elements of X taken one row at a time. Consider a function f which maps E^{nm} into the real line. If f is twice differentiable, we may be interested in the matrix F of second partial derivatives with respect to the elements of X. It is convenient to write this $nm \times nm$ matrix in the block partitioned form

$$F = \frac{\partial^2 f}{\partial(\text{vec } X)\,\partial(\text{vec } X)'} = \begin{bmatrix} F_{11} & F_{12} & & F_{1n} \\ F_{21} & F_{22} & & F_{2n} \\ & & \ddots & \\ F_{n1} & F_{n2} & & F_{nn} \end{bmatrix}$$

where each of the n^2 blocks is an $m \times m$ matrix. The matrix F_{pq} consists of cross partial derivatives with respect to elements of the pth and qth rows of X; it has typical element given by

$$\frac{\partial^2 f}{\partial x_{pi} \, \partial x_{qj}}.$$

When calculating such derivatives, one often notes that the matrix F has a special form where each block F_{pq} is, apart from a scalar multiple, the same matrix. That is,

$$F_{pq} = b_{pq} C$$

where b_{pq} is a scalar and C is a $m \times m$ matrix. Writing the $n \times n$ matrix of elements b_{pq} as B, we then say that F is the Kronecker product of B and C; and we write

$$F = B \otimes C.$$

In general, we may define the Kronecker product of any two (not necessarily square) matrices. Let B be an $r \times s$ matrix and let C be a $u \times v$ matrix. Then we define the $ru \times sv$ matrix $B \otimes C$ to consist of rs blocks with the pq block given by $b_{pq} C$. It can be verified that the following relationships are valid whenever the indicated multiplication or inversion is defined:

$$(A \otimes B)(C \otimes D) = (AC \otimes BD).$$
$$(A \otimes B)^{-1} = (A^{-1} \otimes B^{-1}).$$
$$(A \otimes B)' = (A' \otimes B').$$

THE INVERSE OF A PARTITIONED MATRIX

Another result that will be useful in the following chapters concerns the inversion of partitioned matrices. In general the inverse of a matrix is a complicated function of the elements of the original matrix. However, it is possible to find simple expressions for certain blocks of elements. Consider the inverse of the symmetric partitioned matrix A:

$$A^{-1} = \begin{bmatrix} B & C \\ C' & D \end{bmatrix}^{-1} = \begin{bmatrix} R & S \\ S' & T \end{bmatrix}$$

where B and R are square matrices of order n; D and T are square matrices of order m; and C and S are both $n \times m$. By definition

$$(4.2) \qquad \begin{bmatrix} B & C \\ C' & D \end{bmatrix} \begin{bmatrix} R & S \\ S' & T \end{bmatrix} = \begin{bmatrix} I_n & 0 \\ 0 & I_m \end{bmatrix}.$$

Solving the four equations in (4.2) we have

$$(4.3) \quad \begin{aligned} R &= (B - CD^{-1}C')^{-1} = B^{-1} + B^{-1}C(D - C'B^{-1}C)^{-1}C'B^{-1}, \\ T &= D^{-1} + D^{-1}C'(B - CD^{-1}C')^{-1}CD^{-1} = (D - C'B^{-1}C)^{-1} \end{aligned}$$

as long as B and D are both invertible. If B is invertible but D is not, the right-hand expressions are still valid. For example, if D is the zero matrix, we have

$$R = B^{-1} - B^{-1}C(C'B^{-1}C)^{-1}C'B^{-1}.$$

CHAPTER 2

Exact Prior Information

1. INTRODUCTION

Within the classical framework prior information can be expressed in a number of different ways. In each case either the likelihood function $f_n(y, \theta)$ or the parameter space A is modified by the added information. If, for example, one incorporates knowledge obtained from previous statistical studies, the likelihood function must be changed so as to include the old sample as well as the current one. The parameter space, however, will remain unchanged as long as both samples depend on the same parameters. In contrast, if the prior information says that a given parameter must be greater than zero, then the likelihood function is unchanged but the set A is reduced. Since the classical estimation problem is completely characterized by the pair (f_n, A), all prior information can be described by the way it modifies the pair.

In practice we find that most prior information can be classified into one of three general types. The information typically can be described by (1) previous sample evidence, (2) inequality restrictions on the parameter space, or (3) equality restrictions on the parameter space. In the first case the likelihood function is modified; in the latter two cases the parameter space is modified. Our analysis of prior information under the classical approach will be confined to these three cases.

The phrase "information from previous samples" will be used to describe information embodied in a sample of data different from the one currently under analysis. This additional sample is considered to be the realization of some random experiment and possesses a probability law. The probability distribution of the previous sample need not be of the same mathematical form as the probability distribution of the current sample. The only requirement is that it depend, at least in part, on the unknown parameter vector θ. Incorporating prior information into the analysis is done simply by finding the joint probability function of the two samples. In this way the classical theory can handle stochastic prior information without the need of subjective probability distributions.

Inequality restrictions do not affect the likelihood function but merely reduce the set of possible parameter values. This is also true of equality restrictions. In both cases the new (restricted) parameter space is a subset of the original one. In the case of equality restrictions the new parameter space is usually reduced to a lower dimensionality. For example, if it is known that two parameters θ_1 and θ_2 must sum to one, then θ_2 can be replaced by $1 - \theta_1$ in the likelihood function. The number of unknown parameters is effectively reduced by one. In the case of inequality restrictions the new parameter space remains a set of m dimensions. Thus knowledge that θ_1 is greater than zero in no way reduces the number of parameters.

The distinction between information that reduces the dimensionality of the parameter space and information that does not is important. The mathematical tools which are useful in the one case are not useful in the other. Therefore it is natural to treat these two cases separately. Chapter 3 will study the case of "inexact" prior information. This includes information obtained from previous samples and information in the form of inequality restrictions. The information is inexact in the sense that the dimensionality of the parameter space is not reduced. The present chapter will examine exact equality information which does reduce dimensionality.

The literature on estimation with exact information is limited. The only case that has been examined in detail is that of the linear model under linear constraints. A summary of results in this case may be found in the textbooks of GOLDBERGER (1964) and THEIL (1971). MALINVAUD (1970) analyzes the use of constraints in the context of the nonlinear regression model. The most important general study of constrained estimation is presented in a series of articles on the constrained maximum-likelihood estimator by AITCHISON AND SILVEY (1958), (1960) and by SILVEY (1959). The general problem is also discussed by ANDERSON (1951), HAMMERSLEY (1950), KLEIN (1960), and KOOPMANS, RUBIN, AND LEIPNIK (1950). Many of the results that follow are contained in the above-mentioned works, although their implications and generality seem not to have been previously explored.

2. CONSTRAINT EQUATIONS

The simplest type of exact information is the prior knowledge of some elements of θ. This occurs, for example, when the economist believes that interest rates have no effect on aggregate consumption and therefore deletes that variable from his consumption function. If interest rates are highly correlated with variables that do appear in the regression equation, then deleting the interest rate (when it in fact has zero coefficient) will increase the precision of estimating the other parameters. Knowledge of a specific element of the vector θ is just one example of the more general case of information expressed by constraint equations. A more complex example occurs in the estimation of demand functions. If θ is the vector of all price and income elasticities in a many-commodity market, the theory of utility maximization implies that certain weighted sums of these elasticities must equal zero. In the following discussion we shall examine the gain in efficiency that results from such constraint equations.

Suppose that the set of possible values that the unknown parameter vector θ may take is restricted to A_g, the solution set in A of k equations

$$(2.1) \qquad\qquad g_i(\theta) = 0 \qquad\qquad (i = 1, \ldots, k)$$

where k is less than m, the number of unknown parameters. Suppose further that the g_i are continuous and possess partial derivatives of at least the second order. It will be assumed that the matrix of first partial derivatives

$$(2.2) \qquad\qquad G = [g_{ij}] = \left[\frac{\partial g_i}{\partial \theta_j}\right]$$

has full row rank k when evaluated at the true parameter θ^0. That is, the equations (2.1) are functionally independent in a neighborhood of θ^0.

If the information contained in (2.1) has value, then there exists an estimator using the constraints that has a covariance matrix lower than any estimator that does not use the constraints. We already know that the Cramér-Rao inequality gives a lower bound for the covariance matrix of any unbiased estimator in the absence of prior information. It is natural to seek a lower bound for estimators that use the information in (2.1). The reduction in the lower bound due to the constraints can be used as a measure of the value of that information.

The derivation of a lower bound for the variance of an unbiased estimator proceeds as follows. Since A_g is not a set of full dimension in m-space, the standard Cramér-Rao theorem is not applicable. However, it can easily be modified. For any unbiased estimator $t(Y_n)$,

$$(2.3) \qquad\qquad \int_S (t_i - \theta_i) f_n(y, \theta)\, dy = 0 \qquad\qquad (i = 1, \ldots, m)$$

for all θ in the restricted parameter space A_g. Proceeding along the same

lines as our earlier proof, we obtain for any nonstochastic vector
$c = (c_1, \ldots, c_m)'$

(2.4) $\qquad \int \sum_i c_i(t_i - \theta_i^0) f_n(y,\theta^0) \dfrac{f_n(y, \theta^0 + \xi) - f_n(y, \theta^0)}{f_n(y, \theta^0)} dy = \sum_i c_i \xi_i$

where θ^0 is the true parameter and $\xi = (\xi_1, \ldots, \xi_m)'$ is any vector such that
$\theta^0 + \xi$ lies in A_g.

Since (2.4) is valid for all $\theta^0 + \xi$ in A_g, it is also valid in the limit as ξ
approaches zero along a path within the restricted parameter space.
Consider an infinite sequence of nonzero vectors $\xi^1, \xi^2, \xi^3, \ldots$ converging
to zero such that each $\theta^0 + \xi^s$ is in A_g. By our continuity assumptions such
a sequence exists. Let

$$x^s = \frac{\xi^s}{|\xi^s|} \qquad\qquad (s = 1, 2, \ldots).$$

Then there is a subsequence of $x^1, x^2, x^3, \ldots$ that converges to a vector x.
Equation (2.4) becomes

(2.5) $\qquad \int \sum_i c_i(t_i - \theta_i^0) \sqrt{f_n} \cdot \sum_j \dfrac{\partial \log f_n}{\partial \theta_j} x_j \sqrt{f_n}\, dy = \sum_i c_i x_i$

and again the Cauchy-Schwartz inequality yields the result:

(2.6) $\qquad\qquad\qquad\qquad c'Vc \geq \dfrac{(c'x)^2}{x'R_n x}.$

As in the case of unconstrained estimation, there is an inequality relating
the covariance matrix V of any unbiased estimator and the information
matrix R_n.

The inequality (2.6) is valid only for those vectors x that are possible
limits of the sequence $x^1, x^2, x^3, \ldots$. Since $\theta^0 + \xi^s$ is constrained to
remain in the restricted parameter space, the set of permitted x-values is in
general not the entire unit sphere in m-space. In fact, the set of limit points
is the set of vectors having unit length and satisfying

(2.7) $\qquad\qquad\qquad\qquad G^0 x = 0$

where G^0 is the matrix (2.2) evaluated at θ^0. This follows from the mean
value theorem which says that each x^s in the sequence must satisfy the
equation

(2.8) $\qquad\qquad\qquad\qquad G^* x^s = 0$

where G^* is the matrix (2.2) with each row evaluated at some point between θ^0 and $\theta^0 + \xi^s$. In the limit ξ^s approaches zero and (2.8) approaches (2.7). A lower bound for $c'Vc$ is obtained by finding the maximum value the right hand side of (2.6) may take. Changing the normalization constraint slightly, we are led to the following extremal problem:

$$\text{maximize}_{x} \quad (c'x)^2$$

subject to

$$G^0 x = 0$$

$$x'R_n x = 1.$$

This problem can be solved using the method of Lagrange multipliers. The inequality (2.6) becomes $c'Vc \geq c'P_n c$ where P_n is given by[1]

$$(2.9) \qquad P_n = R_n^{-1} - R_n^{-1}G'(GR_n^{-1}G')^{-1}GR_n^{-1},$$

a matrix having rank $m - k$.[2] This maximum is attained when x is a multiple of $P_n c$.

This result can be expressed more simply in terms of the bordered information matrix

$$(2.10) \qquad \begin{bmatrix} R_n & G' \\ G & 0 \end{bmatrix}$$

and its conformably partitioned inverse

$$(2.11) \qquad \begin{bmatrix} R_n & G' \\ G & 0 \end{bmatrix}^{-1} = \begin{bmatrix} P_n & * \\ * & * \end{bmatrix}.$$

Thus the Cramér-Rao bound for the variance of an unbiased estimator when prior constraints are used is given by the $m \times m$ northwest submatrix of the inverted bordered information matrix. The decrease in the bound due to the prior information is given by

$$(2.12) \qquad R_n^{-1} - P_n = R_n^{-1}G'(GR_n^{-1}G')^{-1}GR_n^{-1},$$

a positive semidefinite matrix having rank equal to the number of constraints k.

---

1. For notational convenience the superscript on G^0 is dropped. In the sequel all derivatives are evaluated at the true parameter θ^0 unless otherwise stated.

2. Writing R_n^{-1} as $D'D$ and defining $B = DG'$, we see that P_n has the same rank as the idempotent matrix $I - B(B'B)^{-1}B'$.

Given the constraint equations, it is possible to relax the assumption that R_n is nonsingular. The extremal problem just solved is the same as the problem

$$\text{maximize}_{x} \quad (c'x)^2$$

$$\text{subject to}$$

$$Gx = 0$$

$$x'(R_n + G'G)x = 0.$$

If the matrix $R_n + G'G$ is nonsingular, then equations (2.9) through (2.12) remain valid if R_n is replaced by $R_n + G'G$. The lower bound is then given by the appropriate submatrix of

$$\begin{bmatrix} R_n + G'G & G' \\ G & 0 \end{bmatrix}^{-1} = \begin{bmatrix} \bar{P}_n & * \\ * & * \end{bmatrix}.$$

In this case the availability of a priori information makes estimation possible. Without the information the parameters could not be estimated at all.

THE ATTAINABILITY OF THE BOUND

Typically, no unbiased estimator can be found with a covariance matrix equal to P_n. From the above derivation, it is seen that the bound is attainable only if the Cauchy-Schwartz inequality when applied to (2.5) remains an equality for $x = P_n c$ and all c. This will occur if and only if, for all y, f_n is of the form

(2.13) $$P_n \frac{\partial \log f_n}{\partial \theta} = t - \theta$$

where t does not depend on θ. Although it does not seem possible to state more useful necessary conditions for this to hold, it is possible to present an interesting set of sufficient conditions.

Suppose that there exists an MVB estimator $s(Y_n)$ when there is no prior information. This means that the likelihood function can be written as

(2.14) $$\frac{\partial \log f_n}{\partial \theta} = R_n(s - \theta).$$

Suppose further that the constraints (2.1) are linear so that they take the form $G\theta = a$. In that case we can write

$$P_n \frac{\partial \log f_n}{\partial \theta} = [I - R_n^{-1}G'(GR_n^{-1}G')^{-1}G]R_n^{-1}\frac{\partial \log f_n}{\partial \theta}$$

(2.15)
$$= [I - R_n^{-1}G'(GR_n^{-1}G')^{-1}G](s - \theta)$$

$$= s - R_n^{-1}G'(GR_n^{-1}G')^{-1}(Gs - a) - \theta$$

where neither G nor s depends on θ. Then, if R_n is independent of θ except for at most a scalar multiple, (2.15) is of the form needed for an attainable bound. The MVB estimator is given by

(2.16) $$s^* = s - R_n^{-1}G'(GR_n^{-1}G')^{-1}(Gs - a).$$

The results obtained above may be summarized as follows:

In the presence of prior knowledge expressed by a set of k independent constraint equations, the matrix $P_n = R_n^{-1} - R_n^{-1}G'(GR_n^{-1}G')^{-1}GR_n^{-1}$ is a lower bound to the covariance matrix of any unbiased estimator of θ. The difference in lower bounds $R_n^{-1} - P_n$ is a positive semidefinite matrix of rank k. A sufficient (but not necessary) condition for P_n to be attainable is that
  1) *R_n^{-1} is attainable when the constraints are ignored,*
  2) *R_n can be written as the product of a matrix which does not depend on θ and a scalar which may depend on θ, and*
  3) *the constraints $g_i(\theta)$ are linear.*

3. THE ASYMPTOTIC BOUND

The asymptotic extension of these results has a similar form. It is merely necessary to define

(3.1) $$P = \lim_{n \to \infty} \frac{1}{n}P_n = R^{-1} - R^{-1}G'(GR^{-1}G')^{-1}GR^{-1},$$

which is the $m \times m$ northwest submatrix of

(3.2) $$\lim_{n \to \infty} \begin{bmatrix} \frac{1}{n}R_n & G' \\ G & 0 \end{bmatrix}^{-1} = \begin{bmatrix} R & G' \\ G & 0 \end{bmatrix}^{-1}.$$

Then one can state:

In the presence of prior information expressed by a set of constraint equations, the matrix P is essentially a lower bound for the asymptotic *covariance matrix of any consistent estimator of θ. The efficiency gain $R^{-1} - P$ is a positive semidefinite matrix having rank k. The bound is attained by the constrained maximum-likelihood estimator.*

A complete proof of this proposition is lengthy and difficult. Fortunately, however, the classical proofs of the asymptotic Cramér-Rao inequality can be applied with only minor modification. It is necessary to show that the likelihood function defined on the restricted parameter space A_g satisfies the usual regularity assumptions. This has been done by AITCHISON AND SILVEY (1958) in the course of deriving the asymptotic distribution of the constrained maximum-likelihood estimator.

The method of maximum likelihood is by no means unique in giving estimators with optimal large-sample properties. Another general principle of estimation—the method of minimum chi-square—also gives rise to asymptotically efficient estimators.[3] Consider the quadratic form

(3.3) $$\varphi(\theta) = (t - \theta)'\hat{R}(t - \theta)$$

where t is an estimator of θ that is asymptotically normal and efficient when there are no constraints; $\hat{R}$ is the asymptotic information matrix R evaluated at $\theta = t$. The estimator t might be, for example, the unconstrained maximum-likelihood estimator. In any case, t is an estimator that is asymptotically normal with mean θ and covariance matrix R^{-1}. The variable $n\varphi$ converges in distribution to a chi-square variate as n approaches infinity. The minimum-chi-square estimator of θ in the presence of the prior information is given by $\hat{\theta}$, the solution to the following extremal problem:

$$\underset{\theta}{\text{minimize}} \quad (t - \theta)'\hat{R}(t - \theta)$$
$$\text{subject to}$$
$$g(\theta) = 0.$$

The linearized minimum-chi-square estimator is given by $\hat{\theta}^*$, the solution to the modified extremal problem:

$$\underset{\theta}{\text{minimize}} \quad (t - \theta)'\hat{R}(t - \theta)$$
$$\text{subject to}$$
$$g(t) + \hat{G}(\theta - t) = 0$$

3. The minimum-chi-square method or some variant of it is used by MALINVAUD (1970), pp. 283–6, who refers to it as the minimum-distance method, and by BASMANN (1963), who refers to it as the generalized classical estimating method. For further discussion of the general principle see FERGUSON (1958). Our interpretation of this estimation method differs somewhat from these authors since they do not use the information matrix.

where $\hat{G}$ is the Jacobian matrix G evaluated at $\theta = t$. The solution to the first extremal problem cannot be given explicitly. The solution to the second problem, however, is easily obtained as

$$(3.4) \qquad \hat{\theta}^* = t - R^{-1}G'(GR^{-1}G')^{-1}g(t)$$

where, for ease in notation, the "hat" has been omitted from R and G.

The basic theorem of the minimum-chi-square method is that both $\hat{\theta}$ and $\hat{\theta}^*$ are asymptotically efficient. The argument for the case of $\hat{\theta}^*$ follows; the reader may refer to CHIANG (1956) and FERGUSON (1958) for the complete proof. Using the mean value theorem, we can write (3.4) as

$$(3.5) \qquad \hat{\theta}^* - \theta^0 = [I - R^{-1}G'(GR^{-1}G')^{-1}G^*](t - \theta^0)$$

where G^* is the matrix G evaluated at some point between t and θ^0. The expression in square brackets converges in probability to the matrix PR. Hence, $\sqrt{n}(\hat{\theta}^* - \theta^0)$ has the same asymptotic distribution as $PR\sqrt{n}(t - \theta^0)$. But the latter random variable is asymptotically normal with mean zero and covariance matrix P. Hence $\hat{\theta}^*$ has an asymptotic variance equal to the Cramér-Rao lower bound.

It is important to emphasize that the optimality of the minimum-chi-square estimator depends crucially on the assumption that the unconstrained estimator t has an asymptotic covariance matrix equal to R^{-1}. Only if such an estimator t can be easily calculated will the minimum-chi-square approach be a practical method. Fortunately, for many problems met in practice an easy-to-calculate, efficient estimator for the unconstrained problem exists.

4. AN EXAMPLE

An important example where the bound P_n is attainable in finite samples is the normal linear regression model with linear constraints.[4] Consider the regression equation

$$(4.1) \qquad y = X\beta + u$$

where y is an n-dimensional vector of observations on a random variable, X is an $n \times m$ matrix of nonstochastic variables, β is a vector of m unknown parameters, and u is a vector of n independent normal random errors with

---

4. This case has been treated by THEIL (1961), pp. 331–33 and by CHIPMAN AND RAO (1964).

zero mean and constant variance σ^2. The likelihood function for the sample is

(4.2) $\qquad f_n(y, \beta, \sigma^2) = (2\pi\sigma^2)^{-\frac{1}{2}n} \exp\{-\frac{1}{2}\sigma^{-2}(y - X\beta)'(y - X\beta)\}.$

The logarithmic derivatives are

(4.3) $\qquad\qquad\qquad \dfrac{\partial \log f_n}{\partial \beta} = \dfrac{1}{\sigma^2} X'X(b - \beta),$

(4.4) $\qquad\qquad\qquad \dfrac{\partial \log f_n}{\partial \sigma^2} = \dfrac{n}{2\sigma^4}\left(\dfrac{u'u}{n} - \sigma^2\right)$

where $b = (X'X)^{-1}X'y$ is the least-squares estimator. The information matrix for β and σ^2 is the $(m + 1) \times (m + 1)$ matrix

(4.5) $\qquad\qquad R_n = \begin{bmatrix} \dfrac{1}{\sigma^2}X'X & 0 \\ & \\ 0 & \dfrac{n}{2\sigma^4} \end{bmatrix}.$

Because R_n is block diagonal, the Cramér-Rao bound for β may be examined separately from that for σ^2. It is apparent that (4.3) is of the form (2.14); however, equation (4.4) is not since $u'u/n$ depends on the parameter β. Thus, as is usual with the normal distribution, the Cramér-Rao bound is not attainable for σ^2. No unbiased estimator has a variance as low as $2\sigma^4/n$. However, the least-squares estimator b does have the covariance matrix $\sigma^2(X'X)^{-1}$ and hence is an MVB estimator of β.

Suppose that the prior constraints are of the form

$$G\beta = a.$$

Since the information matrix for (β, σ^2) is block diagonal and the constraints do not involve σ^2, attention can be focused solely on β. The constrained least-squares estimator is found by the use of Lagrange multipliers to be

$$\hat{\beta} = b - (X'X)^{-1}G'[G(X'X)^{-1}G']^{-1}(Gb - a)$$

and the covariance matrix for $\hat{\beta}$ is

$$P_n = \sigma^2\{(X'X)^{-1} - (X'X)^{-1}G'[G(X'X)^{-1}G']^{-1}G(X'X)^{-1}\}.$$

Hence $\hat{\beta}$ is an MVB estimator in the presence of the a priori information.

Under plausible conditions on $X'X$, $\hat{\beta}$ is also asymptotically efficient; but that is a much weaker result. It is easy to verify that the constrained least-squares estimator $\hat{\beta}$ is also the constrained maximum-likelihood and minimum-chi-square estimator.

The analysis can be extended to the case of the linear model with random X matrix or nonlinear constraints on β by considering the asymptotic bound. Again the constrained least-squares estimator is found to be asymptotically efficient under weak regularity conditions. An interesting application of this approach is provided by DURBIN (1960) in the context of the regression model with autocorrelated errors. Consider the simple time-series model

$$(4.6) \qquad y_t = \alpha x_t + u_t \qquad (t = 1, \ldots, n)$$

where the x_t are nonrandom and α is an unknown scalar parameter. The u_t constitute a stationary autoregressive process

$$(4.7) \qquad u_t = \rho u_{t-1} + v_t$$

where $|\rho| < 1$ and the v_t are independent, identically distributed normal random variables with zero mean and variance σ^2.

Equations (4.6) and (4.7) may be combined to form the model

$$(4.8) \qquad y_t = \rho y_{t-1} + \alpha x_t - \alpha \rho x_{t-1} + v_t \qquad (t = 1, \ldots, n).$$

Conditional on y_0, (4.8) may be treated as a normal regression model with independent errors. The likelihood function has the same form as (4.2) where X is now the $n \times 3$ matrix consisting of observations on y_{t-1}, x_t, and x_{t-1}. The parameter vector β consists of the three elements $\beta_1 = \rho$, $\beta_2 = \alpha$, and $\beta_3 = -\alpha\rho$. The unconditional likelihood function is obtained by multiplying (4.2) by the density function for y_0. However, this term becomes insignificant when n approaches infinity and can be ignored for the present asymptotic analysis. Thus our time-series model is a special case of the normal regression model with random explanatory variables and a constrained parameter space. The constraint can be expressed by the nonlinear equation

$$g(\beta_1, \beta_2, \beta_3) = \beta_1 \beta_2 + \beta_3 = 0$$

with matrix of partial derivatives given by

$$G = [\beta_2 \quad \beta_1 \quad 1] = [\alpha \quad \rho \quad 1].$$

The information matrix, in terms of the unconstrained parameter β, is given by (4.5) with $X'X$ replaced by its expectation. Again ignoring the row and column corresponding to σ, we find

$$R = \lim \frac{1}{\sigma^2 n} \mathscr{E} X'X = \frac{M}{\sigma^2} \begin{bmatrix} \alpha^2 + \dfrac{\sigma^2}{M(1-\rho^2)} & \alpha r & \alpha \\[3mm] \alpha r & 1 & r \\[3mm] \alpha & r & 1 \end{bmatrix}$$

and

$$R^{-1} = \begin{bmatrix} 1-\rho^2 & 0 & -\alpha(1-\rho^2) \\[2mm] 0 & \dfrac{\sigma^2}{M(1-r^2)} & \dfrac{-r\sigma^2}{M(1-r^2)} \\[3mm] -\alpha(1-\rho^2) & \dfrac{-r\sigma^2}{M(1-r^2)} & \alpha^2(1-\rho^2) + \dfrac{\sigma^2}{M(1-r^2)} \end{bmatrix},$$

where $M = \lim \Sigma x_t^2/n$ and $r = \lim \Sigma x_t x_{t-1}/nM$.

If the constraint that $\beta_1\beta_2 + \beta_3 = 0$ is ignored and least squares is applied to (4.8), there is no unique way to obtain estimates of ρ and α from the estimates of β. However, if one should choose to estimate ρ by $\hat{\beta}_1$ and α by $\hat{\beta}_2$ (and hence ignore β_3 entirely), the resulting consistent estimator will have an asymptotic covariance matrix V given by the northwest submatrix of R^{-1}:

$$(4.9) \qquad V = \begin{bmatrix} 1-\rho^2 & 0 \\[3mm] 0 & \dfrac{\sigma^2}{M(1-r^2)} \end{bmatrix}.$$

If the constraint is imposed, then the constrained least-squares estimator of ρ and α will have an asymptotic covariance matrix V^* given by the northwest submatrix of $P = R^{-1} - R^{-1}G'(GR^{-1}G')^{-1}GR^{-1}$:

$$(4.10) \qquad V^* = \begin{bmatrix} 1-\rho^2 & 0 \\[3mm] 0 & \dfrac{\sigma^2}{M(1-2r\rho+\rho^2)} \end{bmatrix}.$$

Comparing V and V^*, we see that the imposition of the constraint lowers the asymptotic variance of $\hat{\alpha}$ but does not affect the asymptotic variance of $\hat{\rho}$ at all. That is, the unconstrained least-squares estimator of ρ is fully efficient. Since $R^{-1} - P$ is a matrix of rank one, there are always linear combinations of β whose variance remains the same when constraints are imposed. In this case, there turns out to be a very interesting linear combination, namely the parameter ρ itself. Durbin uses this result to construct a simple, efficient method of estimating α: first, perform an unconstrained regression of y_t on y_{t-1}, x_t, x_{t-1}; then regress $y_t - \hat{\rho} y_{t-1}$ on $x_t - \hat{\rho} x_{t-1}$ where $\hat{\rho}$ is the least-squares estimate $\hat{\beta}_1$. The coefficient from the second regression has the same asymptotic distribution as the constrained least-squares estimator and requires no nonlinear minimization techniques. Of course, there are many other ways of efficiently estimating α—including the linearized minimum-chi-square estimator given in equation (3.4)—all having the same asymptotic distribution.

5. Constraint Parameters

Another way of expressing exact prior information is to assume that the elements of θ are related functionally to a second set of parameters. Let α be a vector of r unknown parameters. Suppose that the statistician knows that each θ_i is a given function of the elements of α. That is,

$$(5.1) \qquad \theta_i = h_i(\alpha) \qquad (i = 1, \ldots, m)$$

where each h_i possesses bounded partial derivatives of at least the second order. It is assumed that the matrix of first partial derivatives

$$(5.2) \qquad H = [h_{ij}] = \left[\frac{\partial h_i}{\partial \alpha_j}\right]$$

has constant rank ρ in an open neighborhood containing the true parameter α^0. It is further assumed that the set of possible values that α may take is an open set in r-dimensional Euclidean space.

Under these conditions it will generally be the case that, in a neighborhood of θ^0, $m - \rho$ of the θ_i can be expressed as functions of the remaining ρ. That is, it is possible to convert the m equations (5.1) and the r new variables into $m - \rho$ constraint equations involving only the θ_i. Hence, the case being considered here is essentially equivalent to the case presented in the previous sections. However, for a number of problems (of which the simultaneous equations problem is an important example), the form (5.1) is more natural and more easily interpreted than the derived constraint equations. Moreover, it will be possible here to derive covariance matrices for estimates of both α and θ.

We begin by assuming that α^0 is identifiable. That is, if θ^0 is the true value of θ, then α^0 is the unique solution of

(5.3) $$\theta^0 = h(\alpha).$$

This implies that H^0, the matrix (5.2) evaluated at α^0, has full rank r. Furthermore, we assume that the distance $|h(\alpha) - h(\alpha^0)|$ is bounded from below by a positive number in any closed set not containing α^0. That is, not only is α^0 the unique solution of (5.3), but in addition there are no "almost" solutions distant from α^0. These identifiability assumptions will be dropped later.

The derivation of the variance bound for this case can be split into two parts. First, a lower bound for V_θ, the covariance matrix of an unbiased estimator of θ, is obtained; then a lower bound for V_α, the covariance matrix of an unbiased estimator of α, is obtained. For the first part, much of the derivation of section 2 is relevant. Equation (2.5) is still valid except that the values of x for which it holds now differ. The parameter $\theta^0 + \xi$ is now constrained to lie not in the set A_g, but rather in A_h, the range of (5.1). Since the functions h_i are continuously differentiable, we have for any vector α

$$h(\alpha) = h(\alpha^0) + H^*(\alpha - \alpha^0)$$

where H^* is the Jacobian matrix (5.2) with each element evaluated somewhere between α and α^0. Therefore any θ satisfying the constraints must be of the form $\theta^0 + \xi$ with

$$\xi = H^*(\alpha - \alpha^0).$$

Again considering a sequence $\xi^1, \xi^2, \xi^3, \ldots$ approaching zero and the corresponding sequence of normalized vectors $x^1, x^2, x^3, \ldots$, we see that x is a possible limit point if and only if

(5.4) $$x = H^0 z$$

for some vector z in r-space. Thus, (2.6) remains valid if (2.7) is replaced by (5.4). The lower bound for $c'V_\theta c$ is obtained by solving the constrained extremal problem:[5]

$$\text{maximize} \quad (c'x)^2$$
$$\underset{x}{\text{subject to}}$$
$$x = Hz$$
$$x'R_n x = 1$$

z unrestricted.

5. Again, for notational convenience, the superscript on H^0 will be dropped.

This, however, is the same as the problem:

$$\text{maximize} \quad (c'Hz)^2$$
$$\text{subject to}$$
$$z'H'R_nHz = 1.$$

The solution to the latter problem is obtained using the method of Lagrange multipliers. The objective function is maximized when $z = N_n c$ where

(5.5)
$$N_n = H(H'R_nH)^{-1}H'$$

is a matrix having rank r. The value of the objective function at the maximum is $c'N_n c$. Hence, the Cramér-Rao inequality becomes

(5.6)
$$c'V_\theta c \geq c'H(H'R_nH)^{-1}H'c.$$

The decrease in the bound due to the constraints $R_n^{-1} - N_n$ is a positive semidefinite matrix of rank $m - r$.

The second part of the problem is to find a lower bound for V_α. Here the procedure is quite simple. Since the functions f_n and h are continuously differentiable, the compound function

$$f_n[y, h(\alpha)] = f_n^*(y, \alpha)$$

is a density function that satisfies the classical regularity assumptions. Hence the information matrix for α is obtained by the chain rule:

(5.7)
$$\frac{\partial \log f_n^*}{\partial \alpha_i} = \sum_k \frac{\partial \log f_n}{\partial \theta_k} \cdot \frac{\partial \theta_k}{\partial \alpha_i},$$

(5.8)
$$\frac{\partial^2 \log f_n^*}{\partial \alpha_i \, \partial \alpha_j} = \sum_k \sum_p \frac{\partial^2 \log f_n}{\partial \theta_k \, \partial \theta_p} \frac{\partial \theta_k}{\partial \alpha_i} \frac{\partial \theta_p}{\partial \alpha_j} + \sum_k \frac{\partial \log f_n}{\partial \theta_k} \frac{\partial^2 \theta_k}{\partial \alpha_i \, \partial \alpha_j}.$$

The second term on the right of (5.8) has zero expectation since

$$\int \frac{\partial \log f_n}{\partial \theta_k} f_n = \int \frac{\partial f_n}{\partial \theta_k} = \frac{\partial}{\partial \theta_k} \int f_n = \frac{\partial}{\partial \theta_k} 1 = 0.$$

Thus

$$-\mathscr{E} \frac{\partial^2 \log f_n^*}{\partial \alpha_i \, \partial \alpha_j} = \sum_k \sum_p h_{ki} r_{kp} h_{pj}$$

and, if H has rank r, the inverted information matrix for α is

(5.9)
$$M_n = (H'R_nH)^{-1}.$$

The Cramér-Rao inequality becomes

(5.10) $c'V_\alpha c \geq c'M_n c = c'(H'R_nH)^{-1}c.$

THE ATTAINABILITY OF THE BOUND

Only under restrictive conditions will there exist an unbiased estimator whose variance equals the lower bound. Again, linearity of the constraints provides the simplest example. Suppose s is an MVB estimator when no constraints are present and hence

(5.11) $\dfrac{\partial \log f_n}{\partial \theta} = R_n(s - \theta).$

If the constraints (5.1) are linear so that they are of the form

(5.12) $\theta = H\alpha + a,$

we can write

$$N_n \frac{\partial \log f_n}{\partial \theta} = N_n R_n(s - H\alpha - a)$$

(5.13)

$$= [H(H'R_nH)^{-1}H'R_n(s - a) + a] - \theta$$

and, using (5.7),

$$M_n \frac{\partial \log f_n^*}{\partial \alpha} = M_n H' \frac{\partial \log f_n}{\partial \theta}$$

(5.14) $$= (H'R_nH)^{-1}H'R_n(s - H\alpha - a)$$

$$= (H'R_nH)^{-1}H'R_n(s - a) - \alpha.$$

But, analogous to (2.13), the bound is attainable if the right-hand sides of (5.13) and (5.14) are the difference between the estimator and the parameter. This is the case if R_n does not depend on θ (except perhaps for a scalar multiple).

In summary we can state the following proposition:

In the presence of prior information expressed by a set of constraint parameters α which are related to θ by the known differentiable equations $\theta = h(\alpha)$, the matrix $N_n = H(H'R_nH)^{-1}H'$ is a lower bound for the covariance matrix of any unbiased estimator of θ and the matrix $M_n = (H'R_nH)^{-1}$ is a lower bound for the covariance matrix of any unbiased estimator of α. The difference in lower bounds $R_n^{-1} - N_n$ is a positive semi-

definite matrix of rank $m - r$. A sufficient (but not necessary) condition for M_n and N_n to be attainable is that

1) R_n^{-1} *is attainable when the constraints are ignored,*
2) R_n *can be written as the product of a matrix which does not depend on θ and a scalar which may depend on θ, and*
3) *the constraints $h_i(\alpha)$ are all linear.*

Again these results can be expressed more simply in terms of a bordered information matrix. Consider the square matrix of order $2m + r$

$$(5.15) \qquad \mathscr{R}_n = \begin{bmatrix} R_n & 0 & -I \\ 0 & 0 & H' \\ -I & H & 0 \end{bmatrix}$$

that is partitioned into three row blocks (the first containing m rows, the second containing r rows, and the third containing m rows) and similarly three column blocks. The four northwest blocks can be interpreted as the information matrix of f_n in terms of θ and α. Since f_n does not depend directly on α, there are blocks of zeros. The matrix $[-I \quad H]$ is simply the Jacobian of the constraint function

$$h(\alpha) - \theta = 0.$$

Thus (5.15) is formed in exactly the same way as (2.10). It is an information matrix of order $m + r$ bordered by a matrix expressing m constraints. This matrix also turns out to be minus the expected value of the second partial derivative matrix of the Lagrangean

$$L(\theta, \alpha, \lambda) = \log f_n(y, \theta) + \sum_{i=1}^{m} \lambda_i[\theta_i - h_i(\alpha)]$$

where the λ_i are taken to have zero expected value. That is,

$$\mathscr{R}_n = -\mathscr{E} \begin{bmatrix} \dfrac{\partial^2 L}{\partial\theta\,\partial\theta'} & \dfrac{\partial^2 L}{\partial\theta\,\partial\alpha'} & \dfrac{\partial^2 L}{\partial\theta\,\partial\lambda'} \\[2ex] \dfrac{\partial^2 L}{\partial\alpha\,\partial\theta'} & \dfrac{\partial^2 L}{\partial\alpha\,\partial\alpha'} & \dfrac{\partial^2 L}{\partial\alpha\,\partial\lambda'} \\[2ex] \dfrac{\partial^2 L}{\partial\lambda\,\partial\theta'} & \dfrac{\partial^2 L}{\partial\lambda\,\partial\alpha'} & \dfrac{\partial^2 L}{\partial\lambda\,\partial\lambda'} \end{bmatrix}.$$

It is easily verified that the conformably partitioned inverse has the form

$$\mathcal{R}_n^{-1} = \begin{bmatrix} N_n & * & * \\ * & M_n & * \\ * & * & * \end{bmatrix}$$

with M_n and N_n on the diagonal. Thus the inverse elements of a suitably bordered information matrix give lower bounds for the covariance matrices of any unbiased estimator of θ and α.

AN ASYMPTOTIC RESULT

The asymptotic extension of our results is straightforward. Defining

$$M = \lim \frac{1}{n} M_n \quad \text{and} \quad N = \lim \frac{1}{n} N_n,$$

which are diagonal blocks of

$$\mathcal{R}^{-1} = \lim \begin{bmatrix} \frac{1}{n} R_n & 0 & -I \\ 0 & 0 & H' \\ -I & H & 0 \end{bmatrix}^{-1} = \begin{bmatrix} N & * & * \\ * & M & * \\ * & * & * \end{bmatrix},$$

we can state the proposition:

In the presence of prior information expressed as (5.1), the matrices N and M are lower bounds for the asymptotic covariance matrices of any consistent estimators of θ and α. The efficiency gain in estimating θ is given by $R^{-1} - N$, a positive semidefinite matrix of rank $m - r$. The bound is attained by the constrained maximum-likelihood estimator.

Again there are other optimal estimation methods. For example, the minimum-chi-square estimators of θ and α are also asymptotically efficient. These are defined as the solution to the extremal problem

$$\begin{aligned} \underset{\theta}{\text{minimize}} \quad & (t - \theta)' \hat{R}(t - \theta) \\ \text{subject to} \quad & \theta = h(\alpha) \end{aligned}$$

where t is asymptotically normal with mean θ and covariance matrix R^{-1}.

6. IDENTIFICATION

The analysis in the previous section is based on the assumption that α^0 is the unique solution of

(6.1) $$\theta^0 = h(\alpha).$$

It is of interest to examine this assumption in greater detail. The probability law for the sample is uniquely determined by the parameter θ. If there is associated with the true parameter θ^0 more than one vector α satisfying (6.1), then it is not possible to speak of a "true" parameter α^0. Unless there is more a priori information concerning the parameter α, any solution of (6.1) is "true" in the sense that it implies the correct probability distribution of the observable sample. Hence estimation of α is meaningful only if h is a mapping such that θ^0 has a unique image vector α^0.

Yet in practice we often meet problems where it is necessary to estimate α but where it is not known that (6.1) has a unique solution. These problems arise when α can be interpreted as the parameter of some hypothetical experiment that has not been actually performed. If the experiment had been performed, different values of the parameter would be associated with different probability distributions of the resulting sample. Hence it is quite meaningful to talk about a true value of α. Unfortunately, the sample that we are examining comes from some other experiment which depends on the parameter θ. Although θ and α are related by the equations (5.1), it is not necessarily true that the mapping is one-to-one.

A simple example of this type of problem arises under the permanent income theory of consumer behavior. Suppose that individuals make their consumption decisions on the basis of long-run expected income. Therefore the marginal propensity to consume out of permanent income may be an interesting parameter related to the experiment of drawing random individuals and observing their consumption and their permanent income. This experiment is only hypothetical since most budget studies record actual, not permanent, income. If the observations are normally distributed, then the observed sample has a distribution described by five parameters: the mean and variance of consumption, the mean and variance of income, and the correlation coefficient between consumption and income. These basic parameters (like our θ) completely characterize the probability law for the observed sample. But the structural parameters of economic interest, including the marginal propensity to consume out of permanent income, are related to θ in a complex way depending on how expected income is related to actual income. Often it is a difficult question to determine whether estimation of the structural parameter α from the given data is even possible.

This problem of estimating a structural parameter α when the likelihood function is in terms of another parameter θ is the essence of the famous identification problem in statistical inference.[6] It will arise in chapter 4 when we turn to the simultaneous equations model. Although it would take us too far afield to discuss the identification problem at length, it is useful to see how it fits into our analysis. A parameter is said to be identifiable if different numerical values of the parameter are associated with different probability laws for the sample. In our classical estimation problem, the nonsingularity of R_n guarantees that, at least locally, different values of θ can be distinguished by the sample. In fact, we have made the stronger assumption that every θ in the parameter space A is identifiable. Thus the question of the identifiability of the structural parameter α^0 rests on the properties of h. If the functions are linear, then H is a matrix of constants. In this case the question of identification is quite simple. If H has rank equal to r, then there can exist but one solution to equation (6.1); thus the analysis of section 5 is applicable. If H has rank less than r, then α^0 is not identifiable. There are an infinite number of α vectors that give rise to the same θ^0 and hence the same probability distribution of the sample. Estimation of α^0 is impossible.

If the functions relating θ and α are not linear, the problem becomes more complex. If H has rank r when evaluated at α^0, then the true structural parameter is at least locally identifiable. That is, there exists a neighborhood in which α^0 is the unique solution of $\theta^0 = h(\alpha)$. If, however, in a neighborhood of α^0 the matrix H has constant rank less than r, then there will exist an infinite number of solutions to the equation $\theta^0 = h(\alpha)$. Hence if H nowhere has full column rank, then α^0 will generally not be identifiable. If H everywhere has full rank, then α^0 is at least locally identifiable and may possibly be globally identifiable.[7] The notion of local identification is important because we usually possess rough inequality information about α. Thus we can often restrict our attention to some small region in r-space. If α^0 is locally identifiable, suitable inequality constraints will allow us to estimate the structure. If it is not locally identifiable, no amount of inequality information will permit us to estimate α.

---

6. See, for example, FISHER (1966) and ROTHENBERG (1971).

7. It is possible to state conditions for global identification in the nonlinear case, but they are rather complicated. For details, see FISHER (1966), pp. 157–60.

PARAMETER CONSTRAINTS WITHOUT IDENTIFIABILITY

There remains the question of estimating θ. Is it possible to use the information in (5.1) to increase the efficiency of estimating θ even if α is not identifiable?[8] The answer in general is yes. The derivation in section 5 depends on the fact that x is constrained. If an equation like (5.4) is valid (with H^0 having rank less than m), then the parameter space of θ is reduced to a lower-dimensional space. Again the analysis is simple when the functions h are linear. If the rank ρ of H is less than r and also less than m, then the parameter α^0 is clearly not identifiable. But (5.4) is still valid since $H^* = H^0 = H$. In the derivation of the lower bound for V_θ, the function $(c'x)^2$ was maximized over the set of all x values in the column space of H. If H has rank less than r, then the column space is spanned by a subset H_1 of the columns of H. Then (5.6) is valid if H is replaced by H_1. This is equivalent to replacing the inverse of $H'RH$ by its generalized inverse. The prior information increases efficiency in estimating θ as long as ρ is less than m.

Even if the equations are not linear, a similar result applies. If there is more than one value of α satisfying the equation $\theta^0 = h(\alpha)$, then the matrix H^0 in equation (5.4) is not well defined. Nevertheless, it will still be the case that θ is unrestricted if H *everywhere* has rank m. And if H everywhere has rank less than m, the parameter space for θ is necessarily restricted. In the latter case, it will be possible to obtain estimates of θ that are more efficient than the unconstrained estimates if the restrictions do not depend on the unidentifiable α. This will occur if the column space of $H(\alpha)$ is the same for all α satisfying $\theta^0 = h(\alpha)$. In other words, the result given in equation (5.6) is still valid as long as N depends only on θ. Of course, the inverse in (5.6) must be interpreted as a generalized inverse.

The above discussion should make it clear that the identifiability of α and the existence of restrictions on θ are two separate questions. The answers depend on the rank ρ of H, but in different ways. If H has constant rank for all values near α^0, we can summarize the various possibilities as follows:

	$\rho = r$	$\rho < r$
$\rho = m$	α locally identifiable θ unrestricted	α not identifiable θ unrestricted
$\rho < m$	α locally identifiable θ restricted	α not identifiable θ restricted

8. For convenience, the superscript will often be dropped and the phrase "α is identifiable" used in place of "α^0 is identifiable".

IDENTIFICATION OF A SUBSET OF THE PARAMETERS

One further possibility that should be examined is that some elements of α may be identifiable while the others are not. Again the matrix H is the basis of the analysis. Suppose the vector α is partitioned into two parts, α_1 and α_2. Consider the equation

$$(6.2) \qquad \begin{bmatrix} H_{11} & H_{12} \\ H_{21} & H_{22} \end{bmatrix} \begin{bmatrix} d\alpha_1 \\ d\alpha_2 \end{bmatrix} = \begin{bmatrix} 0 \\ 0 \end{bmatrix}$$

that is obtained by differentiating (6.1). The partitioning of H into two row blocks can be done in many different ways. Suppose, however, that there exists a partitioning such that H_{11} has full column rank and H_{12} is a matrix of zeros. If this is the case, $d\alpha_1$ has the unique solution zero even if the full matrix H does not have full column rank. Since multiplying (6.2) by a nonsingular matrix is permissible, the following result can be stated. If H factors into AB where A is nonsingular and B is of the form

$$\begin{bmatrix} B_{11} & 0 \\ B_{21} & B_{22} \end{bmatrix}$$

with B_{11} having full column rank, then α_1 is locally identifiable. If α_1 is identifiable, it may be estimated by an estimator whose covariance matrix is no less than the appropriate submatrix of $(H_1' R H_1)^{-1}$ where H_1 contains the independent columns of H, including all those associated with α_1.

7. A GENERALIZATION

If the two types of constraints considered in this chapter are combined, a more general treatment is possible. Suppose that, as before, the likelihood function is uniquely determined by a vector θ. Suppose, however, that in addition to the set of equations relating θ to α, there are also constraint equations on α. We have

$$(7.1) \qquad \begin{aligned} \theta_i &= h_i(\alpha) & (i = 1, \ldots, m) \\ \psi_i(\alpha) &= 0 & (i = 1, \ldots, k). \end{aligned}$$

Again assuming that all the functions are continuously twice differentiable, we form the Jacobian matrix

$$\begin{bmatrix} -I & H \\ 0 & \Psi \end{bmatrix}$$

where Ψ and H are the $k \times r$ and $m \times r$ matrices

$$\Psi = \left[\frac{\partial \psi_i}{\partial \alpha_j}\right], \qquad H = \left[\frac{\partial h_i}{\partial \alpha_j}\right].$$

The set of α vectors that satisfy the constraint equation $\psi(\alpha) = 0$ will be called the restricted structural parameter space and be denoted by A_ψ. If the k constraints are independent so that Ψ has full row rank when evaluated at the true α^0, then A_ψ is locally an $r - k$ dimensional manifold. We shall assume the Jacobian matrix for the system (7.1) has constant rank for all α in a neighborhood of α^0 in the restricted parameter space A_ψ.

With respect to the problem of parameter estimation, three general questions may be asked of this model: (1) Under what conditions is α identifiable and estimable? (2) When and by how much does the knowledge incorporated in h and ψ increase the efficiency of estimating θ? (3) What are efficient estimators of α and θ? These questions can be answered in terms of the matrix

(7.2)
$$\Phi = \begin{bmatrix} H \\ \Psi \end{bmatrix}$$

and in terms of a suitably bordered information matrix.

The true α^0 is a solution of (7.1) when θ equals the true value θ^0. Then α^0 will be locally identifiable if the vector equation $\Phi d\alpha = 0$ has the unique solution zero. That is, local identification occurs if Φ has full column rank r when evaluated at α^0. If in addition Ψ has full row rank k, then the bordered information matrix will possess an inverse having the form

$$\begin{bmatrix} R_n & 0 & -I & 0 \\ 0 & 0 & H' & \Psi' \\ -I & H & 0 & 0 \\ 0 & \Psi & 0 & 0 \end{bmatrix}^{-1} = \begin{bmatrix} \bar{N}_n & * & * & * \\ * & \bar{M}_n & * & * \\ * & * & * & * \\ * & * & * & * \end{bmatrix}$$

Suppose that α^0 is identifiable. Then using the methods of the preceding sections, we find that the covariance matrix for any unbiased estimator of θ and α must satisfy the following inequalities:

(7.3)
$$\text{Var } \hat{\theta} \geq \bar{N}_n = H\bar{M}_n H',$$
$$\text{Var } \hat{\alpha} \geq \bar{M}_n = C - C\Psi'(\Psi C\Psi')^{-1}\Psi C$$

where

(7.4) $C = (H'R_nH + \Psi'\Psi)^{-1}.$

Again, all matrices are evaluated at the true parameter α^0.

A special case occurs if Ψ is of the form

(7.5) $\Psi = [I_k \quad 0].$

In this case we assume that the first k elements of α are known exactly and the remaining elements are unconstrained. Substituting (7.5) into (7.3) and (7.4) we have, after a bit of algebra,

$$\overline{M}_n = (\overline{H}'R_n\overline{H})^{-1},$$
$$\overline{N}_n = \overline{H}(\overline{H}'R_n\overline{H})^{-1}\overline{H}'$$

where $\overline{H}$ is the matrix obtained by deleting the first k columns from H. This, of course, is the same result that was obtained in section 5.

In the special case (7.5) it is easy to verify that $\overline{N}_n$ has rank $r - k$. We can find the rank of $\overline{N}_n$ in general by the following argument. The restricted parameter space has the dimension of the space of vectors $d\theta$ satisfying

(7.6)
$$d\theta = H \, d\alpha$$
$$0 = \Psi \, d\alpha$$

where the matrices are evaluated at the true α^0. If Ψ has full row rank k, the set of $d\alpha$ satisfying the second equation of (7.6) has dimension $r - k$. Furthermore, the set of vectors $d\alpha$ satisfying $\Phi d\alpha = 0$ has dimension $r - \rho$ where ρ is the rank of Φ. Then, using the fact that the dimension of the range of a linear transformation is equal to the dimension of the domain less the dimension of the null space, we have the result that the dimension of permissible $d\theta$ is $\rho - k$. This is valid even if ρ is less than r and α is not identifiable.

Since the case considered here includes the cases presented in the earlier sections of this chapter, it is worth summarizing the results:

For the model defined by (7.1), we have under the previously described regularity conditions:

1) *The structural parameter vector α^0 is (at least) locally identifiable if the rank of Φ^0 equals r, the number of structural parameters. If the rank of Φ is constant in a neighborhood of α^0 in the restricted parameter set A_ψ, this rank condition is also necessary for local identification.*

2) *Suppose* Φ *has constant rank in a neighborhood of* α^0 *in* A_ψ. *The parameter space of* θ *is locally restricted to a manifold of less than m dimensions if and only if the rank of* Φ *is less than* $m + k$. *This will necessarily be the case if* $k > r - m$ (*i.e., if the number of independent constraints plus the number of* θ *parameters exceeds the number of structural parameters*). *If the parameter space is restricted, the minimal covariance matrix of an efficient constrained estimator is smaller than that of the unconstrained estimator, the difference being the positive semidefinite matrix*

$$R_n^{-1} - HC[C^{-1} - \Psi'(\Psi C\Psi')^{-1}\Psi]CH'$$

where C *is the inverse (or generalized inverse) of* $H'R_n H + \Psi'\Psi$. *If the inverse exists,* α *is locally identifiable and can be estimated with covariance matrix no less than*

$$C[C^{-1} - \Psi'(\Psi C\Psi')^{-1}\Psi]C.$$

3) *Unless* ψ *and h are linear in* α, *there is in general no estimator that is minimum variance unbiased. Asymptotically, however, both the constrained maximum-likelihood estimator and the constrained minimum-chi-square estimator are efficient as long as* α *is identifiable. The latter estimator is defined as the pair of functions* $\theta^*(y)$ *and* $\alpha^*(y)$ *that minimize*

$$(\theta - t)'R(\theta - t)$$

subject to the constraints

$$\theta = h(\alpha)$$

$$0 = \psi(\alpha)$$

where t is any estimator of θ *that is asymptotically efficient among the class of unconstrained estimators and where R is evaluated at* $\theta = t$.

8. SOME QUALIFICATIONS

The results of this chapter are for the most part applicable only for large samples. In general the finite-sample bounds will not be attainable. Unfortunately the accuracy of the asymptotic approximation is almost never known. A particularly interesting question arises in the case where the Cramér-Rao bound is attainable when no a priori information is present, but the modified bound is not attainable with the information. Suppose, for example, we wish to estimate the coefficient vector of the regression model (4.1). If no prior information is available, the least-squares estimator is best. If the prior information is in the form of a non-linear constraint equation, the bound P_n will not usually be attainable. But the maximum-likelihood estimator will have a sampling distribution which can be approximated by a distribution that has a covariance matrix P. Since P is smaller than R, one can conclude that the maximum-likelihood estimator $\hat{\beta}$ is better than the least-squares estimator b *as far as the approximation is valid*. But the properties of b are known exactly whereas the properties of $\hat{\beta}$ are known only approximately. It is possible that b is better than $\hat{\beta}$, that using the a priori information on the basis of large-sample theory actually makes things worse. Thus we have the choice of using the estimator b which has known properties or using $\hat{\beta}$ which for large n is definitely better but for small n is perhaps worse.

The answer depends, of course, on how close the approximation is. But it also depends on the loss function. If our loss function is really an unbounded quadratic function (which is the basis presumably for minimum variance estimates), then any estimator whose distribution has thick enough tails will be rejected because of infinite variance. Yet the maximum-likelihood estimator under constraint may very well have infinite variance for every sample size n but, for large n, be approximated by a distribution with finite variance. What is needed to analyze these questions is a more careful theory of the appropriate (truncated) loss function. This issue is touched on by CHERNOFF (1956) but the problem remains unsettled. Until these issues are better clarified in the statistical literature, all asymptotic results, including the ones given here, must be treated with caution. Nevertheless, it is probably useful to treat the asymptotic results as approximately valid until more evidence is available.

CHAPTER 3

Inexact Prior Information

1. INTRODUCTION

The use of exact equality restrictions is limited by the fact that in practice most prior information is vague. Often we are unwilling to place such strong restrictions on the parameter space. An alternative is to express the information in an inexact form. The Bayesian approach provides one way of doing this. By using a prior probability distribution to describe our feeling about the likely values of the parameter, we have great flexibility. Yet it is not necessary to leave the classical statistical framework to incorporate vague information. Inequality restrictions, for example, provide a means of describing imprecise knowledge without introducing subjective probabilities. Such restrictions are easy to formulate and can be made as loose or as tight as we desire. Although it is sometimes difficult to compute estimates which satisfy inequality constraints, they do provide a useful tool when the number of parameters is small.

A second way of incorporating inexact prior knowledge is by means of previous samples. Much of our prior knowledge about economic parameters comes from previous empirical research. If sufficient information about the past research is available, it can be incorporated into the analysis of current data. Indeed, since most economic research is based on previous studies, leaving out the past results is a poor statistical procedure. The intelligent use of past sample evidence can be very important in increasing the precision of estimates based on current samples. We shall begin our discussion of inexact prior information with a study of previous sample evidence. Sections 4 and 5 concern the problem of using inequality restrictions. The Bayesian analysis is delayed until chapter 6.

2. INFORMATION FROM PREVIOUS SAMPLES

Suppose that the statistician has available to him, in addition to the sample Y_n, another independent sample from which he obtains the estimator $\hat{\theta}$. Suppose further that the statistician knows that $\hat{\theta}$ is distributed according to the probability density $f_0(\hat{\theta}, \theta)$. That is, the probability law for $\hat{\theta}$ is a known function of the unknown parameter θ. Then the joint density function for Y_n and $\hat{\theta}$ is given by

$$(2.1) \qquad\qquad f(\hat{\theta}, y, \theta) = f_n(y, \theta) \cdot f_0(\hat{\theta}, \theta)$$

as long as Y_n and $\hat{\theta}$ are independently distributed.

If f_0 and f_n satisfy all the regularity conditions of section 1.3, then f will also. Thus, all the assumptions of the Cramér-Rao inequality are satisfied if we treat f as the density function for the sample $(Y_n, \hat{\theta})$. If the information matrix for f is denoted by $\bar{R}_n$, it follows from the multiplicative form of (2.1) that

$$(2.2) \qquad\qquad \bar{R}_n = R_n + R_0$$

where R_0 is the information matrix associated with f_0. Since all three matrices are positive definite, it follows that $R_n^{-1} - \bar{R}_n^{-1}$ is positive definite. Hence we have the result that the lower bound for the variance of an unbiased estimator is decreased when information from a previous sample is used.

The question of the attainability of the bound in finite samples is difficult to answer in general. Although it does not appear possible to specify easily interpretable necessary conditions for the attainability of the lower bound, an interesting set of sufficient conditions can be established. Recall that the Cramér-Rao bound can be attained if and only if f can be expressed in the form

$$(2.3) \qquad\qquad \frac{\partial \log f}{\partial \theta} = \bar{R}_n(t^* - \theta)$$

where t^* is an estimator independent of θ. Suppose that f_n and f_0 can be written as

$$(2.4) \qquad\qquad \frac{\partial \log f_n}{\partial \theta} = R_n(t - \theta),$$

$$\frac{\partial \log f_0}{\partial \theta} = R_0(s - \theta)$$

where t depends on Y_n and s depends on $\hat{\theta}$. That is, suppose that t is an MVB estimator of θ when only Y_n is available and that s is an MVB estimator when only $\hat{\theta}$ is available.

An expression for the logarithmic derivative of f is obtained by adding the two equations of (2.4):

$$\frac{\partial \log f}{\partial \theta} = \frac{\partial \log f_n}{\partial \theta} + \frac{\partial \log f_0}{\partial \theta}$$

(2.5)
$$= (R_n + R_0)[(R_n + R_0)^{-1}(R_n t + R_0 s) - \theta]$$
$$= \bar{R}_n(t^* - \theta).$$

Thus we have the required form as long as

(2.6)
$$t^* = (R_n + R_0)^{-1}(R_n t + R_0 s)$$

does not depend on θ. It is clear that t^* will be independent of θ if R_n and R_0 do not depend on θ. This is overly strong, however; it is sufficient that R_n and R_0 each factors into a matrix independent of θ and a common scalar which may depend on θ.

The above discussion may be summarized in the following extension of the classical Cramér-Rao inequality:

In the presence of stochastic prior information expressed by an independent estimator of θ, the matrix $\bar{R}_n^{-1} = (R_n + R_0)^{-1}$ is a lower bound for the covariance matrix of any unbiased estimator of θ. The bound is attainable if both f_n and f_0 can be written in the form (2.4) with R_n and R_0 not depending on θ (except perhaps for identical scalar multiples).

AN EXAMPLE

We consider again the normal regression model

(2.7)
$$y = X\beta + u$$

where y is an n-dimensional vector of observations on a random variable, X is an $n \times m$ matrix of nonstochastic variables, β is a vector of m unknown parameters, and u is a vector of n independent normal random errors with zero mean and covariance matrix $\sigma^2 I$. The likelihood function is

(2.8)
$$f_n(y, \beta, \sigma^2) = (2\pi\sigma^2)^{-\frac{1}{2}n} \exp\{-\tfrac{1}{2}\sigma^{-2}(y - X\beta)'(y - X\beta)\}.$$

Suppose now that there exists a previous sample *from the same process.* That is, the statistician has available an observation on an n_0-dimensional normal random vector y_0 and an $n_0 \times m$ matrix X_0 such that $\mathscr{E}[y_0] = X_0\beta$ and $\text{Var}[y_0] = \sigma^2 I$. The likelihood function for the sample y_0 will be of the same form as (2.8) with subscripts on y, n and X. The joint sample

(y, y_0) will have a normal density f such that

$$\frac{\partial \log f}{\partial \beta} = \frac{1}{\sigma^2} X'X(b - \beta) + \frac{1}{\sigma^2} X_0'X_0(b_0 - \beta)$$

$$= \frac{1}{\sigma^2}(X'X + X_0'X_0)(b^* - \beta),$$

$$\frac{\partial \log f}{\partial \sigma^2} = \frac{n + n_0}{2\sigma^4}\left[\frac{u'u + u_0'u_0}{n + n_0} - \sigma^2\right]$$

where $b^* = (X'X + X_0'X_0)^{-1}(X'y + X_0'y_0)$. Hence b^* is an MVB estimator of β with covariance matrix equal to the bound $\sigma^2(X'X + X_0'X_0)^{-1}$, the northwest submatrix of

$$(2.9) \qquad \bar{R}_n^{-1} = \begin{bmatrix} \sigma^2(X'X + X_0'X_0)^{-1} & 0 \\ 0 & \dfrac{2\sigma^4}{n + n_0} \end{bmatrix}.$$

The combined sample gives rise to an efficient estimator for β and an attainable Cramér-Rao bound because both samples come from the same stochastic process. If, however, the second sample came from a process with a different variance, b^* would depend on the unknown σ^2 and the bound would not be attainable. Prior information which is derived from a different stochastic process than that which produces the sample will in general not give rise to an estimator whose variance equals the lower bound.

AN ASYMPTOTIC RESULT

In order to complete the analysis of stochastic prior information, we turn to an extension of the asymptotic Cramér-Rao inequality. Defining the asymptotic information matrix for f by

$$(2.10) \qquad \bar{R} = \lim \frac{1}{n}\bar{R}_n = \lim \frac{1}{n}[R_n + R_0],$$

we can argue as above that, since $\bar{R}$ satisfies the same regularity conditions as R, the classical theorem applies. The only remaining question is the value of $\bar{R}$. This, of course, depends on the value of

$$(2.11) \qquad \lim \frac{1}{n}R_0.$$

If it is supposed that the prior information does not change as the sample Y_n gets larger, then R_0 is a fixed matrix and the limit in (2.11) is simply the zero matrix. As the sample gets larger, the prior information plays a smaller role. In the limit, it is of absolutely no value.

A more interesting case arises when the prior information is of the same order of magnitude as the sample information. In other words, it can be "assumed" that the limit in (2.11) is a positive definite matrix $\bar{R}_0$. This fiction should be interpreted as follows: We are interested in an approximation to $\bar{R}_n$ that is valid for "large" n. By "large" one means a sample size small enough to occur in practice, but large enough to make the approximation error reasonably small. For such a sample, R_0/n may very well be much larger than the approximation error. In such cases it is convenient to accept the fiction that R_0 is a function of n and that (2.11) possesses a nonzero limit $\bar{R}_0$. Then we can conclude that stochastic information reduces the bound for the asymptotic covariance matrix of a consistent estimator. These results can be summarized in the following:

In the presence of stochastic prior information expressed by an independent estimator, the matrix $\bar{R}^{-1}$ defined in (2.10) is essentially a lower bound for the asymptotic covariance matrix of any consistent estimator of θ. This lower bound is attained by the maximum-likelihood estimator (where f is the relevant likelihood function). The matrix $\bar{R}^{-1}$ differs from R^{-1} only if the prior information is of the same order of magnitude as the sample information. If the prior information is independent of n there is no gain in asymptotic efficiency.

3. Some Extensions

The preceding results depend on the assumption that $\hat{\theta}$ and Y_n are independently distributed. In practice this is not always the case. Current research often uses some of the data that was used in past research. Nevertheless, as long as the previous sample contains some independent information, it has value. If $\hat{\theta}$ and Y_n are dependent, (2.1) must be written as

$$(3.1) \qquad f(\hat{\theta}, y, \theta) = f_n(y, \theta) \cdot f_0(\hat{\theta}, y, \theta)$$

where f_0 is now interpreted as the conditional density of $\hat{\theta}$ given Y_n. The information matrix for f is still $R_n + R_0$ if R_0 is defined to be the expected conditional information matrix for $\hat{\theta}$. That is,

$$R_0 = -\mathscr{E}_y \mathscr{E}_{\hat{\theta}|y} \left[\frac{\partial^2 \log f_0}{\partial \theta_i \, \partial \theta_j} \right].$$

This matrix is necessarily positive semidefinite. It will be nonzero as long as the conditional density of $\hat{\theta}$ for given Y_n has a nonzero information matrix.

Another practical problem is that the previous and current samples may not depend on the same set of parameters. For example, cross-section and time-series data are both useful in estimating demand equations. But a model developed for the cross-section data will contain some parameters that do not appear in the time-series model, and vice versa. It is useful to modify our analysis to include this case. Let θ_1 be a vector of parameters relevant only to the current sample. Let θ_2 be a vector of parameters relevant to both samples. Let θ_3 be a vector of parameters relevant only to the previous sample. Then the joint density (assuming independence) is

(3.2) $$f_n(y, \theta_1, \theta_2) \cdot f_0(\hat{\theta}_2, \hat{\theta}_3, \theta_2, \theta_3).$$

If we define the two information matrices in terms of the combined vector $\theta = (\theta_1, \theta_2, \theta_3)$, there will be blocks of zeros whenever a particular parameter does not appear in the density. For example, R_n and R_0 can be expressed in partitioned matrix form as

$$R_n = \begin{bmatrix} A_{11} & A_{12} & 0 \\ A_{21} & A_{22} & 0 \\ 0 & 0 & 0 \end{bmatrix}, \qquad R_0 = \begin{bmatrix} 0 & 0 & 0 \\ 0 & B_{22} & B_{23} \\ 0 & B_{32} & B_{33} \end{bmatrix}.$$

We are interested in the upper left part of $(R_n + R_0)^{-1}$ since that is the lower bound for the covariance matrix of efficient estimates of the parameters (θ_1, θ_2) relevant to the current sample. Using again the notation for partitioned matrices, we wish to have an expression for the northwest corner of

$$(R_n + R_0)^{-1} = \begin{bmatrix} A_{11} & A_{12} & 0 \\ A_{21} & A_{22} + B_{22} & B_{23} \\ 0 & B_{32} & B_{33} \end{bmatrix}^{-1}.$$

Upon application of the rules for inverting partitioned matrices we find that the covariance bound for (θ_1, θ_2) is

$$\begin{bmatrix} A_{11} & A_{12} \\ A_{21} & A_{22} + C \end{bmatrix}^{-1}$$

where C is the matrix $B_{22} - B_{23}B_{33}^{-1}B_{32}$. If θ_2 and θ_3 are relevant to f_0 and identifiable, then C will necessarily be positive definite. In that case the prior information is valuable in lowering the covariance for θ_2. Furthermore, if A_{12} is not zero, then the prior information helps in estimating θ_1 as well as θ_2. (This despite the fact that the information is not directly relevant to θ_1.)

In all of our discussion in the past two sections we have assumed that the likelihood function f_0 describes the probability law of some actual sample. Some authors, however, have suggested that f_0 might be used to describe prior information that is obtained from *any* source. Suppose, for example, a statistician has inexact information about θ that arises from introspection. He might feel that his information is equivalent (in the sense of being just as convincing) as that obtained in a sample having likelihood f_0. Thus, he might use the above analysis even though f_0 reflects no actual sample but merely his subjective beliefs. This approach is due to THEIL AND GOLDBERGER (1961), who use the name "mixed estimation" to describe their procedure for combining subjective information and data. By expressing subjective beliefs in the form of pseudosamples, it is possible to incorporate probabilistic subjective information without using the formal apparatus of Bayesian decision theory. Whether there is any advantage to this approach over the Bayesian one remains to be seen.

4. INEQUALITY CONSTRAINTS

Perhaps the simplest way to express a priori information about an unknown parameter vector is by means of a set of inequalities. For example, we might know that θ_1 is greater than zero and that θ_2 lies between zero and one. This information can be expressed by the system of linear inequalities

$$\begin{bmatrix} 1 & 0 \\ 0 & 1 \\ 0 & -1 \end{bmatrix} \begin{bmatrix} \theta_1 \\ \theta_2 \end{bmatrix} > \begin{bmatrix} 0 \\ 0 \\ -1 \end{bmatrix},$$

which is a special case of the general matrix form $B\theta > b$. There is no need, however, to restrict ourselves to linear inequalities. The quadratic inequality $\theta_1^2 + \theta_2^2 < 1$ might naturally arise in the study of dynamic systems where the prior knowledge is that the system is stable. Thus, we shall use the term "inequality constraint" to mean any information that reduces the parameter space A to a full-dimensional subset of A. More precisely, we assume that the inequalities describe a set A^* which is either open or is an open set augmented by some of its boundary points. We exclude only those sets that have lower dimensionality than the original parameter space. Given this definition of inequality constraints, we now explore the gain in efficiency that can result from using such constraints in estimation procedures.

Since inequality information surely has value, it would seem that the use of inequality constraints should reduce the Cramér-Rao lower bound for the variance of an unbiased estimator. In fact, however, this is not the case. The Cramér-Rao inequality was derived for an arbitrary full-dimensional parameter space A. Since the lower bound does not depend on the parameter space, restricting it to A^* cannot lower the bound. A similar argument also applies to the asymptotic Cramér-Rao inequality. Putting this more formally we have:

Despite the presence of a priori information that restricts θ to a subset of A, the lower bound for the variance of an unbiased estimator of θ remains R_n^{-1} as long as the restricted parameter space has full dimension. Furthermore, the unconstrained maximum-likelihood estimator remains asymptotically efficient with covariance matrix R^{-1}.

In other words, inequality constraints are of no value in increasing efficiency as long as the requirement that estimators be unbiased is maintained. Furthermore, even if the assumption of unbiasedness is dropped, it remains true that, asymptotically, inequality constraints do not help. For large n the probability that the maximum-likelihood estimator violates the constraints is almost zero; hence there is nothing to gain by maximizing subject to constraint.[1]

To interpret the above to mean that inequality constraints are worthless would be a serious error. Rather, it points out that the classical theory, which is based on unbiasedness on the one hand and asymptotic approximations on the other, has important weaknesses. Nonstochastic prior information, according to this theory, increases efficiency only if it reduces the dimensionality of the parameter space. Since inequality constraints do not reduce dimensionality, they cannot increase efficiency. But this result crucially depends on the use of unbiasedness in the classical definition of efficiency. A quite different answer is obtained if we evaluate estimators (biased or not) on the basis of mean square error. Although there is no general theory of estimation available when the unbiasedness assumption is dropped, it is possible to make some statements concerning the improvement of estimation precision with inequality constraints using the mean square error criterion.

1. This argument is valid only if the true θ^0 is an interior point of A^*. However, since the boundary of A^* has zero measure, the asymptotic Cramér-Rao inequality is still relevant.

A natural multiparameter measure of the dispersion of an estimator around the true value is the mean square error matrix

(4.1) $$\mathscr{E}(t - \theta)(t - \theta)'.$$

If t is unbiased, this is simply the covariance matrix. An estimator s could be said to be better than an estimator t if the difference in their mean square error matrices were negative definite. This would imply that s had lower expected loss for any quadratic loss function; that is,

(4.2) $$\mathscr{E}(s - \theta)'Q(s - \theta) \leq \mathscr{E}(t - \theta)'Q(t - \theta)$$

for all possible θ and all positive semidefinite Q. One is tempted to try to find Cramér-Rao type bounds using the mean square error matrix in place of the covariance matrix. This turns out not to be fruitful since the only lower bound is the zero matrix. However, it is still possible to compare any two estimators using the mean square error criterion.

AN IMPROVED ESTIMATOR

Suppose t is an unbiased estimator of θ that does not use the inequality information. Its mean square error matrix must be at least as large as R_n^{-1}. If we can construct an estimator s that uses the inequality information and has a mean square error matrix less than R_n^{-1}, then we will have demonstrated that the information has value. Unfortunately, it does not seem possible in general to construct such an estimator. However, if we allow the estimator to depend on the weight matrix Q, it is possible to find an estimator which has lower expected loss than any other estimator t which does not use the information.

Consider the estimator z which is defined as that point in (or on the boundary of) A^* that is closest to t using the metric Q. That is, z is the solution of

(4.3) $$\underset{\theta \in \bar{A}}{\text{minimize}}\,(t - \theta)'Q(t - \theta)$$

where $\bar{A}$ is the closure of A^*. If A^* is convex, then the problem defined by (4.3) has a unique solution. In general it will depend on the set A^* and on the matrix Q. We have the following result:

If A^* is convex, the estimator z is better than the estimator t in the sense that

$$\mathscr{E}[(z - \theta)'Q(z - \theta)] \leq \mathscr{E}[(t - \theta)'Q(t - \theta)]$$

for all θ in A^*. Furthermore, the inequality is strict if Q is nonsingular and $\Pr[t \in \bar{A}]$ is not equal to one.

The assumption that A^* is convex is crucial. If A^* is not convex, there is no way to use the prior information which necessarily is an improvement over ignoring it. Although restrictive, the assumption of convexity is often met in practice. Linear inequalities, for example, always give rise to convex sets. Finding the estimator z will often be a difficult problem. In two dimensions graphical methods are possible. In higher dimensions quadratic programming techniques can be used if the constraints are linear inequalities. In general, however, it will not be easy to find z.

It should be noted that z is not necessarily an optimal estimator. All we can show is that it is better than t. Its major weakness is that it depends on the matrix Q. Two statisticians with the same data and the same constraints need not obtain the same estimate if they weight the various components of error differently. This is in contrast to the classical case of unbiased estimation where the weight function never enters the solution.

To prove the result consider first the following:

LEMMA. *Let $\bar{A}$ be a closed convex set in n-dimensional Euclidean space. Let d be a distance function. Let t be a point exterior to $\bar{A}$ and let z be a point in $\bar{A}$ such that*

$$(4.4) \qquad\qquad d(z, t) \le d(s, t)$$

for all points s in $\bar{A}$. Then,

$$(4.5) \qquad\qquad d(z, \theta) < d(t, \theta)$$

for all θ in $\bar{A}$.

Proof. Suppose the lemma is false and that y is a point in $\bar{A}$ such that $d(z, y) \ge d(t, y)$. Then let r be that point on the line segment zy such that $d(r, y) = d(t, y)$. Due to the convexity of $\bar{A}$, r is in $\bar{A}$ and hence r is distinct from t. Construct the triangle (see figure 3.1) that has vertices at r, t, and y.

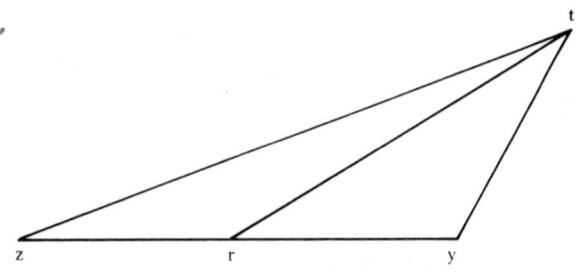

FIGURE 3.1

Since $d(t, y) = d(r, y)$ the angle *try* must be strictly less than 90°. (It may even be zero if r, t, and y are collinear.) Hence the angle *zrt* must necessarily be greater than 90°. Thus the line segment zt is the longest side of the obtuse triangle *ztr*. But this means that r is a point in $\bar{A}$ such that $d(r, t) < d(z, t)$. Since the assumption that $d(z, y) \geq d(t, y)$ leads to the violation of (4.4), we must conclude that no such point y exists.

This lemma can be applied to the case considered in our proposition. If Q is nonsingular, we may let the distance function be

(4.6) $$d(s, \theta) = (s - \theta)'Q(s - \theta).$$

Then the point z defined by (4.3) satisfies (4.4). Since $\bar{A}$ is convex, it follows that

(4.7) $$(t - \theta)'Q(t - \theta) > (z - \theta)'Q(z - \theta)$$

as long as t is exterior to $\bar{A}$. If this occurs with positive probability, then

$$\mathscr{E}[(t - \theta)'Q(t - \theta)] > \mathscr{E}[(z - \theta)'Q(z - \theta)]$$

and the proposition is proved. If Q is singular, then (4.6) is not strictly a distance function. However, the argument is still valid if the strict inequality in (4.7) is replaced by a weak inequality.

5. The Linear Model with Inequality Restrictions

Up to this point we have always assumed that the statistician knew, except for a few unknown parameters, the probability density function for the random sample. Without this assumption we can say little about efficient estimation procedures, with or without prior information. However, in the case of the linear regression model it is possible to prove some results without specifying the mathematical form of the density. Therefore we shall in this section digress slightly and discuss the problem of using inequality restrictions in the regression model where the error distribution is not specified. In that case we are naturally led to the constrained least-squares estimator.

The problem of estimating the parameters of the linear regression model with inequality constraints has been discussed by ZELLNER (1961), JUDGE AND TAKAYAMA (1966), and others. These authors have typically considered only linear inequalities, but the theory holds for the more general case of any convex constrained parameter space. Most of the previous literature is concerned with the computational problem of minimizing the sum of squared residuals when the estimator is constrained to satisfy the inequalities. When the inequalities are linear, this turns out to be a quadratic programming problem. There seems to be little known about the optimality properties of this constrained estimator. A few examples have been presented to show that the constrained estimator has lower mean square error than the unconstrained estimator. One might conjecture that this is so under general conditions. The following example demonstrates that this is false.

THE BEST LINEAR UNBIASED ESTIMATOR

Let y be a vector of n random variables that can be written in the form

$$(5.1) \qquad\qquad y = X\beta + u$$

where X is an $n \times m$ matrix of fixed numbers and β is an m-dimensional vector of unknown parameters. The n-dimensional random error term u has mean zero and covariance matrix $\sigma^2 I$. Without loss of generality we may assume $\sigma = 1$. The matrix X has full rank m. The unrestricted parameter space for β is E^m.

If there were no further restrictions, the best linear unbiased estimator of β would be obtained (according to the Gauss-Markov theorem) by minimizing the sum of squared residuals. For any arbitrary estimator $\hat{\beta}$ this sum may be written as

$$(5.2) \qquad S = (y - X\hat{\beta})'(y - X\hat{\beta}) = (b - \hat{\beta})'X'X(b - \hat{\beta}) + y'My$$

where $b = (X'X)^{-1}X'y$ and $M = I - X(X'X)^{-1}X'$. If $\hat{\beta}$ is unrestricted, S is minimized by the least-squares estimator b. This estimator has an expected value equal to β and a covariance matrix equal to $(X'X)^{-1}$.

The least-squares estimator b is best in the sense that it has the "smallest" covariance matrix out of the class of linear unbiased estimators. That is, if $\hat{\beta}$ is linear in y and has expectation equal to β, then its covariance matrix V will satisfy the inequality

$$c'Vc \geq c'(X'X)^{-1}c$$

for arbitrary vector c. Alternatively, we may describe the optimality of b by noting that, among the class of linear unbiased estimators, it minimizes

$$(5.3) \qquad\qquad \mathscr{E}(\hat{\beta} - \beta)'Q(\hat{\beta} - \beta)$$

for all positive semidefinite matrices Q. These are equivalent statements and are summarized as: b is the best linear unbiased estimator.

Suppose the statistician has information that β lies in A^*, some nonempty convex subset of E^m. We shall assume that A^* has full dimension m.

Linear inequalities, of course, give rise to such a set. Suppose that the a priori information is correct; that is, β does in fact lie in A^*. The question then is to find the best way of using the information.

Since the least-squares estimator does not use the fact that β lies in A^*, one would think that a better estimator could be found. If we use the traditional criteria, this is not true. We have the following proposition:

Despite the presence of a priori information that restricts the parameter space, the unconstrained least-squares estimator b remains best linear unbiased as long as the restricted parameter space has full dimension.

This proposition follows from the standard proof of the Gauss-Markov theorem. Any linear estimator can be written in the form

$$\hat{\beta} = b + Cy = b + CX\beta + Cu.$$

If $\hat{\beta}$ is to be unbiased, we must have $CX\beta = 0$ for all β in the restricted parameter space A^*. Since A^* contains an open subset, this implies $CX = 0$. A little algebra yields the expression

$$\mathcal{E}(\hat{\beta} - \beta)(\hat{\beta} - \beta)' = (X'X)^{-1} + CC'.$$

Hence the best estimator is still obtained by setting $C = 0$.

CONSTRAINED LEAST SQUARES

The previous argument depends on the fact that only local unbiasedness is used in the Gauss-Markov theorem. Thus our result is exactly the same as that found in section 4. It is natural, then, to proceed as we did there and to drop the unbiasedness assumption and evaluate estimators by the mean square error criterion. And a natural estimator to examine is the constrained least-squares estimator.

Let $\bar{A}$ be the closure of the set A^*. Then we may define the constrained least-squares estimator as that function of the sample that minimizes the sum of squared residuals S subject to the constraint that the estimator lies in $\bar{A}$. If A^* is convex, then there will exist a unique solution b^* to the problem. Using (5.2) we may write the problem as

$$(5.4) \qquad \underset{\hat{\beta} \in \bar{A}}{\text{minimize}}\ (\hat{\beta} - b)'X'X(\hat{\beta} - b).$$

If b satisfies the constraints, then the constrained least-squares estimator b^* equals b. If b violates the constraints, then b^* lies on the boundary of the constraint set. The constrained least-squares estimator may be interpreted as a minimum-distance estimator where distance is defined in terms of the least-squares precision matrix $X'X$.

It is natural to suppose that the constrained least-squares estimator is necessarily better than the unconstrained estimator. This however is not true. We have the following rather surprising result given by LOVELL AND PRESCOTT (1970) and ROTHENBERG (1968):

The constrained least-squares estimator can, for some β and some loss matrix Q, be worse than the unconstrained estimator b.

A simple example demonstrates this proposition. Although it is highly artificial, the example does satisfy all of the traditional least-squares assumptions. Let y, u, and β all be two-dimensional vectors and let X be given by

$$X = \begin{bmatrix} 1 & 1 \\ 1 & -1 \end{bmatrix}, \qquad X'X = \begin{bmatrix} 2 & 0 \\ 0 & 2 \end{bmatrix}.$$

Suppose u_1 and u_2 are independent random variables, each having the same two-point distribution

$$\Pr[u_i = 1] = \tfrac{1}{2}, \qquad \Pr[u_i = -1] = \tfrac{1}{2}.$$

It is simple to verify that $\mathscr{E}u = 0$ and $\mathscr{E}uu' = I$.

The ordinary least-squares estimator for this problem is

$$\begin{bmatrix} b_1 \\ b_2 \end{bmatrix} = \tfrac{1}{2}\begin{bmatrix} y_1 + y_2 \\ y_1 - y_2 \end{bmatrix} = \begin{bmatrix} \beta_1 \\ \beta_2 \end{bmatrix} + \tfrac{1}{2}\begin{bmatrix} 1 & 1 \\ 1 & -1 \end{bmatrix}\begin{bmatrix} u_1 \\ u_2 \end{bmatrix}.$$

If it is known that

(5.5) $2\beta_1 + \beta_2 \leq 1$,

then the constrained least-squares estimator is found by minimizing

$$(b_1 - \beta_1)^2 + (b_2 - \beta_2)^2$$

for β satisfying (5.5). Suppose the true parameter vector is $\beta = (0, 0)$. Then the sample space for the least-squares estimator (b_1, b_2) is given by the four points $(1, 0)$, $(0, 1)$, $(-1, 0)$, and $(0, -1)$. Each point occurs with probability of one-fourth. Only the first point violates the constraints. Solving the constrained least-squares problem for $b = (1, 0)$ we obtain the value $b^* = (0.6, -0.2)$. Thus, the constrained least-squares estimator has a sample space given by the four points $(0.6, -0.2)$, $(0, 1)$, $(-1, 0)$, and

$(0, -1)$. By simple calculation we obtain the mean square error matrices

$$M = \mathscr{E}[(b - \beta)(b - \beta)'] = \begin{bmatrix} 0.50 & 0 \\ 0 & 0.50 \end{bmatrix},$$

$$M^* = \mathscr{E}[(b^* - \beta)(b^* - \beta)'] = \begin{bmatrix} 0.34 & -0.03 \\ -0.03 & 0.51 \end{bmatrix}.$$

Comparing M and M^*, we see that using the constraint lowers substantially the mean square error for β_1 but raises slightly the mean square error for β_2. Thus $M - M^*$ is not positive semidefinite. If our loss matrix Q puts most of its weight on β_2, then the constrained estimator is worse than the unconstrained estimator.

Although this example is very special, it does illustrate the basic point: When inequality restrictions are present, constrained least squares may be worse than unconstrained least squares. It should be emphasized that the assumption of a discrete distribution for u is not crucial to the argument; a smooth density function with two rather peaked modes at $+1$ and -1 gives the same result. Also, the fact that there are no degrees of freedom is inconsequential. These assumptions were made to simplify the arithmetic.

Although the above example satisfies all the traditional least-squares assumptions, it is obviously not typical. The question remains whether in practice such cases will ever occur. It appears that as the probability distribution for b becomes smoother and more bell-shaped, it becomes more difficult to construct cases where b is better than b^*. If one assumes that the errors are normally distributed, no such paradoxical example seems possible. As a general proposition it appears that, if b is normally distributed and A^* is convex, the constrained estimator b^* is necessarily better than b. If this is the case, then there is little chance in practice of having b^* worse than b. For moderately large samples, b will be approximately normal and the paradoxical case ruled out. Thus, constrained least squares is probably a good estimation method in practice. Finally, we note that our counterexample cannot occur when β is a scalar. Thus, in the one-parameter case we can conclude that constrained least squares is an improvement over ordinary least squares. As we have seen, this does not generalize to the case of multiparameter estimation.

The constrained least-squares estimator does not make use of any loss function or of any special properties of the error distribution. It depends only on the data and the constraint set A^*. If we modified our estimator to take the weight matrix Q into account, we could always find an improvement over the unconstrained least-squares estimator. Suppose we define the alternative estimator b^{**}, which is the solution of the problem

$$\text{minimize}_{\hat{\beta} \in \bar{A}} (\hat{\beta} - b)' Q (\hat{\beta} - b).$$

This estimator does not have the property of minimizing the sum of squared residuals S and therefore is not properly a constrained least-squares estimator. It is, however, an estimator that uses the prior information and, for a quadratic loss function with weight matrix Q, has lower expected loss than the unconstrained least-squares estimator. This follows directly from our results in section 4.

6. SUMMARY

We have seen in these two chapters how a priori information can be incorporated into the classical theory of estimation. In most cases both finite-sample and asymptotic results were possible. Unfortunately, the last case pointed out the difficulty of the classical approach. Finite-sample results depend crucially on the unbiasedness assumption, a criterion that is not easily defended. Asymptotic results are necessarily only approximately valid in application and the accuracy of the approximation is almost never known. Thus the results of this chapter, like all those of classical statistics, must not be overstated. We shall return to a discussion of the usefulness of the classical approach to inference in Chapter 6.

Our analysis of the general theory of constrained estimation is now completed. Of the various classical ways of expressing a priori information that have been discussed, perhaps the most interesting to econometricians is the use of constraint parameters. This is because the celebrated "simultaneous equations problem" is an example of this case. It is on this important example that the remaining chapters of our study will concentrate.

CHAPTER 4

Efficient Estimation of Simultaneous Equation Systems

1. INTRODUCTION

One of the important stochastic models used in econometric research is the system of linear equations commonly known as the simultaneous equations model. This model, in its simplest form, relates a vector of random variables y linearly to a vector of predetermined variables x and an additive random error vector u:

$$By + \Gamma x = u.$$

The matrices B and Γ are unknown parameters; the error vector u is usually assumed to be normally distributed with mean zero and covariance matrix Σ. A major econometric problem is to estimate the structural parameters B, Γ, and Σ (or certain functions of them) based on a random sample on x and y. In particular, often the aim is to estimate the so-called reduced-form parameters $\Pi = -B^{-1}\Gamma$ and $\Omega = B^{-1}\Sigma B'^{-1}$ which completely characterize the conditional distribution of y given x.

If B, Γ, and Σ are entirely unknown, the statistical analysis of the model is elementary. The structural parameters are unidentified and cannot be estimated; the reduced-form parameters can be estimated by the method of least squares which yields minimum-variance unbiased estimates. However, the traditional treatment of the simultaneous equations model usually assumes that certain elements of B, Γ, and Σ are known a priori and need not be estimated. In this case, if enough structural information is known, it is possible to estimate B, Γ, and Σ; furthermore, it is possible to use the information to obtain reduced-form estimates more efficient than those given by least squares.

In its traditional form, the simultaneous equations problem is a special case of the following general statistical problem: We wish to estimate an unknown parameter vector θ that determines the probability distribution of a set of sample data; however, it is known a priori that θ belongs to some lower-dimensional subset of the possible parameter space. (In the simultaneous equations model, θ consists of the elements of Π and Ω; the restrictions on θ result from the a priori information on B, Γ, and Σ.) This, of course, is the general problem that we examined in chapter 2. Our purpose here is to apply the earlier analysis to the simultaneous equations problem in an attempt to give a unified classical treatment of that topic. The value of overidentifying restrictions in increasing the efficiency of reduced-form estimation is analyzed in some detail. In addition, the well-known identification problem is viewed in a new light. In chapter 7 we shall return to the simultaneous equations problem and analyze it from a Bayesian point of view.

2. THE MODEL*

Let y_t be a G-dimensional vector of random endogenous variables which are related to the K-dimensional vector of predetermined variables x_t by a system of G linear equations with additive random errors u_t:

$$(2.1) \qquad\qquad By_t + \Gamma x_t = u_t.$$

The $G \times G$ matrix B and the $G \times K$ matrix Γ contain unknown parameters which are to be estimated from the sample that consists of n observations on the $G + K$ variables y_t and x_t. The matrix B is assumed to be non-singular. The error vectors $u_1, \ldots, u_n$ are assumed to be independently distributed normal random variables each with mean vector zero and nonsingular covariance matrix Σ. The assumption that Σ is nonsingular means that the equation system (2.1) can contain no identities. This assumption is made solely for the ease of exposition. The derivations that follow are easily modified to include systems containing identities (see appendix B).

The predetermined variables x_t are characterized by the fact that they are distributed independently of the error vectors u_s for $t \leq s$. That is, the errors are independent of current and past values of the predetermined variables. The predetermined variables may be generated by a completely different process from that which generates the errors (in which case they are called exogenous variables) or they may be past values of the endo-

---

* For a more complete description of the model, see KOOPMANS, RUBIN, AND LEIPNIK (1950). Our approach follows closely the methods used in this classic article. Indeed a major part of this chapter consists of rederiving and finding an explicit expression for their equation (3.127). An alternative derivation of some of the results that follow may be found in ROTHENBERG AND LEENDERS (1964).

genous variables which happen to be distributed independently of the future errors.

Since B is nonsingular, the structural form (2.1) may be written in the reduced form

(2.2)
$$y_t = -B^{-1}\Gamma x_t + B^{-1}u_t$$
$$= \Pi x_t + v_t$$

where Π is a $G \times K$ matrix and v_t is a normally distributed vector with mean zero and nonsingular covariance matrix Ω. The reduced-form parameters (Π, Ω) are related to the structural parameters (B, Γ, Σ) by the equations

(2.3)
$$\Pi = -B^{-1}\Gamma$$
$$\Omega = B^{-1}\Sigma B'^{-1}.$$

The joint conditional density function for $y_1, y_2, \ldots, y_n$ given $x_1, x_2, \ldots, x_n$ is[1]

(2.4) $f(y, \Pi, \Omega) = (2\pi)^{-\frac{1}{2}nG}|\Omega|^{-\frac{1}{2}n} \exp\left\{-\frac{1}{2}\sum_t (y_t - \Pi x_t)'\Omega^{-1}(y_t - \Pi x_t)\right\}.$

This can be written more conveniently in terms of the observation matrices X, an $n \times K$ matrix of observations on the K predetermined variables, and Y, an $n \times G$ matrix of observations on the G endogenous variables. We shall assume that

$$X'X = \sum_{t=1}^{n} x_t x_t',$$

the matrix of sums of squares and cross products of the predetermined variables, is nonsingular. The density function can then be written in logarithmic form as

(2.5)
$$\log f = \kappa - \tfrac{1}{2}n \log \det \Omega - \tfrac{1}{2} \text{tr}[\Omega^{-1}(Y' - \Pi X')(Y - X\Pi')]$$
$$= \kappa - \tfrac{1}{2}n \log \det \Omega - \tfrac{1}{2} \text{tr}\, \Omega^{-1}[(\Pi - P)X'X(\Pi - P)' + nS]$$

---

1. More precisely, (2.4) is the conditional density for the endogenous variables given those elements of $x_1, \ldots, x_n$ that are either exogenous or lagged values y_t with $t \leq 0$. For a derivation of (2.4) see KOOPMANS, RUBIN, AND LEIPNIK (1950), pp. 72–73.

where κ is a constant and P and S are the matrices

$$P = Y'X(X'X)^{-1}$$

(2.6)

$$S = \frac{1}{n}Y'[I - X(X'X)^{-1}X']Y.$$

The probability law for the endogenous variables (given X) is uniquely determined by the parameter matrices (Π, Ω). Yet for any pair (Π^0, Ω^0) there are an infinite set of different matrices (B, Γ, Σ) that satisfy (2.3) Hence the structure is not identifiable unless some a priori constraints are placed on the parameters. We shall concentrate on the case where the identification restrictions take the form of knowing specific elements of B, Γ, and Σ. The case of more general restrictions is treated briefly in section 8. Knowledge of specific elements of (B, Γ, Σ) will be referred to as a "zero-order" restrictions. The knowledge that a given element of $(B, \Gamma, \Sigma$ is *zero* will be called a homogeneous zero-order restriction. The knowledge that a parameter is a given *nonzero* number will be called a nonhomogeneous zero-order restriction.

Let α be a column vector consisting of those elements of (B, Γ, Σ) that are *not* known a priori. We assume that α may take on any real value such that B is nonsingular. Let θ be a vector consisting of *all* the elements of (Π, Ω). Then (2.3) is a set of equations of the form

(2.7) $\theta = h(\alpha),$

and (2.4) is a probability function expressed in terms of θ alone. We are therefore in a position to apply the results of chapter 2 concerning the efficient estimation of the basic parameters θ and the constraint parameter α. Specifically, the purpose of the present chapter is to use the general theory of constrained estimation to answer the following questions: (1 What increase in efficiency is gained in estimating the reduced-form parameters θ by imposing the restrictions (2.7)? (2) Of what value are restrictions on the elements of Σ? (3) When will the structural parameters be identifiable? (4) What methods of estimation yield efficient estimates of and α?

It will be convenient to distinguish between those elements of α and θ that refer to the coefficients (B, Γ, Π) and those elements that refer to the covariance matrices (Σ, Ω). Hence, the column vectors α and θ are partitioned as

(2.8) $\alpha = \begin{bmatrix} \delta \\ \sigma \end{bmatrix}, \qquad \theta = \begin{bmatrix} \pi \\ \omega \end{bmatrix}$

where δ is an r-dimensional vector of all the *unknown* elements of B and Γ; σ is an r^*-dimensional vector of all the *unknown* elements of Σ; π is a GK-dimensional vector of all the elements of Π; and ω is a G^2-dimensional vector of all the elements of Ω.[2]

When forming vectors out of the elements of matrices, we must specify the order in which the elements are listed. It will be convenient to follow the convention of first taking the elements of the first row, then the elements of the second row, then the elements of the third row, etc. Any matrix element that is known a priori will simply be omitted. Let π_i be the transpose of the ith row of Π and let ω_i be the transpose of the ith row of Ω. Let β_i, γ_i, and σ_i be column vectors consisting of the *unknown* elements of the ith row of B, Γ, and Σ, respectively. Then π, ω, δ, and σ may be written as

$$\pi = \begin{bmatrix} \pi_1 \\ \cdot \\ \cdot \\ \cdot \\ \pi_G \end{bmatrix}, \quad \omega = \begin{bmatrix} \omega_1 \\ \cdot \\ \cdot \\ \cdot \\ \omega_G \end{bmatrix}, \quad \delta = \begin{bmatrix} \delta_1 \\ \cdot \\ \cdot \\ \delta_G \end{bmatrix}, \quad \sigma = \begin{bmatrix} \sigma_1 \\ \cdot \\ \cdot \\ \sigma_G \end{bmatrix}$$

where δ_i is the vector of unknown coefficients in the ith structural equation:

$$\delta_i = \begin{bmatrix} \beta_i \\ \gamma_i \end{bmatrix}.$$

In this study we shall concentrate on the efficient estimation of δ and π, treating σ and ω as nuisance parameters.

3. Efficient Estimation: Structural Restrictions Ignored

Before examining the usual situation where a number of structural parameters are known a priori, we shall first consider the case where B, Γ, and Σ are completely unrestricted. In this case structural estimation is impossible since the structure is not identified. Furthermore, equations (2.3) impose no restrictions on the reduced-form parameter space. Thus the density (2.4) may be considered as the likelihood function for (Π, Ω) with the structure completely ignored.

In order to study the efficiency of unconstrained reduced-form estimation, we need only to recall the general results of classical estimation theory

2. Due to symmetry there are really only $\frac{1}{2}G(G+1)$ different unknown elements of Ω. However, as explained in appendix A, the derivations that follow are considerably simplified if the symmetry is ignored. The final results are not affected by this convenient simplification.

presented in chapter 1. By the Cramér-Rao inequality, a lower bound to the covariance matrix of any unbiased estimator of θ that does not use a priori restrictions is given by R_n^{-1} where

$$(3.1) \qquad R_n = -\mathcal{E}\left[\frac{\partial^2 \log f}{\partial \theta_i \, \partial \theta_j}\right]$$

is the information matrix for f. Furthermore, a lower bound to the *asymptotic* covariance matrix of any consistent estimator of θ is given by R^{-1} where

$$(3.2) \qquad R = \lim_{n \to \infty} \frac{1}{n} R_n$$

is the asymptotic information matrix. Under independent sampling and certain regularity conditions the maximum-likelihood and minimum-chi-square estimators are asymptotically efficient; that is, their asymptotic covariance matrices are equal to the lower bound R^{-1}.

The information matrix for the reduced-form parameters can be derived from (2.5). The details are given in appendix A. Partitioning according to π and ω, we obtain the square matrix of order $GK + G^2$

$$
R_n = -\mathcal{E}
\begin{bmatrix}
\dfrac{\partial^2 \log f}{\partial \pi \, \partial \pi'} & \dfrac{\partial^2 \log f}{\partial \pi \, \partial \omega'} \\[2ex]
\dfrac{\partial^2 \log f}{\partial \omega \, \partial \pi'} & \dfrac{\partial^2 \log f}{\partial \omega \, \partial \omega'}
\end{bmatrix}
$$

$$(3.3)$$

$$
= \begin{bmatrix}
\Omega^{-1} \otimes \mathcal{M}_n & 0 \\
0 & \frac{1}{2}n(\Omega^{-1} \otimes \Omega^{-1})
\end{bmatrix}
$$

where $\otimes$ represents the Kronecker product and where $\mathcal{M}_n = \mathcal{E}(X'X)$. The asymptotic information matrix is given by

$$(3.4) \qquad R = \begin{bmatrix} R_{11} & R_{12} \\ R_{21} & R_{22} \end{bmatrix} = \begin{bmatrix} \Omega^{-1} \otimes \mathcal{M} & 0 \\ 0 & \frac{1}{2}(\Omega^{-1} \otimes \Omega^{-1}) \end{bmatrix}$$

where

$$(3.5) \qquad \mathcal{M} = \lim \frac{1}{n} \mathcal{M}_n = \lim \frac{1}{n} \mathcal{E}(X'X).$$

We shall assume that the stochastic process that generates X is sufficiently regular to insure that $\mathcal{M}$ is finite, positive definite, and equal to plim $X'X/n$.[3]

The least-squares estimator $P = Y'X(X'X)^{-1}$ is unbiased and has a covariance matrix given by $\Omega \otimes \mathcal{E}(X'X)^{-1}$. If X is nonstochastic, this covariance matrix is equal to the lower bound given by the inverted information matrix. In fact, with other arguments, it can be shown that P is also efficient when X is stochastic. An unbiased estimator for Ω is given by

$$S^* = \frac{n-K}{n}S = \frac{1}{n-K}Y'[I - X(X'X)^{-1}X']Y.$$

Although its covariance matrix is slightly larger than the Cramér-Rao bound, it also can be shown to be efficient. The least-squares estimators P and S (which are also the unconstrained maximum-likelihood estimators) are asymptotically efficient with asymptotic covariance matrix given essentially by[4]

(3.6)
$$R^{-1} = \begin{bmatrix} \Omega \otimes \mathcal{M}^{-1} & 0 \\ 0 & 2(\Omega \otimes \Omega) \end{bmatrix}.$$

4. Efficient Estimation: Structural Restrictions Utilized

If the information that some structural parameters are known a priori is utilized in estimating θ, the asymptotic covariance matrix of the optimal estimator may be less than R^{-1}. Furthermore, if there are enough restrictions put on the structure, the structural parameter α can also be estimated. These results concerning simultaneous equation systems follow from the general theory of constrained estimation presented in chapter 2, section 5. The relevant results obtained there may be summarized as follows.

If it is known that the true θ^0 satisfies the equation

$$\theta = h(\alpha)$$

where α is a vector of unknown parameters, then, under certain regularity

3. See, for example, Koopmans, Rubin, and Leipnik (1950), pp. 133–36. This assumption implies that, if X contains lagged endogenous variables, the difference equation system (2.2) is stable.

4. Because we ignore the symmetry constraint on Ω, R_{22}^{-1} must be reinterpreted before it is actually the covariance matrix for S. See appendix A for details.

conditions, the following hold:

1) The structural parameter α is locally identifiable if the matrix H of partial derivatives has full column rank when evaluated at the true α^0. If α is also globally identifiable, it can be consistently estimated. The lower bound for the asymptotic covariance matrix of any consistent estimator of α is given by

$$M = (H'RH)^{-1}.$$

2) The reduced-form parameter space is restricted if the rank of H is less than the dimension of θ. A lower bound for the asymptotic covariance matrix of any consistent estimator of θ is given by[5]

$$N = H(H'RH)^{-1}H'.$$

3) The bounds M and N are attained by the asymptotic covariance matrices of the constrained maximum-likelihood and minimum-chi-square estimators.

4) The gain in reduced-form efficiency due to imposing the constraints is given by the positive semidefinite matrix $R^{-1} - N$. This matrix is nonzero as long as the rank of H is less than the dimensionality of θ.

Our analysis of the simultaneous equations model will involve the evaluation of M and N for the process having likelihood function (2.4) and the constraints implied by (2.3). The asymptotic information matrix R has already been given in (3.4). The remaining task is to derive the partial derivative matrix for the transformation that relates the reduced-form parameters θ to the structural parameters α. Partitioning according to (2.8), we define the $(GK + G^2) \times (r + r^*)$ matrix

(4.1)
$$H = \begin{bmatrix} \dfrac{\partial \pi}{\partial \delta'} & \dfrac{\partial \pi}{\partial \sigma'} \\[2mm] \dfrac{\partial \omega}{\partial \delta'} & \dfrac{\partial \omega}{\partial \sigma'} \end{bmatrix} \equiv \begin{bmatrix} H_{11} & H_{12} \\ H_{21} & H_{22} \end{bmatrix}$$

where H is evaluated at the true parameter vector α^0.

If H has full column rank, the matrix M can be partitioned according to (δ, σ) and written as

(4.2)
$$\begin{bmatrix} M_{11} & M_{12} \\ M_{21} & M_{22} \end{bmatrix} = \left(\begin{bmatrix} H'_{11} & H'_{21} \\ 0 & H'_{22} \end{bmatrix} \begin{bmatrix} R_{11} & 0 \\ 0 & R_{22} \end{bmatrix} \begin{bmatrix} H_{11} & 0 \\ H_{21} & H_{22} \end{bmatrix} \right)^{-1}$$

$$= \begin{bmatrix} H'_{11}R_{11}H_{11} + H'_{21}R_{22}H_{21} & H'_{21}R_{22}H_{22} \\ H'_{22}R_{22}H_{21} & H'_{22}R_{22}H_{22} \end{bmatrix}^{-1}$$

5. Even if H does not have full column rank, θ will be restricted if H has less than full row rank. In that case, the inverse in N should be interpreted as a generalized inverse.

where use is made of the fact that R_{12}, R_{21}, and H_{12} are all zero matrices. The matrix N can be written in partitioned form as

$$(4.3) \quad \begin{bmatrix} N_{11} & N_{12} \\ N_{21} & N_{22} \end{bmatrix} = \begin{bmatrix} H_{11} & 0 \\ H_{21} & H_{22} \end{bmatrix} \begin{bmatrix} M_{11} & M_{12} \\ M_{21} & M_{22} \end{bmatrix} \begin{bmatrix} H'_{11} & H'_{21} \\ 0 & H'_{22} \end{bmatrix}.$$

Thus the lower bound for the asymptotic covariance matrix of a consistent estimator of π is given by the $GK \times GK$ matrix

$$(4.4) \quad N_{11} = H_{11}M_{11}H'_{11},$$

and the lower bound for the asymptotic covariance matrix of a consistent estimator of δ is given by the $r \times r$ matrix[6]

$$(4.5) \quad \begin{aligned} M_{11} &= [H'_{11}R_{11}H_{11} + H'_{21}R_{22}H_{21} \\ &\quad - H'_{21}R_{22}H_{22}(H'_{22}R_{22}H_{22})^{-1}H'_{22}R_{22}H_{21}]^{-1} \\ &\equiv [M^{(1)} + M^{(2)} + M^{(3)}]^{-1}. \end{aligned}$$

In order to derive explicit expressions for M_{11} and N_{11} we must calculate the matrix H. Before we turn to that task, however, it will be useful to examine the form of equation (4.5). If H_{11} has full column rank r, then $M^{(1)} = H'_{11}R_{11}H_{11}$ is strictly positive definite. The sum $M^{(2)} + M^{(3)}$, however, may be singular and in an important special case is in fact zero.

Suppose that there is no a priori information on the elements of Σ except that the matrix is positive definite. In that case the equation $\Omega = B^{-1}\Sigma B'^{-1}$ is a one-to-one transformation from the G^2-dimensional parameter space of Σ to the G^2-dimensional parameter space of Ω. The matrix H_{22} will be nonsingular and the messy expression for $M^{(2)} + M^{(3)}$ given in (4.5) collapses to the zero matrix. Thus, if Σ is unrestricted, the analysis is greatly simplified. The structural parameters will be identified only if H_{11} has full column rank r. In this case, a lower bound for the asymptotic covariance matrix of a consistent estimator of δ is given by

$$(4.6) \quad M_{11} = (H'_{11}R_{11}H_{11})^{-1},$$

and a lower bound for the asymptotic covariance matrix of a consistent estimator of π is given by

$$(4.7) \quad N_{11} = H_{11}(H'_{11}R_{11}H_{11})^{-1}H'_{11}.$$

The case in which there are no restrictions on the structural covariance matrix Σ is perhaps the most important one in econometric practice.

---

6. To obtain (4.5) we have used the formula for the inverse of a partitioned matrix given in section 4 of chapter 1. This formula is valid only if H'_{22} has full row rank; it is shown in appendix A that this is necessarily the case.

Whereas economic theory often suggests that certain regression coefficients are zero, rarely does the economist possess reliable prior information on the error variances and covariances. Nevertheless, it is possible that in some instances it is known that certain covariance terms are zero. For example, it might be argued that two structural equations describing two separated sectors have independently distributed error terms. In such cases it is important to realize that the asymptotic efficiency of the estimates of δ and π can be increased by making use of the Σ-restrictions. Suppose that H_{11} has full column rank so that the structure is identified on the basis of restrictions on B and Γ alone. Then, by (4.5), M_{11} is the inverse of a matrix that is the sum of a positive definite matrix and a positive semi-definite matrix. The restrictions on Σ will increase the efficiency of estimating δ and π as long as the second matrix is nonzero.[7]

For the next two sections we shall concentrate on the case where there are no Σ-restrictions. The matrices M_{11} and N_{11} are formed using (4.6) and (4.7) after an explicit expression for H_{11} is found. In section 7 we return to the case of Σ-restrictions (which require the evaluation of H_{21} and H_{22}). There it will be proven that a priori information on the structural covariance matrix does indeed improve the efficiency in estimating the coefficients δ and π.

5. The Derivation of H_{11}

The matrix H depends on the exact nature of the a priori restrictions placed on the structure. We begin by describing the restrictions on the coefficient matrices B and Γ. Consider the ith structural equation. Suppose that β_i, the vector of unknown coefficients of endogenous variables, consists of g_i elements and that γ_i, the vector of unknown coefficients of predetermined variables, consists of k_i elements so that δ_i consists of $r_i = g_i + k_i$ unknown parameters. It will be convenient to define the following matrices:

C_i = the $g_i \times G$ matrix obtained by striking from a $G \times G$ identity matrix the rows corresponding to the endogenous variables whose coefficients in the ith equation are known. (E.g., the pth row of I_G is removed if β_{ip} is known a priori.)

D_i = the $k_i \times K$ matrix obtained by striking from a $K \times K$ identity matrix the rows corresponding to the predetermined variables

---

7. All of the results in this chapter concern asymptotic covariance matrices and asymptotic efficiency. When there is no possibility for confusion, however, we shall occasionally drop the adjective "asymptotic" to simplify an already complex terminology.

whose coefficients in the ith equation are known. (E.g., the pth row of I_K is removed if γ_{ip} is known a priori.)

$\Pi_i = C_i\Pi =$ the matrix of reduced-form regression coefficients corresponding to the endogenous variables whose coefficients in the ith equation are unknown.

Finally, it is useful to define the $r_i \times K$ matrix

$$(5.1) \qquad W_i = \begin{bmatrix} C_i\Pi \\ D_i \end{bmatrix} = \begin{bmatrix} \Pi_i \\ D_i \end{bmatrix},$$

which summarizes all the prior information on the coefficients of the ith structural equation.

The matrix H_{11} is obtained by differentiating the GK equations

$$(5.2) \qquad \pi_{rs} = -\sum_i \beta^{ri}\gamma_{is}$$

with respect to the elements of δ. Upon calculation one finds

$$(5.3) \qquad \frac{\partial \pi_{rs}}{\partial \beta_{pq}} = -\sum_i \frac{\partial \beta^{ri}}{\partial \beta_{pq}}\gamma_{is} = \sum_i \beta^{rp}\beta^{qi}\gamma_{is} = -\beta^{rp}\pi_{qs}$$

for all β_{pq} not known a priori and

$$(5.4) \qquad \frac{\partial \pi_{rs}}{\partial \gamma_{pq}} = \begin{cases} -\beta^{rp} & \text{if } s = q, \\ 0 & \text{if } s \neq q \end{cases}$$

for all γ_{pq} not known a priori.[8] Thus the rp block of the partitioned matrix H_{11} is given by

$$(5.5) \qquad \frac{\partial \pi_r}{\partial \delta'_p} = -\beta^{rp}W'_p.$$

The complete matrix H_{11} is given by

$$
H_{11} = \frac{\partial \pi}{\partial \delta'} = \begin{bmatrix} \dfrac{\partial \pi_1}{\partial \delta'_1} & & \dfrac{\partial \pi_1}{\partial \delta'_G} \\ & \ddots & \\ \dfrac{\partial \pi_G}{\partial \delta'_1} & & \dfrac{\partial \pi_G}{\partial \delta'_G} \end{bmatrix} = -\begin{bmatrix} \beta^{11}W'_1 & & \beta^{1G}W'_G \\ & \ddots & \\ \beta^{G1}W'_1 & & \beta^{GG}W'_G \end{bmatrix}
$$

$$(5.6)$$

$$
= -\begin{bmatrix} \beta^{11}I_K & & \beta^{1G}I_K \\ & \ddots & \\ \beta^{G1}I_K & & \beta^{GG}I_K \end{bmatrix} \begin{bmatrix} W'_1 & 0 & 0 \\ 0 & W'_2 & \\ & & \ddots & 0 \\ 0 & 0 & W'_G \end{bmatrix}.
$$

8. Cf. GOLDBERGER (1964), pp. 370–71.

If we define W to be the block diagonal matrix with the W_i as diagonal blocks, we can rewrite (5.6) in a more convenient form. The partial derivative matrix H_{11} is given by the $GK \times r$ matrix

$$(5.7) \qquad H_{11} = -(\mathbf{B}^{-1} \otimes I_K)W'$$

where $r = \Sigma r_i$ is the total number of structural coefficients to be estimated.

If there are no other restrictions on the structural parameters, the possibility of structural estimation and the existence of restrictions on π depend on ρ, the rank of H_{11}. From (5.7) it is clear that the rank of H_{11} is equal to the rank of W since $(\mathbf{B}^{-1} \otimes I_K)$ is nonsingular. Furthermore, because of the block diagonal form of W, the rank of W is the sum of the ranks of the W_i. Of course, the rank of W depends on the (unknown) value of the structural parameter δ. For our rank conditions to be useful, it must be assumed that ρ is constant for all δ in a neighborhood of the true δ^0.

The reduced-form coefficients π are restricted by the prior information on the structure if ρ is less than GK. Since each matrix W_i has a rank no greater than its column dimension K, if any W_i has rank less than K then π is surely restricted. But it is also true that the rank of W_i cannot exceed its row dimension Π_i. Thus the reduced-form coefficients are necessarily restricted if one (or more) structural equation has less than K unknown coefficients.

The structural coefficients are locally identifiable if and only if W has rank r. In fact, since the relation between structure and reduced form can be written as the linear equation $\mathbf{B}\Pi^0 + \Gamma = 0$, this condition is also valid for global identification. The block diagonal form for W indicates that, under the zero-order constraints considered here, each structural equation can be studied separately as far as identification is concerned. The structural coefficients of the ith equation are identifiable if W_i has full row rank r_i; and, if W_i has less than full row rank, at least one of the coefficients of the ith equation is not identifiable. Since the rank of W_i cannot be larger than K, a necessary condition for identifiability is that the number of unknown coefficients in the ith equation be less than or equal to the total number of exogenous variables in the system. Moreover, since multiplying all of the coefficients of the ith equation by a constant does not affect Π, at least one of the restrictions must be nonhomogeneous.

An interesting special case occurs if W_i is square and nonsingular. Since its rank will equal both r_i and K, each of the coefficients of the ith structural equation is identifiable, but no reduced-form restrictions are imposed by the information on that equation. In such a case the structural equation is said to be *exactly identified*. If there were one less structural restriction so that δ_i consisted of $r_i + 1$ coefficients, then δ_i would not be identifiable. Suppose, instead, W_i is rectangular with $r_i < K$ and possesses full rank r_i. Then there is a surplus of information in the sense that one of the structural restrictions could be relaxed without destroying the identifiability of δ_i. In this case the equation is said to be *overidentified*. It is easy to verify that the reduced form is necessarily restricted if any structural equation is overidentified and that the reduced form is unrestricted if all the structural equations are exactly identified.

A difficulty with these results is that the matrix W depends on the true parameter matrix Π^0. It is rare that the econometrician has much intuitive feeling about the true value of Π. Of course, Π can always be estimated. Nevertheless, it is often desirable to have the above rank conditions for restrictions and identifiability expressed in terms of the structural matrices B and Γ about which economists have more information. Consider the matrix identity

$$\begin{bmatrix} B & \Gamma \\ C_i & 0 \\ 0 & D_i \end{bmatrix} \begin{bmatrix} B^{-1} & \Pi \\ 0 & I_K \end{bmatrix} = \begin{bmatrix} I_G & 0 \\ * & W_i \end{bmatrix}$$

where the $(r_i + G) \times (G + K)$ matrix on the left is denoted by T_i. Since the second matrix is nonsingular and the third matrix is block triangular, the rank of T_i equals G plus the rank of W_i. Now the bottom part of T_i consists of r_i rows taken from a $G + K$ identity matrix. Each row corresponds to one of the elements of δ_i. Consider the matrix $(B_i \quad \Gamma_i)$ which is formed by deleting from the true structural coefficient matrix $(B^0 \quad \Gamma^0)$ the columns associated with these r_i elements. Thus $(B_i \quad \Gamma_i)$ consists of the structural coefficients for those variables which appear in the ith equation with a known coefficient. Since T_i can be put in block triangular form by reordering the columns, its rank must equal r_i plus the rank of $(B_i \quad \Gamma_i)$. We conclude, therefore, that the rank of W_i equals $r_i - G$ plus the rank of $(B_i \quad \Gamma_i)$.

We can summarize the results of this section as follows:

The matrix H_{11} is given by $-(B^{-1} \otimes I_K)W'$ and has the same rank as W. The matrix W is block diagonal with the ith block given by the $r_i \times K$ matrix

$$W_i = \begin{bmatrix} \Pi_i \\ D_i \end{bmatrix}.$$

If there are no other types of structural constraints, then the reduced-form coefficients are restricted if and only if at least one of the W_i has rank less than K. Furthermore, the ith structural equation is identified if and only if W_i has rank r_i. Since the rank of W_i equals $r_i - G$ plus the rank of $(B_i \quad \Gamma_i)$, these conditions can also be stated in terms of the true structural coefficient matrices.

6. The Variance Bound

We may now evaluate M_{11} and N_{11} to obtain the lower bounds on the covariance matrices of efficient estimates of δ and π. From (4.6), (5.7), and (3.4) we can write

$$
\begin{aligned}
M_{11} &= (H'_{11} R_{11} H_{11})^{-1} \\
(6.1) \qquad &= [W(B^{-1} \otimes I_K)'(\Omega^{-1} \otimes \mathcal{M})(B^{-1} \otimes I_K)W']^{-1} \\
&= [W(\Sigma^{-1} \otimes \mathcal{M})W']^{-1}
\end{aligned}
$$

where use is made of the fact that $\Sigma = B\Omega B'$. Hence

$$
\begin{aligned}
N_{11} &= H_{11}(H'_{11} R_{11} H_{11})^{-1} H'_{11} \\
(6.2) \qquad &= (B^{-1} \otimes I_K)W'[W(\Sigma^{-1} \otimes \mathcal{M})W']^{-1} W(B^{-1} \otimes I_K)'.
\end{aligned}
$$

The matrix M_{11} may be rewritten in a somewhat more meaningful way. Using (3.5) we can write

$$
(6.3) \quad W(\Sigma^{-1} \otimes \mathcal{M})W' = \lim \frac{1}{n} \mathscr{E}
\begin{bmatrix}
W_1 X'X W'_1 \sigma^{11} & & W_1 X'X W'_G \sigma^{1G} \\
& \cdot & \\
& & \cdot \\
W_G X'X W'_1 \sigma^{G1} & & W_G X'X W'_G \sigma^{GG}
\end{bmatrix}.
$$

But, by the definition of W_i,

$$
\begin{aligned}
XW'_i &= X[\Pi'_i \quad D'_i] \\
(6.4) \qquad &= [Y_i - V_i \quad X_i] \equiv \bar{Z}_i
\end{aligned}
$$

where Y_i is the matrix of current endogenous variables that appear in the ith equation with unknown coefficients, V_i is the corresponding matrix of reduced-form errors, and X_i is the matrix of exogenous variables that appear in the ith equation with unknown coefficients. Hence $\bar{Z}_i$ is the "purified" matrix of variables which appear in the ith structural equation with unknown coefficients. Then

$$(6.5) \qquad M_{11} = \operatorname{plim} n \begin{bmatrix} \bar{Z}_1' \bar{Z}_1 \sigma^{11} & \bar{Z}_1' \bar{Z}_G \sigma^{1G} \\ & \cdot \\ & \cdot \\ \bar{Z}_G' \bar{Z}_1 \sigma^{G1} & \bar{Z}_G' \bar{Z}_G \sigma^{GG} \end{bmatrix}^{-1},$$

a form equivalent to the covariance matrix given by ZELLNER AND THEIL (1962) for the three-stage least-squares estimator.

Equations (6.1) and (6.2) express compactly the covariance matrices of asymptotically efficient estimators of the structural and reduced-form coefficients. These expressions are derived under the assumption that (1) every structural equation is identified, and (2) there is no a priori information on Σ. It is of some interest to consider the question of relaxing these assumptions.

The problem of underidentification can easily be handled. Suppose that the first structural equation is underidentified; that is, the rank of W_1 is ρ_1 which is less than r_1. Then δ_1 cannot be estimated consistently. Let W_1^* be the matrix consisting of ρ_1 independent rows of W_1. Then, if W_1^* replaces W_1 in W, equation (6.2) is still valid for the lower bound on the covariance matrix of an estimator of π. Furthermore, if the first ρ_1 rows and columns of M_{11} are ignored and W_1^* replaces W_1, (6.1) remains valid for the lower bound on the covariance matrix for an estimator of $(\delta_2, \ldots, \delta_G)$. If W_1^* should be nonsingular (i.e., if $\rho_1 = K$), then the $K \times K$ identity matrix will serve for W_1^* since both will span the same space. These observations follow from the discussion in section 6 of chapter 2.

The assumption that there is no a priori information on Σ is quite crucial to the derivation of (6.1) and (6.2). As was pointed out in section 4, in the presence of Σ-restrictions the expressions for M_{11} and N_{11} become much more complicated. An examination of this case follows.

7. COVARIANCE RESTRICTIONS

Although a priori information concerning elements of the structural covariance matrix is probably rare in practice, it is still of some interest to examine the effects of such information on estimation efficiency. If it turns out that Σ-restrictions are very valuable in increasing the efficiency of estimating δ and π, then it would seem that more attention ought to be placed on learning about the variances and covariances of the structural disturbances. In any case, from a purely logical point of view, it is quite asymmetric to limit oneself to coefficient restrictions in a theoretical study of the simultaneous equations problem.

There are, of course, many ways to express a priori information about Σ. The most natural extension of the analysis in the previous sections is to consider the zero-order restrictions of knowing the numerical values of some of the σ_{ij}. The constrained Cramér-Rao bound for δ can be calculated from (4.5) after expressions for H_{21} and H_{22} are found. These expressions are relatively simple although the derivations are rather tedious and are given in appendix A. Although there is no difficulty in evaluating H for the general case of zero-order restrictions, the resulting expressions are not very illuminating. For any given set of restrictions, equation M_{11} can be evaluated numerically; but general algebraic expressions for the Cramér-Rao bound are not interpretable. However, for two special cases of zero-order Σ-restrictions, an algebraic analysis is quite useful. The first case assumes that the statistician knows *every* element of Σ. The second case assumes that the matrix Σ is known to be *diagonal*.

Σ COMPLETELY KNOWN

The assumption that Σ is known a priori is, on the face of it, very implausible. It is difficult to imagine many real-world problems where the econometrician knows the true value of Σ but not the true values of B and Γ. Consider, however, the following case: A structure has been estimated in the past from a large sample so that very precise estimates of B, Γ, and Σ have been obtained. Because of certain technological changes, however, some elements of B and Γ have shifted. It is now desired to reestimate the model on a new (small) sample. Those elements of B, Γ, and Σ that have not shifted (and these might include every element of Σ) may be assumed to be known. The problem then is to efficiently estimate the remaining parameters under the assumption that Σ and certain other parameters are known.

Another justification for studying the case of a known Σ is to be able to compare the results with other problems involving covariances as nuisance parameters. It is well known that in the "traditional" normal linear regression model, prior information on the covariance matrix does *not* increase the efficiency of estimating the regression coefficients. This is a result of the block diagonal form of the information matrix. For example, in the unconstrained reduced form (3.3), the least-squares estimator is best regardless of whether Ω is known or unknown. This is not the case with simultaneous equations. Prior knowledge of Σ *does* improve the efficiency of estimating B, Γ, and Π. The best estimator of Π when Σ is unknown is not the best estimator when Σ is known. Thus one purpose of the present discussion is to shed light on this difference between the traditional regression model and the "simultaneous equations" case.

Our task is to find expressions for the Cramér-Rao bounds M_{11} and N_{11} when, in addition to the restrictions imposed on B and Γ, there is also the restriction that Σ is known. The Jacobian matrix for the transformation (2.3) is now

$$(7.1) \qquad H = \begin{bmatrix} H_{11} \\ H_{21} \end{bmatrix} = \begin{bmatrix} \dfrac{\partial \pi}{\partial \delta'} \\ \dfrac{\partial \omega}{\partial \delta'} \end{bmatrix}$$

since Σ is known. If H has full column rank, the asymptotic variance bound for δ is

$$(7.2) \qquad \begin{aligned} M_{11} &= (H'RH)^{-1} = (H'_{11}R_{11}H_{11} + H'_{21}R_{22}H_{21})^{-1} \\ &= [M^{(1)} + M^{(2)}]^{-1}. \end{aligned}$$

The matrix $M^{(1)} = H'_{11}R_{11}H_{11}$ has been evaluated in section 6 and is given by the inverse of (6.5). The matrix $M^{(2)} = H'_{21}R_{22}H_{21}$ is derived in appendix A and takes the following form: $M^{(2)}$ is an $r \times r$ matrix consisting of zeros except for those elements corresponding to a pair of endogenous parameters. If $m_{ij}^{(2)}$ is the element of $M^{(2)}$ corresponding to the ith and jth elements of δ, $m_{ij}^{(2)}$ will be nonzero only if both δ_i and δ_j are elements of B. If δ_i is β_{pq} and δ_j is β_{rs}, then

$$(7.3) \qquad m_{ij}^{(2)} = \omega_{qs}\sigma^{pr} + \beta^{qr}\beta^{sp}.$$

From (6.5) we can obtain the corresponding element of $M^{(1)} = H'_{11}R_{11}H_{11}$:

$$(7.4) \qquad \begin{aligned} m_{ij}^{(1)} &= \operatorname{plim} \frac{1}{n}\bar{y}'_q\bar{y}_s\sigma^{pr} = \operatorname{plim} \frac{1}{n}(y_q - v_q)'(y_s - v_s)\sigma^{pr} \\ &= \operatorname{plim} \frac{1}{n}y'_q y_s\sigma^{pr} - \omega_{qs}\sigma^{pr}. \end{aligned}$$

Hence, the matrix M_{11} is obtained by inverting a matrix that is identical to $M^{(1)}$ except for those elements corresponding to a pair of elements of B. For those elements, $m_{ij}^{(1)}$ is replaced by

$$(7.5) \qquad m_{ij}^{(1)} + m_{ij}^{(2)} = \operatorname{plim} \frac{1}{n}y'_q y_s\sigma^{pr} + \beta^{qr}\beta^{sp}.$$

If the structural parameters are identified by the coefficient restrictions alone, then these parameters can be estimated even if the Σ-restrictions are ignored. In that case the minimal asymptotic covariance matrix for δ is given by the inverse of $M^{(1)}$. Thus using the fact that Σ is known reduces this covariance matrix as long as at least one element of $M^{(2)}$ is nonzero. Examining (7.3) we see that the diagonal elements corresponding to unknown elements of B are necessarily positive. Hence knowledge of Σ will always increase the efficiency of an optimal estimator of the structural parameter δ as long as there exists at least one unknown element of B. Similarly, the efficiency of an optimal estimator of the reduced-form parameter π is also increased since the covariance matrix is now

$$H_{11}[M^{(1)} + M^{(2)}]^{-1}H'_{11}.$$

If the coefficient restrictions taken by themselves are not sufficient to identify the structural parameters, then the knowledge of Σ may enable one to estimate parameters that otherwise would not be estimable. In this case, however, there is the possibility that the efficiency in estimating π is unaffected. If the structure is identified without the Σ-constraints, then the addition of these constraints necessarily increases the efficiency of estimating the structural and reduced-form regression coefficients.

AN EXAMPLE

Since the formulas for efficiency gain under covariance restrictions are rather complicated, it is useful to consider an example. We take the simple consumption function model

$$C_t = \alpha Y_t + u_t$$

$$C_t = Y_t - Z_t$$

where C_t is consumption in year t, Y_t is income, and Z_t is exogenous demand (all measured as deviations from their sample means). The reduced-form equation

$$Y_t = \pi Z_t + v_t$$

has as parameter the multiplier

$$\pi = h(\alpha) = \frac{1}{1 - \alpha}.$$

If the marginal propensity to consume α and the structural error variance σ^2 are both unknown, the reduced-form parameter space is unrestricted. Hence the asymptotic variance bound for estimating π is given by the reciprocal of the information term. If the u_t are normal and independent, this may be written as

$$R^{-1} = \frac{\omega^2}{\mathcal{M}} = \frac{\sigma^2}{(1 - \alpha)^2 \mathcal{M}}$$

where ω^2 is the variance of v_t and $\mathcal{M}$ is given by

$$\mathcal{M} = \lim \frac{1}{n}\Sigma Z_t^2.$$

The asymptotic variance bound for estimating α is given by

$$(H'RH)^{-1} = \left[\frac{1}{(1-\alpha)^4}\frac{(1-\alpha)^2\mathcal{M}}{\sigma^2}\right]^{-1} = \frac{\sigma^2(1-\alpha)^2}{\mathcal{M}}.$$

If σ is known a priori, these variance bounds drop. Using (7.5) and the results in appendix B concerning systems containing identities, we have for the bound on estimating α

$$[M^{(1)} + M^{(2)}]^{-1} = \frac{\sigma^2(1-\alpha)^2}{\mathcal{M} + 2\sigma^2}.$$

The variance bound for estimating π now becomes

$$\frac{\sigma^2}{(1-\alpha)^2(\mathcal{M}+2\sigma^2)}.$$

In either case the percent decrease in asymptotic variance is given by

$$\frac{2\sigma^2}{\mathcal{M}+2\sigma^2} = 2\frac{1-R^2}{2-R^2}$$

where R^2 is the population squared correlation coefficient for the reduced-form equation. If $R^2 = 0.9$, then there is an 18 percent reduction in variance due to the prior information. If $R^2 = 0.5$, then there is a 66 percent reduction. In practice, of course, exogenous demand is highly correlated with income and hence the efficiency gain is relatively small. Furthermore, this very simple model with only one error term probably exaggerates the value of knowing the error variances. Nevertheless, the gain from Σ-restrictions is clearly not negligible. This is in sharp contrast to the classical regression model where knowledge of the error variances has no value whatever. In our model, for example, knowing the value of σ is important, but knowing the value of ω is not. These results all follow from the fact that the information matrix $H'RH$ does not have the block diagonal form of R.

Σ KNOWN TO BE DIAGONAL

A more realistic form of a priori information is the knowledge that Σ is a diagonal matrix. Although we rarely know the entire Σ matrix, we sometimes know that the errors of two structural equations are uncorrelated. This assumption has been made in a number of econometric models (e.g., BASMANN [1963] and KLEIN [1950]), although it is perhaps mathematical convenience rather than economic realism that has been the motivation. It is, however, probably the case that the zero-covariance assumption can often be justified in practice. We shall examine the effects of making this assumption without further justification.

The task is similar to the one of the previous subsection. We must find expressions for the Cramér-Rao bounds M_{11} and N_{11} when, in addition to the zero-order restrictions imposed on B and Γ, there is also the restriction that Σ is an unknown *diagonal* matrix. The asymptotic variance bound for δ is of the form (4.5). That is, assuming that H has full column rank,

$$
\begin{aligned}
(7.6) \quad M_{11} &= [H'_{11}R_{11}H_{11} + H'_{21}R_{22}H_{21} \\
&\quad - H'_{21}R_{22}H_{22}(H'_{22}R_{22}H_{22})^{-1}H'_{22}R_{22}H_{21}]^{-1} \\
&= [M^{(1)} + M^{(2)} + M^{(3)}]^{-1}.
\end{aligned}
$$

Since $M^{(1)}$ and $M^{(2)}$ have been evaluated already, the remaining task is to evaluate $M^{(3)}$. Again, the algebraic derivation has been placed in appendix A. The result is that $M^{(3)}$ is an $r \times r$ matrix of zeros except for those elements corresponding to a pair of elements of B. If the ith element of δ is β_{pq} and the jth element is β_{rs}, then

$$
(7.7) \qquad m^{(3)}_{ij} = \begin{cases} 0 & \text{if } p \neq r, \\ -2\beta^{qp}\beta^{sp} & \text{if } p = r. \end{cases}
$$

To form the matrix M_{11} we add the three matrices $M^{(1)} + M^{(2)} + M^{(3)}$ and invert. It can be demonstrated that $M^{(2)} + M^{(3)}$ is nonzero as long as there is at least one unknown element in B and B is not diagonal. Thus knowledge that Σ is diagonal makes M_{11} and N_{11} smaller than they would be if only the restrictions on B and Γ were used. Again this conclusion is based on the assumption that the structure is identifiable even without the Σ-restrictions.

8. Σ-RESTRICTIONS AND IDENTIFICATION

We may now summarize some results on structural identification. When the zero-order restrictions involve only the elements of B and Γ, the identifiability of the elements of δ depends on the matrix H_{11}. When there are Σ-restrictions in addition to the restrictions on B and Γ, the entire H matrix must be examined. Recall that H is the $(GK + G^2) \times (r + r^*)$ matrix

$$H = \begin{bmatrix} H_{11} & 0 \\ H_{21} & H_{22} \end{bmatrix}.$$

The submatrix H_{11} is given in equation (5.7); typical elements of H_{21} and H_{22} are given in appendix A. Applying the general theory developed in chapter 2, section 6, we can conclude that the complete set of structural parameters $\alpha = (\delta, \sigma)$ is locally identifiable if H has full column rank. The question of identification for simultaneous equation systems is thus one concerning the rank of the Jacobian matrix H.

The rank of H_{11} has been analyzed already in section 5. In appendix A it is shown that H_{22} always has full column rank under zero-order restrictions (given that B is assumed to be nonsingular). Hence, a sufficient condition for the identifiability of the complete set of structural parameters is that H_{11} have full column rank. However, depending on the number of Σ-restrictions, this condition is not always necessary.

When there are no restrictions on Σ, H_{22} is nonsingular. In that case H_{11} having full column rank is both necessary and sufficient for the local identifiability of α. With Σ-restrictions, however, the condition is no longer necessary. It is possible for H to have full rank $r + r^*$ while H_{11} has rank less than r. For this to be the case, it is clear that H must have no more rows than columns. Hence a necessary condition for identification is that $r + r^* \leq GK + G^2$. Or

$$(GK + G^2 - r) + (G^2 - r^*) \geq G^2;$$

the number of coefficient restrictions plus the number of covariance restrictions must be at least as great as the number of structural equations squared.

An analysis of sufficient conditions for identifiability is difficult when Σ-restrictions are present. Since identifiability is not the major topic of this study, we shall not pursue the matter further. FISHER (1966), using a different approach, has studied the topic extensively. Further results may be found in ROTHENBERG (1971), WEGGE (1965), and in section 10 below.

9. EFFICIENT ESTIMATORS

Up to now we have described the asymptotic covariance matrix of efficient estimators under various types of a priori information, but we have not discussed the problem of finding an efficient estimator. It is not our purpose to present new estimators or to develop computational algorithms for old ones. All that will be done in this section is to determine which of the previously proposed estimators of δ and π are asymptotically efficient.

Returning to the general notation of section 2, we write the likelihood (2.4) as

$$(9.1) \qquad\qquad\qquad f(\pi, \omega)$$

and the constraints (2.3) as

$$(9.2) \qquad\qquad\qquad \pi = h_1(\delta)$$

$$(9.3) \qquad\qquad\qquad \omega = h_2(\delta, \sigma).$$

As before π and ω are vectors consisting of *all* the elements of Π and Ω; δ and σ are vectors consisting of only the *unknown elements* of B, Γ, and Σ. The unconstrained least-squares estimators of Π and Ω are

$$(9.4) \qquad P = Y'X(X'X)^{-1}, \qquad S = \frac{1}{n}Y'[I - X(X'X)^{-1}X']Y,$$

and may be written in vector form as

$$(9.5) \qquad\qquad\qquad p = \text{vec } P, \qquad s = \text{vec } S.$$

The matrices $\hat{R}_{11}$ and $\hat{R}_{22}$ are the asymptotic information matrices R_{11} and R_{22} evaluated at $\pi = p$ and $\omega = s$. It is assumed that H has full column rank and the structural parameters (δ, σ) are identifiable.

Since reduced-form estimates can easily be obtained using (9.2) and (9.3), we shall discuss only structural estimation. Specifically, we shall consider the following estimators: (1) full-information maximum likelihood, (2) linearized maximum likelihood, (3) minimum chi-square, and (4) three-stage least squares. Single equation methods, such as two-stage least squares, are generally not efficient and will not be considered.

FULL-INFORMATION MAXIMUM LIKELIHOOD

The maximum-likelihood estimator of (δ, σ) is the solution to the extremal problem

$$(9.6) \qquad\qquad \underset{\delta,\,\sigma}{\text{maximize}}\; f[h_1(\delta), h_2(\delta, \sigma)],$$

which, under our assumption of normality, is equivalent to

(9.7)
$$\text{maximize } 2n \log|\det B| - n \log \det \Sigma$$
$$\underset{\delta,\,\sigma}{} - \text{tr}[\Sigma^{-1}(BY' + \Gamma X')(YB' + X\Gamma')].$$

If there are no Σ-restrictions, the maximum-likelihood estimator of δ can be expressed as the solution of the "concentrated" extremal problem[9]

(9.8)
$$\underset{\delta}{\text{minimize}} \frac{|(BY' + \Gamma X')(YB' + X\Gamma')|}{|B|^2}.$$

The maximum-likelihood estimator of (δ, σ) given by (9.7) is consistent and asymptotically efficient as long as *all* of the structural restrictions are taken into account. That is, the function (9.7) is to be maximized only with respect to the *unknown* elements of (B, Γ, Σ). In particular, if Σ is restricted, the solution of (9.8) is *not* efficient. The maximum-likelihood estimator of (π, ω) can be obtained from the maximum-likelihood estimator of (δ, σ) by using (9.2) and (9.3). These reduced-form estimates are efficient as long as the structural estimates are.

LINEARIZED MAXIMUM LIKELIHOOD

The maximum-likelihood estimators are difficult to compute since the normal equations for (9.7) and (9.8) are nonlinear. Suppose however some consistent, but inefficient, estimator of (δ, σ) is available. An example would be the two-stage least-squares estimator. Then one could linearize the log likelihood function (9.7) around the inefficient estimator and maximize it instead of the true likelihood function. Explicit formulas for the linearized maximum-likelihood estimator are given by ROTHENBERG AND LEENDERS (1964). They also prove that the linearized estimator is asymptotically efficient.

MINIMUM CHI-SQUARE

The minimum-chi-square estimator of (δ, σ) is the solution of the extremal problem[10]

(9.9)
$$\underset{\delta,\,\sigma}{\text{minimize}} \, [p - h_1(\delta)]\hat{R}_{11}[p - h_1(\delta)]$$
$$+ [s - h_2(\delta, \sigma)]'\hat{R}_{22}[s - h_2(\delta, \sigma)],$$

9. See, for example, KOOPMANS AND HOOD (1953), pp. 160–61.

10. The minimum-chi-square approach to constrained estimation is discussed in chapter 2, section 2.

which, upon substitution for $\hat{R}$ and h, is equivalent to

(9.10)
$$\text{minimize}_{\delta, \sigma} \text{tr}[S^{-1}(P + B^{-1}\Gamma)X'X(P + B^{-1}\Gamma)' + (I - S^{-1}B^{-1}\Sigma B'^{-1})^2].$$

If Σ is unrestricted, the second term can be made zero for any estimate $\hat{B}$ by setting $\hat{\Sigma} = \hat{B}S\hat{B}'$. Thus, in the case of no Σ-restrictions, the minimum-chi-square estimator for δ is the solution of

(9.11)
$$\text{minimize}_{\delta} \text{tr}[S^{-1}(P + B^{-1}\Gamma)X'X(P + B^{-1}\Gamma)'].$$

The minimum-chi-square estimator of (δ, σ) given by (9.9) is consistent and asymptotically efficient if all structural restrictions are taken into account. The reduced-form estimates found by using (9.2) and (9.3) are also efficient. These observations follow from the general theory of constrained estimation developed in chapter 2. The solution to (9.11) is called by MALINVAUD (1970) the minimum-distance estimator of δ. It is clear from the preceding discussion that this estimator is efficient only if Σ is unrestricted.

THREE-STAGE LEAST SQUARES

The three-stage least-squares (3SLS) estimator of δ may be expressed as the solution to the problem

(9.12)
$$\text{minimize}_{\delta} \text{tr}[\hat{\Sigma}^{-1}(BP + \Gamma)X'X(BP + \Gamma)']$$

where $\hat{\Sigma}$ is some consistent estimator of Σ (e.g., the two-stage least-squares estimator).[11] Unlike the maximum-likelihood and minimum-chi-square methods, three-stage least squares is computationally convenient since (9.12) is quadratic in δ. It involves only solving a large system of linear equations.

When Σ is unconstrained, 3SLS is consistent and asymptotically efficient. This follows from the discussion in section 6 where the asymptotic bound for δ was found to be (6.5), the same expression as derived by Zellner and Theil for the 3SLS estimator. However, when Σ is constrained, 3SLS is no longer efficient since its asymptotic variance remains unchanged although the asymptotic variance bound decreases.

---

11. This interpretation of three-stage least squares is due to BASMANN (1965). The original presentation is given by ZELLNER AND THEIL (1962).

10. A GENERALIZATION

By assuming that all a priori information takes the form of zero-order structural restrictions, we have been able to derive explicit expressions for the minimum variance bounds M_{11} and N_{11}. We shall now consider more general structural restrictions which include zero-order restrictions as a special case. Unfortunately, it will not be possible to derive results as explicit as those in the previous sections.

Let α now be interpreted as the vector of *all* the elements of (B, Γ, Σ). Then

$$(10.1) \qquad \theta = h(\alpha)$$

is the set of equations (2.3) relating the $G^2 + GK$ reduced-form parameters θ to the $2G^2 + GK$ structural parameters α. The matrix of partial derivatives

$$(10.2) \qquad H = \left[\frac{\partial \theta}{\partial \alpha'} \right]$$

cannot possibly have full column rank since it has more columns than rows. In fact, from the results of section 5 and appendix A, it follows that H has rank $G^2 + GK$ for all permitted α.

Previously we have considered restrictions that set certain elements of α equal to known numbers. A more general assumption is that the restrictions can be represented by a set of equations

$$(10.3) \qquad \psi(\alpha) = 0$$

where ψ is a vector of k differentiable functions. It is clear that zero-order restrictions are a special case of (10.3). We shall assume that the k equations (10.3) are independent. That is, we assume that Ψ, the matrix of partial derivatives of ψ, has full row rank k for all α near the true α^0.

It will be convenient to partition Ψ as

$$(10.4) \qquad \Psi = [\Psi_1 \quad \Psi_2]$$

where

$$\Psi_1 = \left[\frac{\partial \psi}{\partial \delta'} \right], \qquad \Psi_2 = \left[\frac{\partial \psi}{\partial \sigma'} \right]$$

are $k \times G(G + K)$ and $k \times G^2$ matrices. Then we can form the Jacobian matrix

(10.5)
$$\Phi = \begin{bmatrix} H \\ \Psi \end{bmatrix} = \begin{bmatrix} H_{11} & 0 \\ H_{21} & H_{22} \\ \Psi_1 & \Psi_2 \end{bmatrix},$$

which has $G^2 + GK + k$ rows and $2G^2 + GK$ columns. The matrix Φ depends, of course, on the (unknown) value of α. We shall assume that, in a neighborhood of α^0, its rank ρ is constant for all α satisfying (10.3).

From section 7 of chapter 2 we know that the identifiability of the structural parameters α and the existence of restrictions on the reduced-form parameters θ depend on the rank ρ of the matrix Φ. In particular, α is locally identifiable if $\rho = 2G^2 + GK$ (i.e., if Φ has full column rank). Furthermore, θ is restricted if ρ is less than $G^2 + GK + k$ (i.e., if Φ has less than full row rank). By examining the dimensions of Φ we observe that a necessary condition for identifiability is that k be at least as large as G^2. A sufficient condition for θ to be restricted is that k be larger than G^2. These order conditions are simple extensions of the conditions obtained previously for zero-order parameter constraints on the structure.

Using the derivations of section 5 and appendix A, we can write an explicit expression for Φ. Defining $\overline{W}$ to be the $(G + K) \times K$ matrix

$$\overline{W} = \begin{bmatrix} \Pi \\ I_K \end{bmatrix},$$

we have

(10.6)
$$\Phi = \begin{bmatrix} (B^{-1} \otimes \overline{W}') & 0 \\ \Delta & B^{-1} \otimes B^{-1} \\ \Psi_1 & \Psi_2 \end{bmatrix}$$

where Δ is a $G^2 \times G(G + K)$ matrix with typical element given by (A.5). It is shown in ROTHENBERG (1971) that the rank of Φ is equal to $G^2 + GK + \rho^*$ where ρ^* is the rank of the $k \times G^2$ matrix

(10.7)
$$\Phi^* = \Psi_1[I_G \otimes (B \quad \Gamma)'] + \Psi_2[I_G \otimes 2\Sigma].$$

Thus we have the simple identification criterion due to WEGGE (1965): The structural parameter α^0 is locally identifiable if Φ^* has rank G^2 when evaluated at α^0. If the rank is constant in a neighborhood of α^0, then this condition is also necessary for local identifiability. Similarly, we have a simple criterion for the existence of reduced-form restrictions: The reduced-form parameter θ is restricted if Φ^* has constant rank less than k for all α near α^0 that satisfy (10.3).

If θ is restricted, then the asymptotic covariance matrix for an efficient estimator is smaller than that given by the unconstrained Cramér-Rao bound R^{-1}. The minimal covariance matrix for an estimator of θ was derived in chapter 2 and is given by

$$(10.8) \qquad H[C - C\Psi'(\Psi C\Psi')^{-1}\Psi C]H'$$

where C is the inverse (or, if singular, the generalized inverse) of $H'RH + \Psi'\Psi$. For any given problem one can evaluate (10.8) at some estimated value of the structural parameter α.

If none of the constraint equations (10.3) involve Σ, then some simplification occurs. Identification and the existence of restrictions on Π depend on the rank of

$$(10.9) \qquad \begin{bmatrix} H_{11} \\ \Psi_1 \end{bmatrix} = \begin{bmatrix} (\mathbf{B}^{-1} \otimes \overline{W}') \\ \Psi_1 \end{bmatrix}.$$

Equation (10.7) defining Φ^* remains valid with Ψ_2 equal to zero. The minimum covariance matrix for an efficient estimator of the reduced-form regression coefficients π is given by

$$(10.10) \qquad H_{11}[C_{11} - C_{11}\Psi_1'(\Psi_1 C_{11}\Psi_1')^{-1}\Psi_1 C_{11}]H_{11}'.$$

Using the results of section 6, we can write C_{11} as

$$(10.11) \qquad \begin{aligned} C_{11} &= [H_{11}'R_{11}H_{11} + \Psi_1'\Psi_1]^{-1} \\ &= [(\Sigma^{-1} \otimes \mathcal{M}^*) + \Psi_1'\Psi_1]^{-1} \end{aligned}$$

where $\mathcal{M}^*$ is the $(G + K) \times (G + K)$ matrix

$$\mathcal{M}^* = \text{plim} \frac{1}{n} \begin{bmatrix} \overline{Y}'\overline{Y} & Y'X \\ X'Y & X'X \end{bmatrix}.$$

These results on identification and efficiency are, of course, very similar to the ones presented in the earlier sections of the chapter. In the case of zero-order parameter restrictions we were able to derive explicit formulas for the covariance matrices of efficient estimators. Here in the case of more general restrictions we can only give expressions for the form of these matrices. This is the cost of the increased generality.

11. SUMMARY

In this chapter we have applied the theory of efficient estimation with prior information in the form of constraint parameters to the simultaneous equations model. Expressions for the asymptotic variance bound were found for both the reduced-form regression coefficients Π and the structural coefficients B and Γ. In addition, some results on the identifiability of the structural parameters were obtained by examining the Jacobian matrix H of the reduced-form transformation. Finally, we were able to show that the three-stage least-squares estimator and Malinvaud's minimum-distance estimator are asymptotically efficient only if there are no restrictions on the matrix Σ. The maximum-likelihood and minimum-chi-square estimators that take into account all the restrictions are both asymptotically efficient.

The algebra produced in this chapter yields only very modest qualitative results. The important question is whether the efficiency increases due to a priori restrictions are numerically important. The formulas derived here must be applied to some actual econometric problems in order to answer this question. That task is begun in chapter 5.

Appendix A

We shall derive expressions for some of the important matrices used in this chapter. The information matrix R_n is obtained by taking derivatives of the logarithmic likelihood function (2.5). If π_{pq} and π_{rs} are elements of Π, then a typical element is

A.1)
$$-\mathscr{E}\frac{\partial^2 \log f}{\partial \pi_{pq} \partial \pi_{rs}} = \mathscr{E}\omega^{pr}\sum_t x_{tq}x_{ts}$$

and the limiting matrix R_{11} has the form $\Omega^{-1} \otimes \mathscr{M}$. Each cross partial derivative with respect to an element of Π and an element of Ω is linear in $P - \Pi$ and hence has zero expected value. Thus, $R_{12} = R'_{21} = 0$.

The matrix R_{22} is somewhat more difficult to derive. Let $a_{ij,kl}$ be the element of the information matrix obtained by differentiating with respect to ω_{ij} and ω_{kl}. Since Ω is symmetric this submatrix should be of order $\frac{1}{2}G(G + 1)$ and should consist only of the elements $a_{ij,kl}$ with $i \geq j$ and $k \geq l$. Furthermore, when taking derivatives, we should impose the restriction $\omega_{ij} = \omega_{ji}$. Unfortunately, the resulting matrix is cumbersome and difficult to work with. Therefore, we have used an alternative approach which is considerably more convenient.

Suppose we ignore the symmetry and treat Ω as consisting of G^2 independent elements. Taking derivatives, we obtain

$$\frac{\partial \log f}{\partial \omega_{pq}} = -\frac{1}{2}n\omega^{qr} + \frac{1}{2}\sum_i \sum_j \sum_t v_{tj}v_{ti}\omega^{ip}\omega^{qj},$$

$$-\mathscr{E}\frac{\partial^2 \log f}{\partial \omega_{pq} \partial \omega_{rs}} = -\frac{1}{2}n\omega^{qr}\omega^{sp} + \mathscr{E}\frac{1}{2}\sum_i \sum_j \sum_t v_{tj}v_{ti}(\omega^{ip}\omega^{qr}\omega^{sj} + \omega^{qj}\omega^{ir}\omega^{sp})$$

$$= \frac{n}{2}\omega^{qr}\omega^{sp},$$

since $\mathscr{E}v_{tj}v_{ti}$ is by definition the reduced-form covariance ω_{ji}. But, of course, Ω is symmetric and the limiting matrix of elements can be written as

A.2)
$$R_{22} = \frac{1}{2}(\Omega^{-1} \otimes \Omega^{-1}).$$

If the symmetry of Ω is consistently ignored in all of the calculations, it can be shown that we obtain the same answers as if we had systematically imposed the symmetry constraints at each step. Since the derivations are considerably easier if the constraints are not imposed, we have followed the former procedure. However, we must still interpret the matrix R_{22}. Since there are in fact only $\frac{1}{2}G(G + 1)$ different elements of Ω, the $G^2 \times G^2$ matrix R_{22}^{-1} cannot represent a covariance matrix for an estimator of Ω. The following heuristic interpretation may be helpful. Any symmetric matrix Ω can be written as $\Omega = \frac{1}{2}(B + B')$ where B is not necessarily symmetric. If we ignore the symmetry of Ω we are, in effect, working with B. Suppose one has an estimate $\hat{B}$ of B. Then an estimate of Ω would be $\frac{1}{2}(\hat{B} + \hat{B}')$. The covariance between any two elements of $\hat{\Omega}$ could be written as

$$\text{Cov}(\omega_{pq}, \omega_{rs}) = \text{Cov}\left(\frac{b_{pq} + b_{qp}}{2}, \frac{b_{rs} + b_{sr}}{2}\right)$$

(A.3)

$$= \frac{1}{2}[\text{Cov}(b_{pq}, b_{rs}) + \text{Cov}(b_{pq}, b_{sr})].$$

Thus, if R_{22}^{-1} is thought of as a lower bound to the covariance matrix of an estimator of B, then a lower bound for an estimator of Ω is given by a matrix whose typical element (corresponding to ω_{pq} and ω_{rs}) is

$$\omega_{pr}\omega_{qs} + \omega_{ps}\omega_{qr}.$$

Asymptotically, this bound is attained by the least-squares estimator S.

We shall now derive the typical elements of the Jacobian matrices H_{21} and H_{22} and also of the matrices $H_{21}'R_{22}H_{21}$ and $H_{21}'R_{22}H_{22}$. Finally, for the case where Σ is diagonal, we shall derive an expression for the typical element of the matrix $H_{21}'R_{22}H_{22}(H_{22}'R_{22}H_{22})^{-1}H_{22}'R_{22}H_{21}$. The matrices H_{21} and H_{22} are obtained by differentiating the G^2 elements of Ω,

(A.4)
$$\omega_{rs} = \sum_i \sum_j \beta^{ri}\sigma_{ij}\beta^{sj},$$

with respect to δ and σ.

Each element of the $G^2 \times r$ matrix H_{21} corresponds to an element of Ω and an element of δ. It is clear from (A.4) that the derivative of any ω_{rs} with respect to an element of Γ is zero. Hence H_{21} contains a column of zeros for each element of δ that comes from Γ. The elements of H_{21} corresponding to elements of B take the following form. If β_{pq} is not known a priori, then

$$\frac{\partial \omega_{rs}}{\partial \beta_{pq}} = \sum_i \sum_j \left[\frac{\partial \beta^{ri}}{\partial \beta_{pq}}\sigma_{ij}\beta^{sj} + \beta^{ri}\sigma_{ij}\frac{\partial \beta^{sj}}{\partial \beta_{pq}}\right]$$

(A.5)
$$= -\sum_i \sum_j [\beta^{rp}\beta^{qi}\sigma_{ij}\beta^{sj} + \beta^{ri}\sigma_{ij}\beta^{sp}\beta^{qj}]$$

$$= -(\omega_{sq}\beta^{rp} + \omega_{rq}\beta^{sp}).$$

The matrix H_{22} is of order $G^2 \times r^*$ (where r^* is the number of unknown elements of Σ). If σ_{ab} is unknown, then

(A.6)
$$\frac{\partial \omega_{rs}}{\partial \sigma_{ab}} = \beta^{ra}\beta^{sb}.$$

Hence H_{22} is obtained by striking from $\mathbf{B}^{-1} \otimes \mathbf{B}^{-1}$ the columns that refer to known elements of Σ. Since $B^{-1} \otimes B^{-1}$ has full rank (and therefore G^2 independent columns), H_{22} must necessarily have full column rank.

Each element of the $r \times r$ matrix $H'_{21}R_{22}H_{21}$ corresponds to a pair of structural regression coefficients. The ij element (corresponding to δ_i and δ_j) is zero if either δ_i or δ_j or both are elements of Γ. If $\delta_i = \beta_{pq}$ and $\delta_j = \beta_{p'q'}$, then, using (A.5) and (3.4), we have

$$
\begin{aligned}
(H'_{21}R_{22}H_{21})_{ij} &= \tfrac{1}{2}\sum_{r}\sum_{s}\sum_{r'}\sum_{s'} (\omega_{sq}\beta^{rp} + \omega_{rq}\beta^{sp})\omega^{rr'}\omega^{ss'}(\omega_{s'q'}\beta^{r'p'} + \omega_{r'q'}\beta^{s'p'}) \\
(A.7) \qquad &= \tfrac{1}{2}(\omega_{qq'}\sigma^{pp'} + \beta^{qp'}\beta^{q'p} + \beta^{qp'}\beta^{q'p} + \omega_{qq'}\sigma^{pp'}) \\
&= \omega_{qq'}\sigma^{pp'} + \beta^{qp'}\beta^{q'p}
\end{aligned}
$$

where use has been made of the relation

$$
\sigma^{rs} = \sum_{i}\sum_{j}\beta^{ir}\omega^{ij}\beta^{js}.
$$

Each element of the $r^* \times r^*$ matrix $H'_{22}R_{22}H_{22}$ corresponds to a pair of unknown elements of Σ. The ij element, where i represents σ_{ab} and j represents σ_{cd}, is given by

$$
\begin{aligned}
(H'_{22}R_{22}H_{22})_{ij} &= \tfrac{1}{2}\sum_{r}\sum_{s}\sum_{r'}\sum_{s'} \beta^{ra}\beta^{sb}\omega^{rr'}\omega^{ss'}\beta^{r'c}\beta^{s'd} \\
(A.8) \qquad &= -\tfrac{1}{2}\sigma^{ac}\sigma^{bd}.
\end{aligned}
$$

Hence, $H'_{22}R_{22}H_{22}$ is obtained by striking from $\tfrac{1}{2}\Sigma^{-1} \otimes \Sigma^{-1}$ the rows and columns corresponding to the known elements of Σ.

Each element of the $r \times r^*$ matrix $H'_{21}R_{22}H_{22}$ corresponding to an element of δ and an unknown element of Σ. The rows corresponding to elements of Γ are zero. The other elements are of the following form (where the ith row represents β_{pq} and the jth column represents σ_{ab}):

$$
\begin{aligned}
(H'_{21}R_{22}H_{22})_{ij} &= -\tfrac{1}{2}\sum_{r}\sum_{s}\sum_{r'}\sum_{s'} (\omega_{sq}\beta^{rp} + \omega_{rq}\beta^{sp})\omega^{rr'}\omega^{ss'}\beta^{r'a}\beta^{s'b} \\
(A.9) \qquad &= -\tfrac{1}{2}(\beta^{qb}\sigma^{pa} + \beta^{qa}\sigma^{pb}).
\end{aligned}
$$

An important matrix for considering Σ-restrictions is

$$
M^{(3)} = -H'_{21}R_{22}H_{22}(H'_{22}R_{22}H_{22})^{-1}H'_{22}R_{22}H_{21}.
$$

Unfortunately, although we have an expression for the typical element of $H'_{22}R_{22}H_{22}$, we cannot find a simple expression for its inverse except for special cases. If the prior information is of the form that restricts Σ to be diagonal, then $H'_{22}R_{22}H_{22}$ is a $G \times G$ diagonal matrix with the ii element given by

$$
(A.10) \qquad\qquad (H'_{22}R_{22}H_{22})_{ii} = \tfrac{1}{2}\sigma^{ii}\sigma^{ii}.
$$

The inverse is a $G \times G$ diagonal matrix with the ii element equal to $2\sigma_{ii}^2$. Hence, if

$\delta_i = \beta_{pq}$ and $\delta_j = \beta_{rs}$, we have

$$m_{ij}^{(3)} = -\tfrac{1}{2} \sum_i (\beta^{qi}\sigma^{pi} + \beta^{qi}\sigma^{pi})\sigma_{ii}^2(\beta^{si}\sigma^{ri} + \beta^{si}\sigma^{ri})$$

(A.11)
$$= \begin{cases} 0 & \text{if } p \neq r, \\ -2\beta^{sp}\beta^{qp} & \text{if } p = r. \end{cases}$$

Appendix B

The results in this chapter are based on the assumption that Σ, the matrix of structural error covariances, is nonsingular. This means that all G structural equations are stochastic with nondegenerate random error terms. In most economic models, however, there appear linear identities—nonstochastic equations that contain no unknown parameters. The purpose of this appendix is to show that, after a trivial redefinition of certain matrices, the results of the chapter apply to the case in which there are linear identities.

One way to handle the case of linear identities is simply to "solve them out." That is, the identities can be used to reduce the number of structural equations and the number of endogenous variables so that the reduced system has a nonsingular covariance matrix of structural errors. If the system is linear and B is nonsingular, this can always be done. The trouble with this method is that the a priori constraints will become more complicated. If the original system had only zero-order coefficient restrictions, the process of solving out the identities will introduce restrictions of a higher order. Furthermore, the parameters of the original model are usually easier to interpret than the parameters of the reduced model. For these reasons, therefore, it is desirable to work with models that contain the identities.

Suppose the system contains G' stochastic equations and $G - G'$ identities. We assume that there are no unknown parameters in the identities. The complete system (2.1) can be partitioned as follows:

$$
\text{(B.1)} \qquad \begin{bmatrix} B_{11} & B_{12} \\ B_{21} & B_{22} \end{bmatrix} \begin{bmatrix} y_1 \\ y_2 \end{bmatrix} + \begin{bmatrix} \Gamma_1 \\ \Gamma_2 \end{bmatrix} x = \begin{bmatrix} u_1 \\ 0 \end{bmatrix}
$$

where y_1 is a vector of G' of the dependent variables, y_2 is a vector of the remaining dependent variables, x is the vector of all K endogenous variables, and u_1 is the G'-dimensional vector of disturbances. The matrices B_{21}, B_{22}, and Γ_2 are known a priori. If the matrix B is nonsingular, then there exists some ordering of the endogenous variables for which B_{22} is nonsingular. We assume y_1 and y_2 are chosen so that B_{22} is nonsingular.

The system (B.1) is equivalent (as far as the stochastic part is concerned) to

$$
\text{(B.2)} \qquad B_{11}y_1 + B_{12}[-B_{22}^{-1}B_{21}y_1 - B_{22}^{-1}\Gamma_2 x] + \Gamma_1 x = u_1
$$

or

$$
\text{(B.3)} \qquad \bar{B}y_1 + \bar{\Gamma}x = u_1
$$

where

(B.4)
$$\bar{B} = B_{11} - B_{12}B_{22}^{-1}B_{21},$$
$$\bar{\Gamma} = \Gamma_1 - B_{12}B_{22}^{-1}\Gamma_2.$$

It is easy to verify that $\bar{B}$ is simply the inverse of B^{11}, the $G' \times G'$ upper left submatrix of B^{-1}:

(B.5)
$$B^{-1} = \begin{bmatrix} B_{11} & B_{12} \\ B_{21} & B_{22} \end{bmatrix}^{-1} = \begin{bmatrix} B^{11} & B^{12} \\ B^{21} & B^{22} \end{bmatrix}.$$

The reduced form for (B.3) is

(B.6)
$$y_1 = \Pi_1 x + v_1$$

where

(B.7)
$$\Pi_1 = -\bar{B}^{-1}\bar{\Gamma} = -[B^{11}\Gamma_1 + B^{12}\Gamma_2],$$

(B.8)
$$v_1 = \bar{B}^{-1}u_1 = B^{11}u_1.$$

All of the relevant stochastic information is given by the probability distribution of v_1 since v_1 is uniquely related to the basic error term u_1. The constraint equations relating the reduced-form parameters Π_1 and Ω_{11} to the structural parameters B_{11}, B_{12}, Γ_1, and Σ_{11} are given by

(B.9)
$$\Pi_1 = -[B^{11}\Gamma_1 + B^{12}\Gamma_2],$$
$$\Omega_{11} = B^{11}\Sigma_{11}B^{11'}.$$

But equations (B.9) are simply a subset of the equations (2.3):

(B.10)
$$\Pi = \begin{bmatrix} \Pi_1 \\ \Pi_2 \end{bmatrix} = -\begin{bmatrix} B^{11} & B^{12} \\ B^{21} & B^{22} \end{bmatrix}\begin{bmatrix} \Gamma_1 \\ \Gamma_2 \end{bmatrix},$$
$$\Omega = \begin{bmatrix} \Omega_{11} & \Omega_{12} \\ \Omega_{21} & \Omega_{22} \end{bmatrix} = \begin{bmatrix} B^{11} & B^{12} \\ B^{21} & B^{22} \end{bmatrix}\begin{bmatrix} \Sigma_{11} & 0 \\ 0 & 0 \end{bmatrix}\begin{bmatrix} B^{11} & B^{12} \\ B^{21} & B^{22} \end{bmatrix}'.$$

Hence the derivatives of (B.9) can be obtained by taking a subset of the derivatives of (B.10). But these latter derivatives have already been calculated in section 5 and appendix A. Since these calculations do not depend on the invertibility of Σ, they are valid in the present context. The only change needed is that ω^{ij} and σ^{ij} should be interpreted as being typical elements of Ω_{11}^{-1} and Σ_{11}^{-1}. Elements of the form β^{ij} and ω_{ij} should be interpreted as typical elements of the *full* $G \times G$ matrices B^{-1} and Ω.

The relevant information matrix for (Π_1, Ω_{11}) is

(B.11)
$$\begin{bmatrix} \Omega_{11}^{-1} \otimes \mathcal{M} & 0 \\ 0 & \frac{1}{2}(\Omega_{11}^{-1} \otimes \Omega_{11}^{-1}) \end{bmatrix}.$$

Equation (5.7) becomes

(B.12) $$H_{11} = -(B^{11} \otimes I)W'$$

where W is unchanged. Equation (6.1) becomes

$$
\begin{aligned}
M_{11} &= (H'_{11}R_{11}H_{11})^{-1} \\
&= [W(B^{11} \otimes I)'(\Omega_{11}^{-1} \otimes \mathcal{M})(B^{11} \times I)W']^{-1} \\
&= [W(\Sigma_{11}^{-1} \otimes \mathcal{M})W']^{-1}.
\end{aligned}
$$

(B.13)

CHAPTER 5

The Value of Restrictions

1. INTRODUCTION

The results obtained up to now indicate that under rather general conditions a priori restrictions that reduce the dimensionality of the parameter space result in an increase in estimation efficiency. In this chapter we shall consider the question of how important this increase is in practice. That is, we shall investigate the *magnitude* of the efficiency increase that results from a priori restrictions.

In order to speak of the amount by which efficiency is increased, we must first define some cardinal measure of efficiency. Up to now efficiency has been treated as an ordinal concept. An unbiased estimator t_n has been called more efficient than an unbiased estimator s_n if the difference in covariance matrices $V_s - V_t$ is positive semidefinite for all θ. If θ were a scalar, then this difference in variances would be a perfectly satisfactory measure of efficiency increase. When θ is a vector, however, it is not at all obvious how to measure the "magnitude" of $V_s - V_t$. A common way to measure the size of a covariance matrix is to consider its determinant value.[1] This approach, however, has little intuitive appeal. Furthermore, it cannot be applied to our problem since the covariance matrices involved may be singular; the determinant will give the absurd measure of zero.

The following approach has greater appeal. In the general problem posed in chapter 1, the unknown parameter vector θ must be estimated by a vector function of the sample $t_n = t(Y_n)$. Suppose the statistician possesses a loss function $L(t_n, \theta)$ defined over the possible values the estimator and parameter may take. If this function expresses the importance of various estimation errors, then it is natural to rank estimators according to their *expected* loss. If $L(t_n, \theta)$ is a general quadratic function in the estimation

1. See, for example, ZELLNER AND THEIL (1962), p. 63.

error $t_n - \theta$, it can be written as

(1.1) $$L = (t_n - \theta)'Q(t_n - \theta) + (t_n - \theta)'q_1 + q_0$$

where Q is a positive semidefinite matrix, q_1 is a vector, and q_0 is a scalar. Then, for any unbiased estimator t_n, expected loss is given by tr $QV_t + q_0$. Thus the ranking of unbiased estimators in this case is based on tr QV_t. The estimator t_n is best if tr $QV_t \leq$ tr QV_s for all unbiased s and for all permissible values of θ. The efficiency gain due to using t_n instead of s_n is, according to the approach suggested here, measured by the difference in expected loss

(1.2) $$\text{tr } Q(V_s - V_t).$$

The function tr QV_t is thus a useful measure of the size of a covariance matrix. It has the advantage over the determinant in that it is derivable from decision-theoretic considerations and can be nonzero even when V_t is singular. Furthermore, the cardinal measure (1.2) is consistent with the ordinal measure $V_s - V_t$ as we showed in chapter 1.

The above discussion also is relevant for asymptotic efficiency. In that case, however, t_n is replaced by the random variable t whose distribution approximates that of t_n. Then V_t is the covariance matrix of the approximating distribution (i.e., the asymptotic covariance matrix). The decision-theoretic interpretation is less convincing in this case, however, since $\mathscr{E}L(t_n, \theta)$ need not be finite even though $\mathscr{E}L(t, \theta)$ is finite. This results from the fact, alluded to in section 8 of chapter 2, that an unbounded loss function is not really appropriate for decision-theoretic purposes. Again the theory ought to be conducted with a truncated loss function as suggested by CHERNOFF (1956). Unfortunately very little is known about this extension of classical estimation theory.

The major difficulty with the efficiency measure tr QV is that it depends on an arbitrary matrix Q. This however should not be surprising since it is clear that the statistician's preferences must appear somewhere in the analysis. Indeed, the amazing thing about the classical theory of minimum-variance unbiased estimation is how far one can go before one needs to specify the relative importance of the different elements of θ. All the theorems on the Cramér-Rao bound can be stated in terms of expected quadratic loss, but there is no need to do this. Only when we drop the unbiasedness assumption is it necessary to introduce the matrix Q in order to obtain qualitative results. For quantitative conclusions, however, the loss matrix Q is crucial.

2. A GENERAL RESULT

Consider now the case of constraint parameters presented in section 5 of chapter 2. The asymptotic[2] covariance matrix of an efficient estimator of θ is given by R^{-1} if the constraints are ignored and by $H(H'RH)^{-1}H'$ if the constraints are used. Hence the efficiency gain is measured by

(2.1) $\text{tr}[QR^{-1} - QH(H'RH)^{-1}H']$.

For many purposes it is more interesting to look at the ratio

(2.2) $\eta = \dfrac{\text{tr}[QH(H'RH)^{-1}H']}{\text{tr}[QR^{-1}]}$.

This "efficiency ratio" measures the relative efficiency of the unconstrained estimator with respect to the constrained estimator. It is thus analogous to the traditional one-dimensional notion of relative efficiency. If η is near zero, then the loss due to not using the constraints is very large. An η-value of one-half indicates that loss is cut in half if the constraints are used. An η-value near one indicates that there is little loss which results from ignoring the constraints.

Ideally we would like to get some indication of the size of η that depends on Q, R, and H in a very simple way. In particular since H depends on the constraint parameters that are unknown, it would be desirable to find an expression for η that is not sensitive to the value of H. Unfortunately, it does not appear possible in general to find such an expression for η. In one very special case, however, an amazingly simple answer results. Suppose for a moment that Q and R both are equal to an $m \times m$ identity matrix. That is, (1) expected loss depends only on the sum of the variances and (2) the efficient unconstrained estimator has a covariance matrix with unit variances and zero for all covariances. In that case

$$\eta = \frac{\text{tr}[H(H'H)^{-1}H']}{\text{tr}[I_m]} = \frac{\text{tr}[I_r]}{\text{tr}[I_m]} = \frac{r}{m}.$$

Thus if there are ten elements of θ but only three constraint parameters α, the efficiency of the unconstrained estimator of θ is three-tenths.

---

2. Because the application to simultaneous equation systems involves nonlinear constraints which make the finite-sample variance bound unattainable, the rest of this chapter will concentrate on the asymptotic theory. The adaptation of these results to the finite-sample case is trivial. Again, in order to simplify the terminology, the adjective "asymptotic" will often be dropped.

This very special case generalizes if we are willing to settle for some inequalities. The basic result of this section is given by the following theorem:

The efficiency ratio η satisfies the inequality

$$(2.3) \qquad \frac{r}{m}\frac{\lambda_1}{\bar{\lambda}} \leq \eta \leq \frac{r}{m}\frac{\lambda_m}{\bar{\lambda}}$$

where r is the dimension of α, m is the dimension of θ, λ_1 is the smallest characteristic root of the matrix $R^{-1}Q$, λ_m is the largest root, and $\bar{\lambda}$ is the arithmetic average of the m roots of that matrix.

The proof is straightforward. Since R is positive definite and Q is symmetric, there exists[3] a nonsingular matrix A such that $A'RA = I$ and $A'QA = D$ where D is a diagonal matrix consisting of the characteristic roots of $R^{-1}Q$. Defining $X = A^{-1}H$, we can write the numerator of (2.2) as

$$\text{tr}[QH(H'RH)^{-1}H'] = \text{tr}[(H'RH)^{-1}H'QH] = \text{tr}[(X'X)^{-1}X'DX].$$

But this last term may be written either as

$$\text{tr}[(X'X)^{-1}X'X\lambda_1] + \text{tr}[(X'X)^{-1}X'(D - \lambda_1 I)X]$$

or as

$$\text{tr}[(X'X)^{-1}X'X\lambda_m] - \text{tr}[(X'X)^{-1}X'(\lambda_m I - D)X].$$

In both cases the second trace is nonnegative since both $D - \lambda_1 I$ and $\lambda_m I - D$ are positive semidefinite. Thus,

$$\lambda_1 \text{tr}[I_r] \leq \text{tr}[QH(H'RH)^{-1}H'] \leq \lambda_m \text{tr}[I_r].$$

Furthermore,

$$\text{tr}[QR^{-1}] = \text{tr}[R^{-1}Q] = \sum_{i=1}^{m} \lambda_i = m\bar{\lambda}.$$

Dividing, we obtain (2.3).

If the characteristic roots of $R^{-1}Q$ are not widely dispersed so that λ_1 and λ_m are close to each other, then η must be approximately equal to r/m. If Q should equal R, as is the case if both are identity matrices, then η is exactly r/m. Thus our result suggests that if QR^{-1} is nearly the identity matrix, the efficiency gain due to a reduction in the dimension of the parameter space of θ is roughly proportional to the decrease in dimensionality.

3. See, for example, THRALL AND TORNHEIM (1957), p. 188.

Our inequality gives a precise statement only if the characteristic roots of $R^{-1}Q$ are highly concentrated. In fact, the upper bound need not be less than one. Unfortunately, it is not at all clear that in practice the roots will be highly concentrated. Even if Q is the identity matrix, there is no particular reason to expect the roots of R^{-1} to have any special concentration. Thus our general result is not always useful. It does, however, have a practical use. One is often interested in the size of η in order to decide whether it is worthwhile to go to the extra trouble of estimating θ subject to the constraints. Particularly when one is not entirely sure of the validity of the constraints, one wants to know their potential value (if correct) before risking their use. The inequality (2.3), however, does *not* depend on the matrix H except for the column dimension r. It depends only on the matrices Q and R, the one given by the statistician's loss function, the other estimable without using the constraints at all.

Thus a possible procedure to follow when in doubt about using the a priori constraints is (1) estimate θ and $R(\theta)$ by a method that ignores the constraints, (2) find the characteristic roots of the estimated R and derive the bounds on η, and finally (3) if the upper bound is small enough to suggest a large efficiency gain, reestimate θ using the constraints. Of course, if it is essential to estimate the constraint parameters α, then the question does not even arise.

The purpose of this section has been to get some indication of the size of the efficiency gain due to imposing restrictions. We must conclude, however, that if one really wants a precise measure of this gain, there is no alternative to actually evaluating numerically the matrices R^{-1} and $H(H'RH)^{-1}H'$. Since these matrices depend on the unknown parameters α and θ, one must first estimate these parameters and then use them to estimate the covariance matrices. The general results of this section are suggestive, but practice with specific problems and actual data must be the ultimate test of the value of a priori restrictions. In the following sections we shall look at two small simultaneous equation systems and calculate the various covariance matrices that were derived in chapter 4.

3. EXAMPLE I: AN ARTIFICIAL MODEL

Before we turn to an example which has some "real-world" interpretation, it will be useful to illustrate the results of chapter 4 by an artificial example. This will have the advantage of presenting the basic ideas without our getting lost in a morass of numerical calculation. We shall turn to a model that does try to represent an actual econometric process in the next section.

Consider the two-equation model

(3.1)
$$y_1 + \beta_{12}y_2 + \gamma_{13}x_3 = u_1$$
$$\beta_{21}y_1 + y_2 + \gamma_{21}x_1 + \gamma_{22}x_2 = u_2$$

where y_1 and y_2 are endogenous variables; x_1, x_2, and x_3 are the exogenous variables. The random errors are assumed to be normally distributed with zero mean and *zero* covariance. There are thus six zero-order restrictions:

(3.2)
$$\beta_{11} = 1, \qquad \gamma_{11} = 0,$$
$$\beta_{22} = 1, \qquad \gamma_{12} = 0,$$
$$\sigma_{12} = 0, \qquad \gamma_{23} = 0.$$

The reduced form of this system is

(3.3)
$$y_1 = \pi_{11}x_1 + \pi_{12}x_2 + \pi_{13}x_3 + v_1$$
$$y_2 = \pi_{21}x_1 + \pi_{22}x_2 + \pi_{23}x_3 + v_2.$$

The vectors of reduced-form and unknown structural coefficients are given by

$$\pi = \begin{bmatrix} \pi_{11} \\ \pi_{12} \\ \pi_{13} \\ \pi_{21} \\ \pi_{22} \\ \pi_{23} \end{bmatrix}, \qquad \delta = \begin{bmatrix} \beta_{12} \\ \gamma_{13} \\ \beta_{21} \\ \gamma_{21} \\ \gamma_{22} \end{bmatrix}.$$

We shall consider the estimation of these regression coefficients under four different assumptions about the use of a priori information:

1) If no structural restrictions are used, the structural parameters cannot be consistently estimated. The minimum (asymptotic) variance bound for the unconstrained estimator of π is derived in chapter 4, section 3, and is given by

(3.4)
$$R_{11}^{-1} = \Omega \otimes \mathcal{M}^{-1}$$

where Ω is the 2×2 covariance matrix of reduced-form errors and $\mathcal{M}$ is the 3×3 limiting sample matrix of cross products for the exogenous variables.

2) If the five coefficient restrictions are used (but the constraint $\sigma_{12} = 0$ ignored), the five unknown structural coefficients δ can be efficiently estimated with an asymptotic covariance matrix

$$(3.5) \qquad [M^{(1)}]^{-1} = (H'_{11}R_{11}H_{11})^{-1}$$

where, by equation (5.6) of chapter 4, H_{11} is the 6×5 matrix:

$$H_{11} = - \begin{bmatrix} \beta^{11} & 0 & 0 & \beta^{12} & 0 & 0 \\ 0 & \beta^{11} & 0 & 0 & \beta^{12} & 0 \\ 0 & 0 & \beta^{11} & 0 & 0 & \beta^{12} \\ \beta^{21} & 0 & 0 & \beta^{22} & 0 & 0 \\ 0 & \beta^{21} & 0 & 0 & \beta^{22} & 0 \\ 0 & 0 & \beta^{21} & 0 & 0 & \beta^{22} \end{bmatrix} \begin{bmatrix} \pi_{21} & 0 & 0 & 0 & 0 \\ \pi_{22} & 0 & 0 & 0 & 0 \\ \pi_{23} & 1 & 0 & 0 & 0 \\ 0 & 0 & \pi_{11} & 1 & 0 \\ 0 & 0 & \pi_{12} & 0 & 1 \\ 0 & 0 & \pi_{13} & 0 & 0 \end{bmatrix}.$$

The reduced-form covariance matrix is now

$$(3.6) \qquad H_{11}[M^{(1)}]^{-1}H'_{11} = H_{11}(H'_{11}R_{11}H_{11})^{-1}H'_{11}.$$

3) If the constraint $\sigma_{12} = 0$ is used along with the coefficient restrictions, the covariance matrix for an efficient estimate of δ becomes

$$(3.7) \qquad [M^{(1)} + M^{(2)} + M^{(3)}]^{-1}$$

and that for π becomes

$$(3.8) \qquad H_{11}[M^{(1)} + M^{(2)} + M^{(3)}]^{-1}H'_{11}$$

where, using equations (7.3) and (7.7) of chapter 4,

$$M^{(2)} = \begin{bmatrix} \omega_{22}\sigma^{11} + \beta^{21}\beta^{21} & 0 & \omega_{21}\sigma^{12} + \beta^{22}\beta^{11} & 0 & 0 \\ 0 & 0 & 0 & 0 & 0 \\ \omega_{21}\sigma^{12} + \beta^{22}\beta^{11} & 0 & \omega_{11}\sigma^{22} + \beta^{12}\beta^{12} & 0 & 0 \\ 0 & 0 & 0 & 0 & 0 \\ 0 & 0 & 0 & 0 & 0 \end{bmatrix},$$

$$M^{(3)} = \begin{bmatrix} -2\beta^{21}\beta^{21} & 0 & 0 & 0 & 0 \\ 0 & 0 & 0 & 0 & 0 \\ 0 & 0 & -2\beta^{12}\beta^{12} & 0 & 0 \\ 0 & 0 & 0 & 0 & 0 \\ 0 & 0 & 0 & 0 & 0 \end{bmatrix}.$$

4) Finally, if Σ is assumed to be entirely known, then the covariance matrices for efficient estimates of δ and π become

(3.19) $$[M^{(1)} + M^{(2)}]^{-1},$$

(3.10) $$H_{11}[M^{(1)} + M^{(2)}]^{-1}H'_{11}.$$

All of the above covariance matrices depend on the values of the unknown parameters. In order to see how efficiency is affected by the use of a priori information it is necessary to know the numerical values of these parameters. We shall evaluate the various covariance matrices under the assumption that the true parameters are given by

$$B = \begin{bmatrix} 1 & 1 \\ 2 & 1 \end{bmatrix}, \qquad \Gamma = \begin{bmatrix} 0 & 0 & 1 \\ 1 & 1 & 0 \end{bmatrix},$$

$$\Sigma = \begin{bmatrix} 1 & 0 \\ 0 & 1 \end{bmatrix}, \qquad \mathcal{M} = \begin{bmatrix} 1 & 0 & 0 \\ 0 & 1 & 0 \\ 0 & 0 & 1 \end{bmatrix}.$$

These numerical assumptions were chosen for computational convenience. Since the model is purely artificial, the question of "realistic" values does not have much meaning. On the basis of the above numerical specifications of the structure, it follows that

$$B^{-1} = \begin{bmatrix} -1 & 1 \\ 2 & -1 \end{bmatrix}, \qquad \Pi = \begin{bmatrix} -1 & -1 & 1 \\ 1 & 1 & -2 \end{bmatrix},$$

$$\Omega = \begin{bmatrix} 2 & -3 \\ -3 & 5 \end{bmatrix}, \qquad \Omega^{-1} = \begin{bmatrix} 5 & 3 \\ 3 & 2 \end{bmatrix}.$$

It is of interest to evaluate the upper and lower bounds of the inequality (2.3) before proceeding to actually evaluate the covariance matrices. We shall do this for the simplest case, in which only the five coefficient restrictions are used. If we ignore the estimation of Ω, we have from (2.2) and (3.6)

$$\eta = \frac{\text{tr}[QH_{11}(H'_{11}R_{11}H_{11})^{-1}H'_{11}]}{\text{tr}[QE_{11}^{-1}]}$$

where Q is a 6×6 loss matrix for the six elements of π. If we take Q to be the identity matrix, the evaluation of (2.3) involves only finding the characteristic roots of R_{11}^{-1}. Since the matrix R_{11}^{-1} is of the Kronecker product form, this is easily accomplished. There are three roots equal to 6.85 and three roots equal to 0.15. With $m = 6$ and $r = 5$, the inequality (2.3) becomes

$$0.04 \leq \eta \leq 1.65.$$

It is clear that this inequality tells us nothing and that numerical evaluation of the covariance matrix of the restricted estimators is needed.

The basic matrices necessary for the calculations and the resulting asymptotic covariance matrices for efficient estimates of the parameters are reproduced in the appendix to this chapter. Tables 5.1 and 5.2 present some useful summary measures of the gain in efficiency resulting from the use of correct prior information. In table 5.1 the asymptotic variances of the efficient parameter estimates are given. In table 5.2 the loss measure tr QV_t is evaluated for two alternative quadratic loss functions. In one case the matrix Q is simply an identity matrix and expected loss is expressed as the sum of the variances. In the other case the matrix Q is square with all elements equal to unity. It expresses expected loss as the variance of the sum of all the regression coefficient estimates.

TABLE 5.1   ARTIFICIAL NUMERICAL EXAMPLE:
ASYMPTOTIC VARIANCES OF EFFICIENT ESTIMATES

Parameter	Type of a priori restrictions on structure			
	Case 1 none*	Case 2 B, Γ only	Case 3 Σ diagonal	Case 4 Σ known
		Structure		
β_{12}		0.50	0.40	0.09
γ_{13}		3.00	2.60	1.37
β_{21}		1.00	0.60	0.30
γ_{21}		2.00	1.60	1.30
γ_{22}		2.00	1.60	1.30
Sum		8.50	6.80	4.36
		Reduced form		
π_{11}	2.00	1.50	1.40	1.09
π_{12}	2.00	1.50	1.40	1.09
π_{13}	2.00	2.00	1.60	1.30
π_{21}	5.00	3.00	2.60	1.37
π_{22}	5.00	3.00	2.60	1.37
π_{23}	5.00	5.00	4.60	4.28
Sum	21.00	16.00	14.20	10.50

* Structural parameters not identified.

TABLE 5.2 ARTIFICIAL NUMERICAL EXAMPLE:
MEASURES OF EFFICIENCY GAIN DUE TO STRUCTURAL RESTRICTIONS

Loss function	Type of structural restrictions			
	Case 1 none	Case 2 B, Γ only	Case 3 Σ diagonal	Case 4 Σ known
	Structure			
$\mathrm{tr}[V_\delta]$	–	8.50	6.80	4.36
$\mathrm{tr}[Q_1 V_\delta]$	–	4.50	3.60	3.35
	Reduced form			
$\mathrm{tr}[V_\pi]$	21.00	16.00	14.20	10.50
$\mathrm{tr}[Q_1 V_\pi]$	3.00	3.00	2.60	1.37

NOTE: The matrix Q_1 is a square matrix of appropriate size consisting solely of ones. The matrices V_δ and V_π represent the appropriate minimal covariance matrices for δ and π.

It is seen from these tables that the degree of efficiency gain depends on what loss matrix is used. Some variances drop sharply under a priori information while others hardly change at all. Furthermore, the co-variances are affected considerably by the imposition of structural restrictions. Yet the overall impression is that a priori restrictions are important in increasing efficiency. When Σ is (correctly) assumed to be diagonal and the five structural coefficient restrictions are used, the reduced-form variances are cut by amounts ranging from 8 to 30 percent of their un-restricted values. If Σ is known and the five coefficient restrictions are used, the loss due to reduced-form estimation error (as measured by either loss matrix) is half of that obtained if no structural restrictions are used. Finally, it is interesting to note that adding the assumption that Σ is diagonal to the coefficient restrictions reduces loss by nearly 20 percent in our example.

4. EXAMPLE II: A MACROECONOMIC MODEL

The importance of overidentifying restrictions in increasing the efficiency of reduced form estimation depends on the particular model and data that are used. Since the model presented in the previous section is completely artificial, it cannot tell us much about the value of a priori information in practice. A more fruitful test lies in the use of models and data that are representative of actual econometric applications. For this purpose we shall study a simple, but by no means trivial, macroeconomic model of the United States economy which has been developed by KLEIN (1950). This model, the first of three analyzed in his monograph, has been estimated by various methods and has become a classic in the econometric literature. Our use of Klein's model I and his original data will facilitate comparisons of the present results with those of others who have also used this numerical example.

The system consists of three behavioral structural equations and a number of identities. The precise form in which the system is written is somewhat arbitrary since the identities can be "solved out" in varying degrees. Since the theory of chapter 4 is most easily applied when there are only zero-order restrictions, this will dictate the form of the system we shall use. Specifically, we shall consider a system of seven structural equations in seven current endogenous variables and eight predetermined variables. The variables are listed in table 5.3 and are further described in Klein's study.[4] The system contains three stochastic structural equations. These are a consumption function

$$(4.1) \qquad C = \delta_1 P + \delta_2 W + \delta_3 P_{-1} + \delta_4 + u_1,$$

an investment function

$$(4.2) \qquad I = \delta_5 P + \delta_6 P_{-1} + \delta_7 K_{-1} + \delta_8 + u_2,$$

and a labor demand function

$$(4.3) \qquad W_1 = \delta_9 Y + \delta_{10} t + \delta_{11} Y_{-1} + \delta_{12} + u_3.$$

The 3×3 covariance matrix of the contemporaneous errors u_1, u_2, and u_3 is denoted by Σ and is assumed to be nonsingular. The errors are assumed to be normally distributed with zero means.

The system is completed by four identities

$$(4.4) \qquad \begin{aligned} Y + W_2 &= C + I + G \\ Y &= W_1 + P + T \\ K &= I + K_{-1} \\ W &= W_1 + W_2. \end{aligned}$$

Defining y as the vector of the seven current endogenous variables and x as the vector of the eight predetermined variables, we can write the

4. Our notation differs slightly from Klein's. We use P instead of Π for profits. Further, our Y is $Y + T - W_2$ in Klein's notation (i.e., our Y is net private product whereas his is national income). Our model, however, is identical with his.

TABLE 5.3 VARIABLES IN KLEIN'S MODEL I

Current Endogenous Variables

$y_1 = C$	Consumption
$y_2 = I$	Net private investment
$y_3 = W_1$	Private wage bill
$y_4 = P$	Profits
$y_5 = W$	Total wage bill
$y_6 = Y$	Net private national product
$y_7 = K$	End-of-year capital stock

Predetermined Variables

$x_1 = W_2$	Government wage bill
$x_2 = T$	Business taxes
$x_3 = G$	Government expenditures
$x_4 = t$	Time (1931 = 0)
$x_5 = P_{-1}$	Lagged profits
$x_6 = K_{-1}$	Lagged capital stock
$x_7 = Y_{-1}$	Lagged net private national product
$x_8 = 1$	Unity (dummy variable representing the constant term)

system as

(4.5)
$$By + \Gamma x = u$$

where

(4.6)
$$y' = (C, I, W_1, P, W, Y, K)$$
$$x' = (W_2, T, G, t, P_{-1}, K_{-1}, Y_{-1}, 1)$$
$$u' = (u_1, u_2, u_3, 0, 0, 0, 0).$$

The matrices B and Γ may be partitioned as follows:

$$B = \begin{bmatrix} B_{11} & B_{12} \\ B_{21} & B_{22} \end{bmatrix} = \begin{bmatrix} 1 & 0 & 0 & -\delta_1 & -\delta_2 & 0 & 0 \\ 0 & 1 & 0 & -\delta_5 & 0 & 0 & 0 \\ 0 & 0 & 1 & 0 & 0 & -\delta_9 & 0 \\ 1 & 1 & 0 & 0 & 0 & -1 & 0 \\ 0 & 0 & 1 & 1 & 0 & -1 & 0 \\ 0 & 1 & 0 & 0 & 0 & 0 & -1 \\ 0 & 0 & 1 & 0 & -1 & 0 & 0 \end{bmatrix},$$

$$\Gamma = \begin{bmatrix} \Gamma_1 \\ \Gamma_2 \end{bmatrix} = \left[\begin{array}{cccccccc} 0 & 0 & 0 & 0 & -\delta_3 & 0 & 0 & -\delta_4 \\ 0 & 0 & 0 & 0 & -\delta_6 & -\delta_7 & 0 & -\delta_8 \\ 0 & 0 & 0 & -\delta_{10} & 0 & 0 & -\delta_{11} & -\delta_{12} \\ \hline -1 & 0 & 1 & 0 & 0 & 0 & 0 & 0 \\ 0 & 1 & 0 & 0 & 0 & 0 & 0 & 0 \\ 0 & 0 & 0 & 0 & 0 & 1 & 0 & 0 \\ 1 & 0 & 0 & 0 & 0 & 0 & 0 & 0 \end{array}\right].$$

The reduced form is

(4.7) $\qquad y = -B^{-1}\Gamma x + B^{-1}u = \Pi x + v.$

Although (4.7) consists of seven equations, they are not independent. The last four rows of Π can be derived from the first three by using the four structural identities (4.4). Furthermore, the vector v has a singular normal distribution of rank three. There will be no loss of information, therefore, if we consider only the first three equations of (4.7). The relevant matrices of the reduced-form system are Π_1, the 3×8 matrix obtained by deleting the last four rows of Π, and Ω_{11}, the covariance matrix for v_1, v_2, and v_3. These matrices may be written as

(4.8) $\qquad\qquad \Pi_1 = B^{11}\Gamma_1 + B^{12}\Gamma_2,$

(4.9) $\qquad\qquad \Omega_{11} = B^{11}\Sigma B^{11\prime}$

where B^{11} and B^{12} are submatrices of B^{-1}.

We may now apply the theory of chapter 4 to this simultaneous equations system. The first three reduced-form equations contain twenty-four unknown regression coefficients

$$\pi' = (\pi_{11}, \ldots, \pi_{18}, \pi_{21}, \ldots, \pi_{28}, \pi_{31}, \ldots, \pi_{38})$$

and nine unknown elements of Ω_{11}. If the structural constraints were ignored, these parameters could be estimated by the method of least squares. The resulting estimator of π would have an asymptotic covariance matrix given by

(4.10) $\qquad\qquad R_{11}^{-1} = \Omega_{11} \otimes \mathscr{M}^{-1}$

where $\mathscr{M}$ is the limiting moment matrix of the predetermined variables.

Equations (4.8) and (4.9) relate the thirty-three reduced-form parameters to the structural parameters B, Γ, and Σ. But there are only twenty-one unknown elements of the structure—the twelve coefficients

$$\delta' = (\delta_1, \delta_2, \ldots, \delta_{12})$$

and the nine elements of Σ. Thus the zero-order restrictions on B and Γ impose a number of constraints on the reduced form. If we further impose restrictions on Σ, more constraints are added. We shall consider the estimation of δ and π in the following three cases:

1) If Σ is unrestricted, equation (4.9) may be ignored since it is a one-to-one transformation imposing no constraints on the reduced form. The Jacobian of (4.8) is the 24×12 matrix[5]

$$(4.11) \qquad H_{11} = (B^{11} \otimes I_8)W'$$

where the block diagonal matrix W is presented in table 5A.4 of the appendix. The unrestricted information matrix for π is simply the inverse of (4.10). The asymptotic covariance matrix for an efficient estimator of δ is given by

$$(4.12) \qquad [M^{(1)}]^{-1} = (H'_{11}R_{11}H_{11})^{-1}.$$

The asymptotic covariance matrix for an efficient estimator of π is given by

$$(4.13) \qquad H_{11}(H'_{11}R_{11}H_{11})^{-1}H'_{11}.$$

2) If Σ is known to be diagonal, the asymptotic covariance matrix for an efficient estimator of δ is given by

$$(4.14) \qquad [M^{(1)} + M^{(2)} + M^{(3)}]^{-1}$$

where $M^{(2)}$ amd $M^{(3)}$ are 12×12 matrices containing mostly zeros. The nonzero elements are given in appendix tables 5A.5 and 5A.6. The asymptotic covariance matrix for an efficient estimate of π is given by

$$(4.15) \qquad H_{11}[M^{(1)} + M^{(2)} + M^{(3)}]^{-1}H'_{11}.$$

3) If Σ is known completely, the asymptotic covariance matrix for an efficient estimator of δ is given by

$$(4.16) \qquad [M^{(1)} + M^{(2)}]^{-1}.$$

The asymptotic covariance matrix for an efficient estimator of π is given by

$$(4.17) \qquad H_{11}[M^{(1)} + M^{(2)}]^{-1}H'_{11}.$$

5. Cf. chapter 4, appendix B, equation (B.12).

5. EXAMPLE II: NUMERICAL RESULTS

The covariance matrices given in equations (4.10) through (4.17) are functions of the matrices B, Γ, Σ, and $\mathcal{M}$. In order to compare the efficiency of the various estimators it will be necessary to evaluate the covariance matrices at some assumed "true" values of the unknown parameters. For B and Γ we shall use the two-stage least-squares estimates based on the twenty-one-year sample presented in Klein's monograph.[6] As for Σ, we shall use two alternative specifications. In specification I we use the non-diagonal matrix obtained from the residuals of the two-stage least-squares regression. (No adjustment for degrees of freedom is made.) In specification II we use the same two-stage least-squares estimates of the variances but put all covariances equal to zero. The same B and Γ matrices are used in both cases.

With these assumed "true" structural parameters we can form all of the previously defined covariance matrices as soon as we specify the limiting moment matrix $\mathcal{M}$. For purposes of comparison it is useful to take the $X'X$ matrix of predetermined variables for the twenty-one-year sample presented by Klein. Since the sample sum of squares and cross products $X'X$ is really an estimate of n times $\mathcal{M}$, our calculations yield asymptotic covariance matrices divided by the sample size n. The matrix $X'X$ is reproduced in appendix table 5A.8.

The result of all the calculations is a set of covariance matrices for efficient estimates of δ and π based on alternative specifications as to the true structure and the number of a priori restrictions used in estimating. The following seven different sets of assumptions were used:

    I. True Σ nondiagonal
       A. No structural restrictions
       B. Restrictions on (B, Γ) only
       C. Restrictions on (B, Γ); Σ assumed known
    II. True Σ diagonal
       A. No structural restrictions
       B. Restrictions on (B, Γ) only
       C. Restrictions on (B, Γ); Σ assumed diagonal
       D. Restrictions on (B, Γ); Σ assumed known

---

6. The estimates and some of the summary statistics can be found in GOLDBERGER, NAGAR, AND ODEH (1961), ROTHENBERG AND LEENDERS (1964), and ZELLNER AND THEIL (1962). It should be noted, however, that the calculations in the latter two papers contain some errors. All of the matrices used in the present experiment are given in appendix tables 5A.7–5A.10.

For each of these seven cases a 24 × 24 covariance matrix for an efficient estimator of π was calculated. For each of the five cases where the structure is identified (excluding, therefore, cases I–A and II–A) a 12 × 12 covariance matrix for an efficient estimator of δ was calculated.[7]

To help in summarizing the reduction in sampling variability due to the imposition of structural restrictions, the standard deviations (i.e., the square root of the diagonal elements of the covariance matrices) are presented in tables 5.4 and 5.5. Expected quadratic loss tr QV is evaluated in table 5.6 for each of the covariance matrices. In this latter table the variances and covariances associated with the constant terms are ignored. Thus V_δ is the 9 × 9 matrix of structural covariances after the rows and columns associated with the constant term have been deleted. Similarly, V_π is the 21 × 21 matrix of reduced-form covariances (again ignoring constant terms) and V_π^* is the 7 × 7 northwest submatrix of V_π. Again two alternative loss matrices are used. In the one case we use an identity matrix of appropriate size. In the other case we use Q_1, a matrix consisting solely of ones. Of course, these are but two out of an infinite set of loss matrices that could be used.

A glance at the standard deviations in tables 5.4 and 5.5 indicates reduced-form precision is increased considerably as a result of restrictions on the structural form. This is confirmed by the loss measures presented in table 5.6. The imposition of twelve overidentifying restrictions on B and Γ has a very strong effect on the reduced-form covariance matrix. With either loss function and either specification, loss is reduced by a factor of 50 or more. Of course, the reduction in reduced-form variability is not uniform but rather is concentrated in a few elements of π. The coefficients of W_2 and t seem to be affected much more than the others. Nevertheless, the total impact of the use of prior information is striking.

The effects of restrictions on the matrix Σ are much less striking, although still substantial. The assumption of a completely known Σ cuts expected loss by up to 50 percent when compared to the case in which only coefficient restrictions are used. The assumption that Σ is diagonal cuts loss by up to 25 percent. However, these reductions in expected loss are small when compared to the 98 percent reductions obtained from the restrictions on B and Γ.

---

7. These twelve covariance matrices are reproduced in appendix tables 5A.11–5A.14. Due to their large size, the seven reduced-form matrices are not reproduced in their entirety; instead, only the 8 × 8 submatrices corresponding to the parameters of the first equation are presented. Since the matrices are asymptotic covariance matrices divided by 21, they may serve as approximations to the actual covariance matrices for a sample of that size.

TABLE 5.4   KLEIN'S MODEL I:
STANDARD DEVIATIONS OF EFFICIENT COEFFICIENT ESTIMATORS
(Specification I: Σ nondiagonal)

Equation and coefficient	True parameter value	Type of structural restrictions		
		Case A none*	Case B B, Γ only	Case C Σ known
Structure:				
Consumption				
P	0.017		0.097	0.067
W	0.810		0.036	0.035
P_{-1}	0.216		0.094	0.077
1	16.555		1.281	1.247
Investment				
P	0.150		0.134	0.082
P_{-1}	0.616		0.131	0.095
K_{-1}	−0.158		0.029	0.025
1	20.278		5.927	5.048
Labor demand				
Y	0.439		0.029	0.024
t	0.130		0.027	0.026
Y_{-1}	0.147		0.033	0.029
1	1.500		1.099	1.095
Reduced form:				
Consumption				
W_2	0.684	2.299	0.072	0.063
T	−0.129	0.349	0.248	0.157
G	0.664	0.355	0.206	0.131
t	0.159	0.706	0.028	0.027
P_{-1}	0.769	0.471	0.129	0.126
K_{-1}	−0.105	0.108	0.034	0.026
Y_{-1}	0.179	0.256	0.038	0.035
1	42.830	28.703	7.448	5.782

* Structural parameters not identified.

The efficiency inequality (2.3) again turns out to have no value, at least when Q is the identity matrix. The characteristic roots of R_{11}^{-1}, even when the rows and columns associated with the constant term are deleted, are so widely dispersed that the inequality merely says that efficiency lies between zero and one. It appears, therefore, that the inequality (2.3) cannot be generally relied on for giving insight into the value of a priori restrictions.

TABLE 5.5 KLEIN'S MODEL I:
STANDARD DEVIATIONS OF EFFICIENT COEFFICIENT ESTIMATORS
(Specification II: Σ diagonal)

Equation and coefficient	Type of structural restrictions			
	Case A none*	Case B B, Γ only	Case C Σ diagonal	Case D Σ known
Structure:				
Consumption				
P		0.108	0.097	0.084
W		0.040	0.039	0.039
P_{-1}		0.101	0.095	0.086
1		1.307	1.292	1.281
Investment				
P		0.143	0.127	0.097
P_{-1}		0.139	0.127	0.106
K_{-1}		0.033	0.032	0.030
1		6.776	6.490	6.031
Labor demand				
Y		0.033	0.028	0.027
t		0.029	0.028	0.028
Y_{-1}		0.037	0.033	0.033
1		1.139	1.137	1.137
Reduced form:				
Consumption				
W_2	2.380	0.078	0.074	0.072
T	0.408	0.236	0.191	0.168
G	0.368	0.211	0.173	0.152
t	0.731	0.038	0.038	0.038
P_{-1}	0.488	0.124	0.121	0.120
K_{-1}	0.112	0.035	0.032	0.029
Y_{-1}	0.265	0.045	0.042	0.041
1	29.722	7.643	7.021	6.503

* Structural parameters not identified.

The calculations presented above indicate that the imposition of twelve overidentifying restrictions in Klein's model reduces enormously the variances of the reduced-form estimator. It is natural to ask whether the reduced-form variances would increase much if one or two of the less plausible restrictions were relaxed. That is, suppose we estimated the structure including a few more variables in each equation and then solved

TABLE 5.6   KLEIN'S MODEL I:
EXPECTED QUADRATIC LOSS UNDER ALTERNATIVE STRUCTURAL RESTRICTIONS
Specification I: Σ Nondiagonal

Loss function	Type of structural restrictions		
	Case A none	Case B B, Γ only	Case C Σ known
Structure			
$\text{tr}[V_\delta]$	–	0.0580	0.0299
$\text{tr}[Q_1 V_\delta]$	–	0.0153	0.0119
Reduced form			
$\text{tr}[V_\pi]$	14.0282	0.2765	0.1339
$\text{tr}[V_\pi^*]$	6.3620	0.1290	0.0644
$\text{tr}[Q_1 V_\pi^*]$	3.0529	0.0393	0.0279

Specification II: Σ Diagonal

Loss function	Type of structural restrictions			
	Case A none	Case B B, Γ only	Case C Σ diagonal	Case D Σ known
Structure				
$\text{tr}[V_\delta]$	–	0.0678	0.0559	0.0401
$\text{tr}[Q_1 V_\delta]$	–	0.0105	0.0097	0.0093
Reduced form				
$\text{tr}[V_\pi]$	14.1139	0.2759	0.2009	0.1542
$\text{tr}[V_\pi^*]$	6.8215	0.1266	0.0907	0.0749
$\text{tr}[Q_1 V_\pi^*]$	3.2734	0.0421	0.0349	0.0330

for the reduced form. What is the added cost (in terms of increased reduced-form variability) of fewer restrictions? This question can be answered quite easily. Suppose, for example, someone believes that sales are an important determinant of investment demand. This would suggest that net product Y should have a nonzero coefficient in the investment equation. If the zero constraint is dropped, the model now includes thirteen structural parameters and the matrix H_{11} gets an added column. All of the covariance matrices may now be recalculated with the new H_{11} matrix and compared with the earlier ones.

In order to make the comparisons meaningful, the "true" values of the parameters must remain the same for all calculations. Thus, even though we are relaxing some of the constraints (i.e., estimating more parameters), we will assume that the coefficients really are zero. We are asking the question: What is the cost of relaxing a restriction that really is valid? This is, of course, the same question we asked when comparing the twelve-restriction model with the no-restriction model. The answer, in the case of letting Y appear in the investment equation, is that the cost is modest: the mean reduced-form variance increases 15 percent. (Recall that relaxing twelve constraints increases the mean variance 5000 percent!)

The cost of relaxing a valid constraint depends, of course, on the specific constraint and on the other constraints which are being imposed. For Klein's model we started with Case I–B and removed, one by one, twelve constraints until we arrived at an exactly identified system. At each stage we evaluated the covariance matrix bound (4.15) and calculated its trace and other summary statistics. The order in which constraints are relaxed is somewhat arbitrary, but we tried to relax the more implausible ones first. Table 5.7 presents the order chosen. When all twelve restrictions were removed, the system (4.1–4.3) became the exactly identified system

$$C = \delta_1 W_1 + \delta_2 P + \delta_3 W_2 + \delta_4 t + \delta_5 P_{-1} + \delta_6 K_{-1} + \delta_7 Y_{-1} + \delta_8$$

$$I = \delta_9 P + \delta_{10} Y + \delta_{11} G + \delta_{12} t + \delta_{13} P_{-1} + \delta_{14} K_{-1} + \delta_{15} Y_{-1} + \delta_{16}$$

$$W_1 = \delta_{17} Y + \delta_{18} W_2 + \delta_{19} T + \delta_{20} t + \delta_{21} P_{-1} + \delta_{22} K_{-1} + \delta_{23} Y_{-1} + \delta_{24}.$$

In two cases we also added constraints to see what the effect would be. These results are also presented.

Table 5.7 presents, for each set of imposed constraints, three measures of the variability of the reduced-form estimates. First we have the sum of the variances of the twenty-one coefficient estimates (excluding constant terms). Second we have the sum of the variances of the seven coefficient estimates of the first equation. Finally we have the variance of the sum of the seven coefficient estimates of the first equation. Since each measure indicates the same general result, we will comment only on the first measure.

The table indicates that the reduced-form variances increase moderately when the first new constraints are dropped. Furthermore, the increase is not smooth but is concentrated in one or two constraints. Thus dropping the constraint that private workers and government workers have the same marginal propensity to consume causes an 180 percent increase in the sum of reduced-form variances; and adding a time variable to the investment function causes a 200 percent increase.

These results suggest that, at least in Klein's model, relatively few overidentifying structural restrictions are needed to yield substantial

TABLE 5.7   REDUCED-FORM EXPECTED LOSS AS A FUNCTION OF THE NUMBER OF
OVERIDENTIFYING RESTRICTIONS
(Experiment 1)

Number of overidentifying restrictions	Change	Expected loss		
		tr V_π	tr V_π^*	tr $Q_1 V_\pi^*$
14	Delete t from labor equation	0.264	0.121	0.032
13	Delete W from consumption equation	0.268	0.123	0.032
12	BASIC KLEIN MODEL	0.277	0.129	0.039
11	Add Y to investment equation	0.321	0.143	0.055
10	Add Y_{-1} to investment equation	0.480	0.176	0.080
9	Add P_{-1} to labor equation	0.543	0.198	0.090
8	Add K_{-1} to labor equation	0.714	0.258	0.113
7	Add Y_{-1} to consumption equation	0.862	0.370	0.268
6	Add K_{-1} to consumption equation	1.044	0.492	0.291
5	Add t to consumption equation	1.221	0.631	0.437
4	Replace W by W_1 and W_2 in consumption equation	3.415	2.403	1.154
3	Add G to investment equation	4.327	2.778	1.304
2	Add t to investment equation	12.923	6.347	3.046
1	Add W_2 to labor equation	13.899	6.360	3.053
0	Add T to labor equation	14.028	6.362	3.053

TABLE 5.8   REDUCED-FORM EXPECTED LOSS AS A FUNCTION OF THE NUMBER OF
OVERIDENTIFYING RESTRICTIONS
(Experiment 2)

Number of overidentifying restrictions	Change	Expected loss		
		tr V_π	tr V_π^*	tr $Q_1 V_\pi^*$
0	EXACTLY IDENTIFIED MODEL	14.028	6.362	3.053
1	Delete t from investment equation	4.864	2.811	1.353
2	Replace W_1 and W_2 by W in consumption equation	3.264	1.340	0.705
3	Delete G from investment equation	2.441	1.070	0.600
4	Delete W_2 from labor equation	1.269	1.016	0.583
5	Delete K_{-1} from consumption equation	1.050	0.980	0.567
6	Delete T from wage equation	0.997	0.460	0.311
7	Delete t from consumption equation	0.862	0.310	0.268
12	BASIC KLEIN MODEL	0.277	0.129	0.039

gains in efficiency. This is illustrated in table 5.8 where, beginning with the exactly identified model described above, restrictions are imposed in an order that maximizes efficiency gain. We see that adding just one constraint has an enormous effect on efficiency: the sum of the variances is cut in third. The next few constraints also have a big impact. As a result the first six constraints cause a fourteenfold increase in precision.

6. SUMMARY

By actually evaluating some of the algebraic expressions derived in chapter 4, we have been able to shed some light on the basic question: What is the value of prior structural information? Although the two numerical examples given in this chapter are by no means conclusive, one might conjecture the following:

1) As far as variances are concerned, zero-order restrictions on the structural coefficients B and Γ probably increase reduced-form efficiency more than proportionately. That is, in a model with ten structural coefficients and twenty reduced-form coefficients, use of the restrictions will cut reduced-form variances by more than half.

2) Constraints on Σ are less important than constraints on B and Γ, at least in models with many predetermined variables.

3) Not all constraints are of equal value. A small number of structural restrictions may have an enormous effect on reduced-form precision. The addition of further restrictions may have little value.

4) The greater the collinearity among the predetermined variables, the greater is the gain from imposing structural restrictions.

Appendix

TABLE 5A.1   ARTIFICIAL NUMERICAL EXAMPLE: BASIC MATRICES

$R_{11} = \Omega^{-1} \otimes \mathscr{M}$:

5	0	0	3	0	0
0	5	0	0	3	0
0	0	5	0	0	3
3	0	0	2	0	0
0	3	0	0	2	0
0	0	3	0	0	2

$M^{(1)} = H'_{11} R_{11} H_{11}$:

6	2	0	0	0
2	1	0	0	0
0	0	3	1	1
0	0	1	1	0
0	0	1	0	1

$M^{(2)}$:

9	0	1	0	0
0	0	0	0	0
1	0	3	0	0
0	0	0	0	0
0	0	0	0	0

$M^{(3)}$:

−8	0	0	0	0
0	0	0	0	0
0	0	−2	0	0
0	0	0	0	0
0	0	0	0	0

H_{11}:

$$
\begin{array}{rrrrr}
1 & 0 & 1 & -1 & 0 \\
1 & 0 & 1 & 0 & -1 \\
-2 & 1 & -1 & 0 & 0 \\
-2 & 0 & -1 & 1 & 0 \\
-2 & 0 & -1 & 0 & 1 \\
4 & -2 & 1 & 0 & 0
\end{array}
$$

TABLE 5A.2 ARTIFICIAL NUMERICAL EXAMPLE: ASYMPTOTIC COVARIANCE
MATRICES FOR EFFICIENT STRUCTURAL PARAMETER ESTIMATES

Restrictions on B and Γ only: $[M^{(1)}]^{-1} = (H'_{11}R_{11}H_{11})^{-1}$

$$
\begin{array}{rrrrr}
0.5 & -1.0 & 0 & 0 & 0 \\
-1.0 & 3.0 & 0 & 0 & 0 \\
0 & 0 & 1.0 & -1.0 & -1.0 \\
0 & 0 & -1.0 & 2.0 & 1.0 \\
0 & 0 & -1.0 & 1.0 & 2.0
\end{array}
$$

Restrictions on B, Γ; Σ diagonal: $[M^{(1)} + M^{(2)} + M^{(3)}]^{-1}$

$$
\begin{array}{rrrrr}
0.4 & -0.8 & -0.2 & 0.2 & 0.2 \\
-0.8 & 2.6 & 0.4 & -0.4 & -0.4 \\
-0.2 & 0.4 & 0.6 & -0.6 & -0.6 \\
0.2 & -0.4 & -0.6 & 1.6 & 0.6 \\
0.2 & -0.4 & -0.6 & 0.6 & 1.6
\end{array}
$$

Restrictions on B and Γ; Σ known $[M^{(1)} + M^{(2)}]^{-1}$

$$
\begin{array}{rrrrr}
0.093 & -0.186 & -0.023 & 0.023 & 0.023 \\
-0.186 & 1.372 & 0.047 & -0.047 & -0.047 \\
-0.023 & 0.047 & 0.302 & -0.302 & -0.302 \\
0.023 & -0.047 & -0.302 & 1.302 & 0.302 \\
0.023 & -0.047 & -0.302 & 0.302 & 1.302
\end{array}
$$

TABLE 5A.3   ARTIFICIAL NUMERICAL EXAMPLE: ASYMPTOTIC COVARIANCE
MATRICES FOR EFFICIENT REDUCED-FORM PARAMETER ESTIMATES

No structural restrictions: $R_{11}^{-1} = \Omega \otimes \mathscr{M}^{-1}$

2	0	0	−3	0	0
0	2	0	0	−3	0
0	0	2	0	0	−3
−3	0	0	5	0	0
0	−3	0	0	5	0
0	0	−3	0	0	5

Restrictions on B and Γ only: $H_{11}(H_{11}' R_1^1 H_{11})^{-1} H_{11}'$

1.5	0.5	0	−2	−1	0
0.5	1.5	0	−1	−2	0
0	0	2	0	0	−3
−2	−1	0	3	2	0
−1	−2	0	2	3	0
0	0	−3	0	0	5

Restrictions on B, Γ; Σ diagonal: $H_{11}[M^{(1)} + M^{(2)} + M^{(3)}]^{-1} H_{11}'$

1.4	0.4	0.2	−1.8	−0.8	−0.2
0.4	1.4	0.2	−0.8	−1.8	−0.2
0.2	0.2	1.6	−0.4	−0.4	−2.6
−1.8	−0.8	−0.4	2.6	1.6	0.4
−0.8	−1.8	−0.4	1.6	2.6	0.4
−0.2	−0.2	−2.6	0.4	0.4	4.6

Restrictions on B and Γ; Σ known: $H_{11}[M^{(1)} + M^{(2)}]^{-1} H_{11}'$

1.093	0.093	0.023	−1.186	−0.186	−0.023
0.093	1.093	0.023	−0.186	−1.186	−0.023
0.023	0.023	1.302	−0.023	−0.023	−2.302
−1.186	−0.186	−0.023	1.372	0.372	0.047
−0.186	−1.186	−0.023	0.372	1.372	0.047
−0.023	−0.023	−2.302	0.047	0.047	4.302

TABLE 5A.4   KLEIN'S MODEL I: THE MATRIX W

$$W_1 = \begin{bmatrix} \pi_{41} & \pi_{42} & \pi_{43} & \pi_{44} & \pi_{45} & \pi_{46} & \pi_{47} & \pi_{48} \\ \pi_{51} & \pi_{52} & \pi_{53} & \pi_{54} & \pi_{55} & \pi_{56} & \pi_{57} & \pi_{58} \\ 0 & 0 & 0 & 0 & 1 & 0 & 0 & 0 \\ 0 & 0 & 0 & 0 & 0 & 0 & 0 & 1 \end{bmatrix}$$

$$W_2 = \begin{bmatrix} \pi_{41} & \pi_{42} & \pi_{43} & \pi_{44} & \pi_{45} & \pi_{46} & \pi_{47} & \pi_{48} \\ 0 & 0 & 0 & 0 & 1 & 0 & 0 & 0 \\ 0 & 0 & 0 & 0 & 0 & 1 & 0 & 0 \\ 0 & 0 & 0 & 0 & 0 & 0 & 0 & 1 \end{bmatrix}$$

$$W_3 = \begin{bmatrix} \pi_{61} & \pi_{62} & \pi_{63} & \pi_{64} & \pi_{65} & \pi_{66} & \pi_{67} & \pi_{68} \\ 0 & 0 & 0 & 1 & 0 & 0 & 0 & 0 \\ 0 & 0 & 0 & 0 & 0 & 0 & 1 & 0 \\ 0 & 0 & 0 & 0 & 0 & 0 & 0 & 1 \end{bmatrix}$$

$$W = \begin{bmatrix} W_1 & 0 & 0 \\ 0 & W_2 & 0 \\ 0 & 0 & W_3 \end{bmatrix}$$

TABLE 5A.5   KLEIN'S MODEL I: NONZERO ELEMENTS OF $M^{(2)}$

Number of element	Corresponding parameters	General form	Specification I*	Specification II*
11	$\beta_{14}\beta_{14}$	$\omega_{44}\sigma^{11} + \beta^{41}\beta^{41}$	186.18928	73.69574
12	$\beta_{14}\beta_{15}$	$\omega_{45}\sigma^{11} + \beta^{41}\beta^{51}$	116.51068	51.75721
15	$\beta_{14}\beta_{24}$	$\omega_{44}\sigma^{12} + \beta^{42}\beta^{41}$	−52.91604	21.82293
19	$\beta_{14}\beta_{36}$	$\omega_{46}\sigma^{13} + \beta^{43}\beta^{61}$	248.53375	−13.15615
22	$\beta_{15}\beta_{15}$	$\omega_{55}\sigma^{11} + \beta^{51}\beta^{51}$	136.97282	66.31372
25	$\beta_{15}\beta_{24}$	$\omega_{54}\sigma^{12} + \beta^{52}\beta^{41}$	−28.14636	17.07019
29	$\beta_{15}\beta_{36}$	$\omega_{56}\sigma^{13} + \beta^{53}\beta^{61}$	278.97625	57.70544
55	$\beta_{24}\beta_{24}$	$\omega_{44}\sigma^{22} + \beta^{42}\beta^{42}$	114.11698	60.97878
59	$\beta_{24}\beta_{36}$	$\omega_{46}\sigma^{23} + \beta^{43}\beta^{62}$	−169.98437	−13.15615
99	$\beta_{36}\beta_{36}$	$\omega_{66}\sigma^{33} + \beta^{63}\beta^{63}$	1009.19353	410.43393

* Specification I has a nondiagonal Σ. Specification II has a diagonal Σ. The numbers have been multiplied by the sample size, 21.
NOTE: $M^{(2)}$ is a 12×12 symmetric matrix. Here only the upper part is given.

TABLE 5A.6 KLEIN'S MODEL I: NONZERO ELEMENTS OF $M^{(3)}$

Number of element	Corresponding parameters	General form	Specification II*
11	$\beta_{14}\beta_{14}$	$-2\beta^{41}\beta^{41}$	-43.64586
12	$\beta_{14}\beta_{15}$	$-2\beta^{41}\beta^{51}$	-34.14038
21	$\beta_{15}\beta_{14}$	$-2\beta^{51}\beta^{41}$	-34.14038
22	$\beta_{15}\beta_{15}$	$-2\beta^{51}\beta^{51}$	-26.70507
55	$\beta_{24}\beta_{24}$	$-2\beta^{42}\beta^{42}$	-43.64586
99	$\beta_{36}\beta_{36}$	$-2\beta^{63}\beta^{63}$	-57.26366

* Specification II has a diagonal Σ. The matrix $M^{(3)}$ is irrelevant for Specification I, where Σ is nondiagonal. The numbers have been multiplied by the sample size, 21.

TABLE 5A.7 KLEIN'S MODEL I: "TRUE" STRUCTURAL PARAMETERS

$$B = \begin{bmatrix} 1 & 0 & 0 & -0.0173 & -0.8102 & 0 & 0 \\ 0 & 1 & 0 & -0.1502 & 0 & 0 & 0 \\ 0 & 0 & 1 & 0 & 0 & -0.4389 & 0 \\ 1 & 1 & 0 & 0 & 0 & -1 & 0 \\ 0 & 0 & 1 & 1 & 0 & -1 & 0 \\ 0 & 1 & 0 & 0 & 0 & 0 & -1 \\ 0 & 0 & 1 & 0 & -1 & 0 & 0 \end{bmatrix}$$

$$\Gamma = \begin{bmatrix} 0 & 0 & 0 & 0 & -0.2162 & 0 & 0 & -16.5548 \\ 0 & 0 & 0 & 0 & -0.6159 & 0.1578 & 0 & -20.2782 \\ 0 & 0 & 0 & -0.1304 & 0 & 0 & -0.1467 & -1.5003 \\ -1 & 0 & 1 & 0 & 0 & 0 & 0 & 0 \\ 0 & 1 & 0 & 0 & 0 & 0 & 0 & 0 \\ 0 & 0 & 0 & 0 & 0 & 1 & 0 & 0 \\ 1 & 0 & 0 & 0 & 0 & 0 & 0 & 0 \end{bmatrix}$$

Specification I:

$$\Sigma = \begin{bmatrix} 1.0441 & 0.4379 & -0.3850 \\ 0.4379 & 1.3832 & 0.1926 \\ -0.3850 & 0.1926 & 0.4764 \end{bmatrix}$$

Specification II:

$$\Sigma = \begin{bmatrix} 1.0441 & 0 & 0 \\ 0 & 1.3832 & 0 \\ 0 & 0 & 0.4764 \end{bmatrix}$$

TABLE 5A.8 KLEIN'S MODEL I: SUMS OF SQUARES AND CROSS PRODUCTS OF PREDETERMINED VARIABLES, $X'X$

	x_1	x_2	x_3	x_4	x_5	x_6	x_7	x_8
x_1	626.87	789.27	1200.19	238.00	1746.22	21,683.18	6364.43	107.50
x_2		1054.95	1546.11	176.00	2348.48	28,766.25	8436.53	142.90
x_3			2369.94	421.70	3451.86	42,026.14	12,473.50	208.20
x_4				770.00	−11.90	590.60	495.60	0.00
x_5					5956.29	69,073.54	20,542.22	343.90
x_6						846,132.70	244,984.77	4210.40
x_7							72,200.03	1217.70
x_8								21.00

TABLE 5A.9 KLEIN'S MODEL I: "TRUE" B^{-1} AND Π MATRICES

$$B^{-1} =$$

1.663683	0.663683	1.219449	−0.663683	0.128467	0.000000	−1.347916
0.153115	1.153115	−0.051793	−0.153115	0.175847	0.000000	−0.124054
0.797393	0.797393	1.512484	−0.797393	0.133563	0.000000	−0.646047
1.019405	1.019405	−0.344828	−1.019405	1.170750	0.000000	−0.825922
0.797393	0.797393	1.512484	−0.797393	0.133563	0.000000	−1.646047
1.816798	1.816798	1.167656	−1.816798	0.304314	0.000000	−1.471970
0.153115	1.153115	−0.051793	−0.153115	0.175847	1.000000	−0.124054

$$\Pi =$$

0.684233	−0.128467	0.663683	0.159016	0.768451	−0.104729	−0.178893	42.829782
−0.029061	−0.175847	0.153115	−0.006754	0.743307	−0.181961	−0.007598	25.840167
−0.151345	−0.133563	0.797393	0.197228	0.663510	−0.125829	0.221881	31.639541
−0.193483	−1.170750	1.019405	−0.044966	0.848247	−0.160862	−0.050586	37.030409
0.848655	−0.133563	0.797393	0.197228	0.663510	−0.125829	0.221881	31.639541
−0.344828	−0.304314	1.816798	0.152262	1.511757	−0.286691	0.171295	68.669949
−0.029061	−0.175847	0.153115	−0.006754	0.743307	0.818039	−0.007598	25.840167

TABLE 5A.10   KLEIN'S MODEL I: "TRUE" Ω MATRICES

Specification I: Σ Nondiagonal

$$\Omega = \begin{bmatrix} 3.92422 & 2.40452 & 2.84593 & 3.48280 & 2.84593 & 6.32874 & 2.40452 \\ 2.40452 & 2.00269 & 2.07279 & 2.33442 & 2.07279 & 4.40721 & 2.00269 \\ 2.84593 & 2.07279 & 2.72596 & 2.19277 & 2.72596 & 4.91872 & 2.07279 \\ 3.48280 & 2.33442 & 2.19277 & 3.62445 & 2.19277 & 5.81722 & 2.33442 \\ 2.84593 & 2.07279 & 2.72596 & 2.19277 & 2.72596 & 4.91872 & 2.07279 \\ 6.32874 & 4.40721 & 4.91872 & 5.81722 & 4.91872 & 10.73594 & 4.40721 \\ 2.40452 & 2.00269 & 2.07279 & 2.33442 & 2.07279 & 4.40721 & 2.00269 \end{bmatrix}$$

Specification II: Σ Diagonal

$$\Omega = \begin{bmatrix} 4.20760 & 1.29445 & 2.99579 & 2.50625 & 2.99579 & 5.50205 & 1.29445 \\ 1.29445 & 1.86496 & 1.36199 & 1.79742 & 1.36199 & 3.15941 & 1.86494 \\ 2.99579 & 1.36199 & 2.63318 & 1.72460 & 2.63318 & 4.35778 & 1.36199 \\ 2.50625 & 1.79742 & 1.72460 & 2.57907 & 1.72460 & 4.30367 & 1.79742 \\ 2.99579 & 1.36199 & 2.63318 & 1.72460 & 2.63318 & 4.35778 & 1.36199 \\ 5.50205 & 3.15941 & 4.35778 & 4.30367 & 4.35778 & 8.66145 & 3.15941 \\ 1.29445 & 1.86496 & 1.36199 & 1.79742 & 1.36199 & 3.15941 & 1.86496 \end{bmatrix}$$

TABLE 5A.11 KLEIN'S MODEL I: COVARIANCE MATRICES FOR EFFICIENT ESTIMATES OF δ
(Specification I: Σ Nondiagonal)

```
0.009475 −0.000962 −0.006528 −0.013185  0.005467 −0.004478  0.000085 −0.035957 −0.001023  0.000551  0.001044  0.000889
          0.001325 −0.000594 −0.028997  0.000353 −0.000388  0.000187 −0.037002 −0.000105 −0.000489  0.000058  0.002929
                    0.008857 −0.010163  0.005585 −0.000304  0.052893  0.000779  0.000435 −0.001277  0.027222
                              1.641701 −0.026024  0.000238 −0.004192  0.008870  0.003847  0.000856 −0.600635
                                        0.017895 −0.015090  0.001925 −0.441019  0.000058  0.000277  0.000045 −0.006055
                                                  0.017033 −0.001846  0.345989  0.000109  0.000449  0.000060 −0.010030
Case I–B: Σ unrestricted                                    0.000817 −0.165994 −0.000200  0.000132  0.000236 −0.001703
                                                                     35.127825  0.037242 −0.023846 −0.049073  0.618163
                                                                                0.000837 −0.000182 −0.000782 −0.004902
                                                                                          0.000718 −0.000027  0.012520
                                                                                                    0.001075 −0.015355
                                                                                                              1.207477
```

$$
\begin{array}{cccccccccccc}
0.004480 & -0.00758 & -0.002750 & 0.000826 & 0.001546 & -0.001237 & -0.000084 & 0.011008 & -0.000540 & 0.000371 & 0.000549 & 0.000543 \\
 & 0.001231 & -0.000651 & -0.027598 & -0.000006 & -0.000079 & 0.000127 & -0.024110 & -0.000145 & -0.000457 & 0.000097 & 0.003067 \\
 & & 0.005881 & -0.022864 & -0.001367 & 0.002625 & -0.000115 & 0.003046 & 0.000478 & 0.000531 & -0.000963 & 0.027091 \\
 & & & 1.55066 & -0.003493 & -0.018833 & -0.001980 & 0.785263 & 0.007288 & 0.004008 & 0.002455 & -0.598387 \\
 & & & & 0.006685 & -0.005573 & 0.000641 & -0.150117 & 0.000374 & 0.000069 & -0.000310 & -0.004463 \\
 & & & & & 0.008937 & -0.000727 & 0.093558 & -0.000205 & -0.000256 & 0.000404 & -0.011089 \\
 & & & & & & 0.000613 & -0.121764 & -0.000104 & 0.000085 & 0.000142 & -0.001961 \\
 & & & & & & & 25.481689 & 0.017919 & -0.013958 & -0.029770 & 0.659307 \\
 & & & & & & & & 0.000568 & -0.000086 & -0.000527 & -0.003582 \\
 & & & & & & & & & 0.000672 & -0.000120 & 0.012101 \\
 & & & & & & & & & & 0.000832 & -0.016586 \\
 & & & & & & & & & & & 1.199555 \\
\end{array}
$$

Case I–C: Σ known

TABLE 5A.12 KLEIN'S MODEL I: COVARIANCE MATRICES FOR EFFICIENT ESTIMATES OF δ
(Specification II: Σ Diagonal)

0.011669	−0.001414	−0.007881	−0.009318	0.000000	0.000000	0.000000	0.000000	0.000000	0.000000	0.000000	0.000000
	0.001570	−0.000560	−0.032098	0.000000	0.000000	0.000000	0.000000	0.000000	0.000000	0.000000	0.000000
		0.010180	−0.010418	0.000000	0.000000	0.000000	0.000000	0.000000	0.000000	0.000000	0.000000
			1.709211	0.000000	0.000000	0.000000	0.000000	0.000000	0.000000	0.000000	0.000000
				0.020556	−0.017605	0.002700	−0.600196	0.000000	0.000000	0.000000	0.000000
					0.019445	−0.002586	0.497374	0.000000	0.000000	0.000000	0.000000
						0.001075	−0.218751	0.000000	0.000000	0.000000	0.000000
							45.913945	0.000000	0.000000	0.000000	0.000000
								0.001078	−0.000228	−0.001048	−0.003936
									0.000822	−0.000019	0.014814
										0.001394	−0.017892
											1.296511

Case II–B: Σ unrestricted

0.009448	−0.001252	−0.006265	−0.004997	−0.002776	0.002378	−0.000365	0.081055	0.000125	−0.000026	−0.000122	−0.000456
	0.001504	−0.000619	−0.031129	0.000009	−0.000008	0.000001	−0.000259	−0.000081	0.000017	0.000078	0.000294
		0.008941	−0.014952	0.002229	−0.001909	0.000293	−0.065097	−0.000014	0.000003	0.000013	0.000050
			1.670324	0.009996	−0.008561	0.001313	−0.291870	0.001454	−0.000308	−0.001414	−0.005308
				0.016099	−0.013788	0.002115	−0.470062	0.000136	−0.000029	−0.000133	−0.000498

Case II–C: Σ diagonal

```
0.016175  −0.002085   0.385919  −0.000117   0.000025   0.000114   0.000427
           0.000998  −0.201656   0.000018  −0.000004  −0.000017  −0.000065
                      42.114277  −0.003983   0.000845   0.003874   0.014547
                                  0.000787  −0.000167  −0.000765  −0.002874
                                             0.000809   0.000079   0.014589
                                                        0.001119  −0.018925
                                                                   1.292633
```

```
0.007052  −0.001231  −0.004355   0.003315  −0.001199   0.001027  −0.000157   0.035001   0.000111  −0.000023  −0.000104  −0.000404
           0.001504  −0.000635  −0.031194   0.000002  −0.000000   0.000000  −0.000049  −0.000077   0.000016   0.000075   0.000281
                      0.007418  −0.021586   0.000965  −0.000827   0.000127  −0.028178  −0.000006   0.000001   0.000006   0.000022
                                 1.641293   0.004368  −0.003741   0.000574  −0.127531   0.001420  −0.000301  −0.001382  −0.005188
                                            0.009370  −0.008025   0.001231  −0.273584   0.000080  −0.000017  −0.000078  −0.000293
                                                       0.011239  −0.001328   0.217641  −0.000069   0.000015   0.000067   0.000251
```

Case II–D: Σ known

```
0.000882  −0.175845   0.000011  −0.000002  −0.000010  −0.000039
           36.377440  −0.002343   0.000497   0.002279   0.008557
                       0.000752  −0.000160  −0.000732  −0.002748
                                  0.000808  −0.000086   0.014562
                                             0.001086  −0.019047
                                                        1.292173
```

TABLE 5A.13   KLEIN'S MODEL I: COVARIANCE MATRICES FOR EFFICIENT ESTIMATES OF π_1
(Specification I: Σ Nondiagonal)

Case I–A: No structural restrictions

5.283567	−0.246348	−0.061289	−1.576078	0.426751	0.192752	−0.168432	−60.630595
	0.154936	−0.066984	0.077158	−0.021455	−0.010109	0.011931	2.557263
		0.125987	−0.012511	0.058782	0.008371	−0.043107	−0.620891
			0.498606	−0.105892	−0.059552	0.041787	18.918029
				0.221691	0.031969	−0.115586	−5.959048
					0.011684	−0.016728	−2.896976
						0.065563	2.653334
							823.872798

Case I–B: Restrictions on B and Γ only

0.005119	0.011482	−0.007865	0.000131	−0.002086	0.001289	0.001366	−0.329938
	0.061303	−0.048713	0.001783	0.000345	0.006606	0.001347	−1.401291
		0.042602	−0.001738	0.001032	−0.005892	−0.001873	1.222398
			0.000794	0.000498	0.000355	−0.000265	−0.059523
				0.016571	−0.000620	−0.002497	−0.004089
					0.001158	0.000457	−0.241732
						0.001440	−0.131806
							55.467976

0.004013	0.005684	−0.003236	−0.000057	−0.002069	0.000622	0.001218	−0.188650
	0.024606	−0.018895	0.000701	−0.000565	0.002767	0.000873	−0.605286
		0.017245	−0.000783	0.001112	−0.002569	−0.001103	0.535024
			0.000743	0.000550	0.000198	−0.000318	−0.027041
				0.015921	−0.000496	−0.002170	−0.032057
					0.000651	0.000296	−0.136164
						0.001248	−0.097351
							33.437145

Case I–C: Σ known

TABLE 5A.14 KLEIN'S MODEL I: COVARIANCE MATRICES FOR EFFICIENT ESTIMATES OF π_1
(Specification II: Σ Diagonal)

Case II–A: No structural restrictions

5.665116	−0.264137	−0.065715	−1.689882	0.457568	0.206671	−0.180595	−65.008967
	0.166124	−0.071821	0.082730	−0.023005	−0.010839	0.012793	2.741933
		0.135085	−0.013414	0.063026	0.008975	−0.046219	−0.665728
			0.534617	−0.113539	−0.063853	0.044804	20.284173
				0.237700	0.034277	−0.123933	−6.389374
					0.012528	−0.017936	−3.106178
						0.070298	2.844941
							883.367869

Case II–B: Restrictions on B and Γ only

0.006154	0.012830	−0.009001	0.001419	−0.003084	0.001190	0.002002	−0.333800
	0.055682	−0.046515	0.002972	−0.003881	0.005948	0.003701	−1.326926
		0.044663	−0.002033	0.005787	−0.005835	−0.004424	1.251516
			0.001479	−0.000667	0.000267	0.000081	−0.054664
				0.015448	−0.001043	−0.002529	0.087707
					0.001203	0.000638	−0.249798
						0.001994	−0.193680
							58.408330

0.005432	0.009339	−0.006182	0.001250	−0.003017	0.000869	0.001856	−0.262564
	0.036508	−0.030558	0.002155	−0.003704	0.004198	0.002983	−0.947285
		0.029940	−0.001389	0.004636	−0.004158	−0.003300	0.891803
			0.001439	−0.000664	0.000195	0.000053	−0.038518
				0.014640	−0.000855	−0.002103	0.048301
					0.001006	0.000483	−0.207532
						0.001748	−0.160770
							49.289500

Case II–C: Σ diagonal

0.005165	0.007865	−0.004848	0.001189	−0.002914	0.000691	0.001759	−0.224711
	0.028087	−0.023108	0.001814	−0.003298	0.003213	0.002525	−0.738779
		0.023243	−0.001082	0.004166	−0.003277	−0.002834	0.704702
			0.001425	−0.000641	0.000154	0.000031	−0.029815
				0.014496	−0.000777	−0.002018	0.031390
					0.000844	0.000422	−0.173823
						0.001690	−0.147599
							42.286565

Case II–D: Σ known

CHAPTER 6

The Bayesian Approach to Econometrics

1. INTRODUCTION

The analysis in the previous chapters is based entirely on the classical approach to statistical inference in which the sampling distributions of a suitably restricted class of estimators are compared. It is by no means clear, however, that this classical analysis is the most appropriate for econometric research. Many statisticians in recent years have argued that a more natural basis for econometric inference can be found in a Bayesian decision-theoretic approach. This is particularly the case when the problem is to measure the value of a priori information.

The classical theory may be criticized on a number of grounds. In the first place the theory is based on restrictive assumptions. The exact lower bounds derived in chapter 2 are valid only for unbiased estimators. Attempts to extend the results to the case of biased estimators are not fruitful; the answer always depends on the bias function, about which we know nothing. The remaining results in chapter 2 are of an asymptotic character. These probably give reasonable approximations for moderately large samples but may be very poor when samples are small. Since many econometric studies use short time series, the asymptotic results must be viewed with suspicion. Thus the classical theory, which uses either the unbiasedness assumption or asymptotic approximations, is quite restrictive in the type of answers it can give. The numerical results in chapter 5 are only approximate measures of estimation precision. And the classical constrained estimators are only approximately optimal.

The classical theory can also be criticized for the unrealistic way a priori information is expressed. In practice the statistician possesses imprecise knowledge about the unknown parameters. Rarely can this be expressed in an exact equation of the type studied in chapter 2. Inequality constraints are not always a satisfactory alternative since they ignore the fine detail of our knowledge and, in addition, are inconvenient to use. Often it is more natural to express a priori information in terms of a subjective probability distribution. Thus a Bayesian approach that begins with a prior probability distribution over the entire parameter space is often more convenient than the classical approach of equality or inequality restrictions.

A final objection to the classical approach is that it usually ignores the decision aspect of economic estimation. The value of information is assigned without regard to the use to which the information will be put. Although the classical mean square error measure can be interpreted as expected loss when a decision maker has a quadratic loss function, the classical theory rarely explores the relationship between estimation and decision.

These criticisms suggest that a reformulation of our problem in Bayesian terms may be of value. In the Bayesian framework we shall be able to drop the unbiasedness assumption, allow for a flexible way to describe a priori information, and, in addition, place the entire analysis in a decision context. This chapter begins by presenting the basic features of Bayesian econometric analysis. Then a Bayesian theory of the value of a priori information and its application to the simultaneous equations problem follows in chapter 7.

2. BAYESIAN DECISION THEORY

Statistical decision theory is concerned with the analysis of random experiments for the purpose of making the best decisions under conditions of uncertainty. More formally, "a statistical decision problem arises when we are faced with a set of alternative decisions, one of which must be made, and the degree of preference for the various possible decisions depends on the unknown distribution" of some random variable.[1] Examples of statistical decision problems are easy to find in the economics literature. The familiar stochastic inventory problem is typical. There a firm has available past sales data which can be used in making current inventory decisions. The optimal decision depends both on the costs involved and on future demand. Since future demand is related stochastically to past demands, the problem is to use optimally the sample observations in making ordering decisions.

The inventory problem is only one example of a statistical decision problem in economics. Indeed it may be argued that most econometric problems are of this type. The ultimate purpose of economic research is

1. WALD (1950), p. 2.

to improve economic policy, whether it be the policy of a household, a firm, or a government. The topics and methods of economic research are varied, but the policy aspect is basic to every area. To use the phrase of MARSCHAK (1953), "knowledge is useful if it helps to make the best decisions."

The proposition that econometric research is most usefully viewed as a part of the decision-making process is, of course, not new. The leaders in the development of econometrics have always emphasized the connection between economic research and policy application. Yet, there has been a noticeable gap in connecting the *methods* of econometric research with its *purposes*. The statistical methods of econometrics are only rarely justified on the basis of their value for economic decision making. The econometric techniques discussed in the previous chapters are based on the classical concepts of unbiasedness and minimum variance. The losses involved in actually using these techniques in practice are almost never considered when judging alternative statistical methods.[2]

The traditional way of using data in economic decision problems involves a two-stage process. First, data are collected and point estimates of unknown parameters are made. Second, the point estimates (and perhaps their standard errors) are used by policy makers in making decisions. Decision making and statistical estimation are split into two separate problems. The decision maker does not concern himself with the methods used in obtaining the estimates; and the statistician does not concern himself with the specific uses that will be made of his estimates. Estimation methods are based on certain general principles (e.g., minimum variance unbiasedness) that are presumably of universal validity.

But how universal are these principles? The idea that an estimator ought to have a small variance is very plausible. The second moment may be a somewhat arbitrary measure of dispersion, but without a specific decision problem in mind it is probably as good as any other general measure. The real problem of classical estimation theory lies in the assumption of unbiasedness. Why should we restrict ourselves only to unbiased estimators when seeking the best estimate? There seems to be no answer that is convincing. One is led to accept Savage's remark that "a serious reason to prefer unbiased estimates seems never to have been proposed."[3] Thus if we accept the proposition that statistical methods ought to be

2. Two important exceptions are W. FISHER (1962) and THEIL (1961). Fisher uses a Bayesian approach similar to the one developed here. Theil keeps within the classical framework of unbiased estimators but explicitly develops a decision problem and a loss structure.

3. SAVAGE (1954), p. 244.

appropriate to the decision problem for which they are used, then we must conclude that the traditional point estimates are optimal only by chance. In addition, the value of a priori information as measured in the previous chapters of this monograph may have little relation to the true measure which is based on the improved decisions that are made possible.

Of course not all econometric problems can be usefully considered as decision problems. Often we are interested in estimating economic relationships in order to get a better feeling for the structure of the economy. Although in the long run some policy decisions may rest on our estimates, no immediate decision is intended. In these cases the classical point estimates and covariance matrices may prove to be quite satisfactory. Furthermore, as we shall see, it is often the case that the traditional approach gives answers that closely approximate decision-theoretic ones. Thus, one should view the Bayesian approach not as replacing the classical approach, but rather as providing an attractive alternative for certain classes of problems. Both classical and Bayesian methods have their uses. The problem facing practicing econometricians is to decide which approach is most appropriate for the particular research at hand.

3. THE BAYESIAN ANALYSIS

With these general observations, we shall turn to the technical features of the Bayesian analysis. Only the very basic notation and ideas will be given here. For a more detailed presentation the reader is directed to the books by DEGROOT (1970), LINDLEY (1965), RAIFFA AND SCHLAIFER (1961), and ZELLNER (1971).

The usual analysis of statistical decision theory distinguishes two problems. One is the problem of making the best decision on the basis of a given set of data; the other is the problem of designing the best experiment in order to get information upon which a decision will be based. Both problems are important in most statistical work and the distinction between them is often not emphasized. In this respect, however, econometrics is an exception. In most instances the econometrician does not have the opportunity to design an experiment; his data are given to him as the result of past history and are not under his control. Thus, that aspect of decision theory which is concerned with experimental design is often irrelevant for econometrics. For that reason we shall ignore in this chapter the problems of experimental design and examine only the problem of making terminal decisions.

The problem to be analyzed can be summarized as follows. Given that a random experiment has been performed and the data are before us, a decision must be made. The effects of any action that is taken depend on the unknown state of the world. Furthermore, the data can be thought of as the observed value of a random variable whose probability distribution depends on the true state of the world. How should we use the data to make the best decision?

It is clear that we must specify more carefully what we mean by the "best" decision. Let the state of the world be represented by the parameter vector θ. Suppose that $\{a\}$ is the set of acts that are open to the decision maker. We assume that the set of all pairs (a, θ) can be ranked in order of preference by means of a loss function $L(a, \theta)$. Thus

$$L(a_1, \theta_1) < L(a_2, \theta_2)$$

is equivalent to the statement that (a_1, θ_1) is preferred to (a_2, θ_2). If θ were known, then the best decision would be to select the act that minimizes $L(a, \theta)$. However, θ is not known and hence a decision problem arises.

If an experiment is performed, the decision maker can base his decision on the sample Y_n. The act taken will be a function of the random variable Y_n and hence a random variable itself. The decision function that assigns an act to a sample outcome will be denoted by the symbol d:

$$a = d(Y_n).$$

The problem of making the best decision is thus one of selecting the best decision function. We assume that, for any given θ, the best decision function d is the one with smallest expected loss (sometimes called risk)

$$(3.1) \qquad r(d, \theta) = \int_S L[d(y), \theta] f_n(y, \theta) \, dy$$

where $f_n(y, \theta)$ is, as in the classical theory, the density function of Y_n for given θ; the integration runs over the set S of possible sample values Y_n. Thus, for any *given* θ, a decision function can be judged by examining its risk function. The statistical decision problem is to find the best decision when θ is unknown.

There are a number of solutions that have been proposed for the statistical decision problem. The basic idea of every solution, of course, is to choose the decision rule that has the smallest risk. If there were a decision function d^* which had uniformly minimum risk (i.e., $r[d^*, \theta] \le r[d, \theta]$ for all θ in the parameter space A and for all d), then d^* would be optimal. In general, however, no such function exists and some further criterion is necessary. The various proposed solutions differ with respect to the added criterion that is imposed.

The traditional school solves the problem by restricting the class of decision rules to be considered. If the restrictions are strong enough, there will be a unique decision rule, in the permitted class, that minimizes risk for all θ. In some cases, the restriction of unbiasedness is sufficient to obtain a uniformly best decision rule. If θ and a are m-dimensional vectors and loss is quadratic in $a - \theta$, this traditional approach leads to decision functions that are unbiased and have minimum variance. Thus the classical theory of estimation presented in chapter 1 can be thought of as a restricted solution to a quadratic decision problem. Unfortunately, as already pointed out, the assumption of unbiasedness, although superficially plausible, is quite arbitrary. It has no connection with the loss due to incorrect decisions and, hence, is unsatisfactory from a decision-theoretic point of view.

The *minimax* solution to the statistical decision problem is based on the conservative procedure of avoiding the very worst. For each possible act, focus is put on the largest possible risk. The optimal act is then the one that minimizes this maximum risk. Although much mathematical analysis has been devoted to the minimax solution, few people would probably recommend its use as a general solution to the statistical decision problem.

The most controversial and yet perhaps the most attractive answer to the decision problem is the so-called Bayesian solution. This approach makes use of the decision maker's own prior information about θ. It is based on the commonsense argument that even in the absence of data, decision makers do make reasonable decisions. Hence, some a priori information is already available *before* the experiment is made and this information should be used to make the best decision *after* the data are available.

More specifically, it is assumed that the decision maker's uncertainty can be summarized in a probability function on θ. This probability function represents the "betting odds" that the decision maker would give if he were offered a series of gambles concerning the true value of θ. The Bayesian solution to the statistical decision problem is to select the act that minimizes expected loss where the expectation runs over the joint distribution of Y_n and θ. Thus the Bayesian solution minimizes

$$(3.2) \qquad r^*(d) = \int_A \int_S L(d, \theta) f(y, \theta) D(\theta)\, dy\, d\theta = \int_A r(d, \theta) D(\theta)\, d\theta$$

where $D(\theta)$ is a multivariate density on the parameter space A representing the prior beliefs of the decision maker and $f(y, \theta)$ is now interpreted as the conditional density of Y_n given θ.[4]

The Bayesian solution to the statistical decision problem can be derived from a set of basic principles of consistent behavior. This theory is discussed in detail by SAVAGE (1954) and by PRATT, RAIFFA, AND SCHLAIFER (1964) and need not be reviewed here. However, a few comments on the appropriateness of the Bayesian approach may be of some value. The Bayesian theory is sometimes criticized because it assumes that parameters are random variables while by definition parameters are fixed numbers. This criticism is based on a terminological confusion. The Bayesian analysis does not require θ to represent a random outcome of some actual experiment. We do not have to pretend that the real world was "drawn" from the set of all possible real worlds with a certain probability. Bayesian decision theory merely argues that people who wish to decide consistently in uncertain situations should act *as though* θ were a random variable with a certain distribution function. It is convenient to use the terminology of random experiments when describing θ even if there is no experiment in mind.

The problem of specifying an appropriate subjective probability function $D(\theta)$ is a very real one. It is not easy to express in simple terms rather vague beliefs about parameter values. Furthermore, it is often difficult to find a family of prior distributions that is rich enough to incorporate the decision maker's beliefs but simple enough to be algebraically workable. Yet, considerable prior information about parameters is usually available; using a probability distribution that captures the essence of the information is surely better than ignoring the information entirely.

In practice the rule given in (3.2) is not the most convenient one for analyzing the data after the experiment has been performed. An equivalent and simpler rule can be given as follows. By Bayes's formula the posterior density on θ (i.e., the conditional distribution of θ given $Y_n = y$) is defined as

$$(3.3) \qquad D'(\theta) \equiv D'(\theta|y) = \frac{f(y, \theta)D(\theta)}{f^*(y)}$$

where

$$f^*(y) = \int_A f(y, \theta)D(\theta)\, d\theta$$

4. For notational convenience we drop the subscript n from the density function.

is the marginal density on Y_n. Thus (3.2) can be written as

$$r^*(d) = \int_S \left[\int_A L[d(y), \theta] D'(\theta)\, d\theta \right] f^*(y)\, dy.$$

Since f^* is nonnegative, $r^*(d)$ is minimized if, for every y,

(3.4) $$\int_A L(a, \theta) D'(\theta)\, d\theta$$

is minimized over $\{a\}$. Hence the optimal Bayes decision is that which minimizes expected posterior loss.

We may summarize the above discussion by noting that every Bayesian decision problem can be solved in three steps. First, a loss function that expresses approximately the relative importance of various decision errors is specified. Second, the posterior density function is derived from the prior density and the likelihood function of the process. Third, the optimal act is obtained by minimizing expected loss where the posterior distribution of θ is used in the expectation. If, as is commonly assumed, loss is quadratic in the decision error $a - \theta$, we may write

$$\mathcal{E} L(a, \theta) = \mathcal{E}(a - \theta)' Q(a - \theta)$$
$$= (a - \bar{\theta})' Q(a - \bar{\theta}) + \mathcal{E}(\theta - \bar{\theta})' Q(\theta - \bar{\theta})$$

where $\bar{\theta}$ is the posterior mean of θ. Hence, under quadratic loss the optimal decision for any Q is to choose the mean of the posterior distribution of θ.

4. Specification of the Prior Density

The major problem in any Bayesian analysis is specifying a prior density that represents the decision maker's beliefs and is at the same time convenient to use in deriving the optimal decision. Since the optimal decision will depend on the characteristics of the posterior density function, we should like to begin with a prior that gives rise to a rather simple posterior. Unfortunately, this is often not possible.

By Bayes's formula the posterior density is proportional to the product of the likelihood function and the prior density. Thus we are led to examine functions of the form

(4.1) $$D'(\theta) = D(\theta) f(y, \theta) K(y)$$

where $K(y)$ is a normalizing factor insuring that the area under D' equals one. If θ is a scalar, we may choose any positive function for $D(\theta)$ as long as the product has a finite integral. Even if the resulting posterior is not algebraically convenient, it can always be plotted on paper. Numerical integrations can be used to calculate moments. However, if θ is a vector of many dimensions, we are not so free in choosing the prior density. Unless $D(\theta)$ has a particularly convenient form, the posterior density will be unworkable. Algebraic derivation of moments will be intractable and numerical integrations too costly for practical use.

The problem is to specify a family of prior densities such that (1) any decision maker's prior information can be approximated by a member of the family and (2) any member of the family gives rise to a simple posterior density. The monograph by RAIFFA AND SCHLAIFER (1961) presents one solution to the problem by developing the "natural conjugate" family of distributions. This family may be described as follows. The likelihood function $f(y, \theta)$ is positive for all y in the sample space S and all θ in the parameter space A. Let S^* be the set of y values for which the integral

$$\int_A f(y, \theta)\, d\theta \equiv \frac{1}{K^*(y)}$$

is finite. Then consider the natural conjugate family of functions

(4.2) $$D(\theta) = f(y, \theta)K^*(y)$$

indexed by $y \in S^*$. If y_1 is the actual sample value and y_2 indexes the prior density, the posterior density will be proportional to

(4.3) $$f(y_1, \theta)f(y_2, \theta).$$

But (4.3) can be interpreted as the joint likelihood of two independent samples y_1 and y_2. Hence, if the prior density is a member of the natural conjugate family, the algebra of finding the posterior density is identical to that of finding the distribution of two independent samples from the same process. This latter problem is often very easy, especially if $f(y, \theta)$ is a distribution that possesses a fixed dimensional sufficient statistic. Thus, if the prior beliefs can be expressed in a density function of the form (4.2), the algebra of the Bayesian analysis is greatly simplified.

For a number of econometric problems, the natural conjugate family is very flexible in describing prior beliefs. For example, in the normal linear regression model

$$y = X\beta + u,$$

the likelihood function is proportional to

$$h^{\frac{1}{2}n} \exp\{-\tfrac{1}{2}h(\beta - b)'X'X(\beta - b) - \tfrac{1}{2}hy'[I - X(X'X)^{-1}X']y\}$$

where h is the reciprocal of the error variance σ^2. The natural conjugate prior density for β and h is proportional to

$$h^{\frac{1}{2}a} \exp\{-\tfrac{1}{2}h(\beta - d)'B(\beta - d) - \tfrac{1}{2}hc\}$$

where a and c may be any positive numbers, d may be any vector having the same dimension as β, and B may be any positive definite matrix of the appropriate dimension. This joint density on the parameters can be interpreted as the product of a conditional normal density on β for given h and a marginal gamma distribution on h. The implied marginal density on β is multivariate Student with arbitrary mean vector and covariance matrix. Thus, if the decision maker's information on β can be approximated by a symmetric distribution, the natural conjugate form allows for considerable flexibility. Furthermore, if the natural conjugate family of priors is used, the posterior density on β will have the same algebraic form as the prior. Since the lower-order moments of the Student density are simple functions of the basic parameters, the posterior distribution will be easy to analyze.[5]

Unfortunately, the natural conjugate theory does not always give a convenient family of prior densities. For some very important econometric problems the family defined by (4.2) is very restrictive and often will not fit the prior beliefs of the decision maker. This will in general be the case when we are analyzing systems of regression equations. Consider, for example, the reduced-form system

$$y_t = \Pi x_t + v_t$$

where y_t is a vector of G random variables, x_t is a vector of K nonrandom variables, and v_t is a vector of G random errors. If we assume that v_t has a multivariate normal density with mean zero and covariance matrix Ω, the likelihood function for a random sample of size n is[6]

$$f(\Pi, \Omega) \propto |\Omega|^{-\frac{1}{2}n} \exp\{-\tfrac{1}{2}\operatorname{tr}\Omega^{-1}(Y - X\Pi')'(Y - X\Pi')\}$$

---

5. For details, see RAIFFA AND SCHLAIFER (1961), chapter 13.

6. We shall drop the multiplicative constants (which may depend on the sample data) in writing the likelihood function. The symbol $\propto$ should be read as "is proportional to."

where Y and X are observation matrices. The likelihood function can be rewritten as

(4.4) $f(\Pi, \Omega) \propto |\Omega|^{-\frac{1}{2}n} \exp\{-\frac{1}{2} \text{tr } \Omega^{-1}[(\Pi - P)(X'X)(\Pi - P)' + nS]\}$

where P and S are the least-squares estimates

$$P = Y'X(X'X)^{-1}, \qquad S = \frac{1}{n}(Y - XP')'(Y - XP').$$

If we treat Ω as known, the function (4.4) describes a normal density for Π. Thus the natural conjugate for a reduced-form system is a normal density on the unknown parameters Π. This would seem to be a useful result since typically prior information about the regression parameters can be roughly approximated by a normal distribution. But the catch lies in the fact that (4.4) is not a *general* normal density, but one that forces severe conditions on the variances of our prior beliefs. In particular, a density proportional to (4.4) implies

(4.5) $\text{Var } \pi_{ij} = \omega_{ii} m_{jj}$

where ω_{ii} is a diagonal element of Ω and m_{jj} is a diagonal element of $(X'X)^{-1}$. The form (4.5) implies

$$\frac{\text{Var } \pi_{ri}}{\text{Var } \pi_{si}} = \frac{\text{Var } \pi_{rj}}{\text{Var } \pi_{sj}};$$

that is, the variances of all parameters in the rth equation must be proportional to the variances of the corresponding parameters in the sth equation. Since there is no reason why our a priori beliefs about the π_{ij} should be related in this way, we must conclude that the conjugate family is too restrictive to incorporate our beliefs. Another way of illustrating this point is by expressing the variance formula (4.5) as the matrix

$$V = [v_{ij}] = [\text{Var } \pi_{ij}] = \omega m'$$

where ω is the column vector of the ω_{ii} and m is the column vector of the m_{jj}. The matrix V, representing as it does the prior beliefs of the decision maker, should be free from constraint (except that it must be positive). Yet the conjugate theory forces it to be of rank one. This restriction seems unacceptable.

If Ω is in fact known, we can get around the problem by generalizing the natural conjugate family. Although (4.4) is a very restrictive normal family, replacing it with an arbitrary normal density on Π does not cause any problems. The posterior distribution of Π remains normal and the derivation of posterior moments is elementary. If, however, Ω is unknown, this generalization is not available. An arbitrary normal prior density on Π does not combine with the likelihood function to form a tractable posterior density since Ω enters in a complicated way. The joint conjugate density on Π and Ω derived from (4.4) by replacing the data matrices with arbitrary matrices of constants may be interpreted as the product of a normal density on Π conditional on Ω^{-1} and a Wishart density on Ω^{-1}. This joint density yields a tractable posterior density but the variances of Π are restricted as before.[7] A similar result applies if we consider the structural equations of a simultaneous equations model. Again the prior distribution implied by the natural conjugate theory has unsatisfactory constraints on the choice of prior variances.

The explanation of this result is worth pursuing. The conjugate theory suggests that all prior information arises from previous samples from the same stochastic process. Thus all prior information must satisfy certain constraints that apply to data generated by the process. In economics, however, we do not believe that all our prior information comes from previous samples. We have theoretical arguments that put constraints on our parameters. Also we have access to various sorts of stochastic models referring to the same parameters. For example, we can use both cross-section and time-series data to study demand equations. It is not plausible to assume that our a priori information, based on cross-section analysis, can be formulated *as if* it arose from a time-series sample.

It would appear that, although the Bayesian approach is appropriate for economic decision problems based on econometric models, the notion of a conjugate family of prior densities is not always useful. When *systems* of interrelated equations are analyzed, the conjugate family is not rich enough to incorporate the prior beliefs that economists typically possess.

If instead of using the conjugate theory one simply works with an arbitrary density $D(\Pi, \Omega)$, the posterior density is of the form

$$D'(\Pi, \Omega) \propto D(\Pi, \Omega)|\Omega|^{-\frac{1}{2}n} \exp\{-\tfrac{1}{2}\operatorname{tr}\Omega^{-1}[(\Pi - P)(X'X)(\Pi - P)' + S]\}.$$

In general, this posterior will be very difficult to work with. Some simplification is possible if the prior density is of the form

$$D(\Pi, \Omega) = D_1(\Pi)D_2(\Omega^{-1})$$

---

7. For an analysis of the conjugate normal-Wishart distribution, see DeGroot (1970), pp. 175–80, or Ando and Kaufman (1965).

where D_2 is a Wishart distribution. Then the marginal posterior density on Π can be written as

$$(4.6) \qquad D_1'(\Pi) \propto D_1(\Pi)|S^* + (\Pi - P)X'X(\Pi - P)'|^{-\kappa}$$

where S^* and κ depend on the parameters of D_2. This posterior density is the product of the prior density $D_1(\Pi)$ and a matrix Student density. Except for the special case where $D_1(\Pi)$ is everywhere uniform, the density (4.6) is not easy to handle analytically. Its moments must be determined by numerical approximation methods which are quite complex if Π has many elements.

Under most circumstances the algebra of the Bayesian analysis will not be easy when systems of equations are involved. Covariance matrices are never known in advance, so that some prior density on Ω will be needed. It appears, however, that the marginal posterior distributions of Π are not very sensitive to the prior distributions of Ω. Thus the assumption of a Wishart distribution with large variances might be a reasonable solution. Nevertheless, even with this assumption, the densities are not particularly suited for analytical work. Each problem will have to be examined separately and the appropriate numerical approximation methods applied.

5. A SIMPLE ECONOMETRIC MODEL

In order to illustrate the Bayesian theory, we consider a very simple Keynesian consumption function model. The system contains one behavioral equation that relates consumption expenditure C_t linearly to disposable income Y_t and a stochastic error u_t:

$$(5.1) \qquad C_t = \alpha Y_t + \beta + u_t.$$

The system is closed by the identity

$$(5.2) \qquad Y_t = C_t + Z_t$$

where Z_t, the difference between income and consumption, is called exogenous demand. The reduced form consists of two equations, but there is only one independent relation. We shall be interested in the income equation

$$Y_t = \frac{1}{1-\alpha}Z_t + \frac{\beta}{1-\alpha} + \frac{1}{1-\alpha}u_t$$
$$(5.3)$$
$$= \pi Z_t + \rho + v_t$$

where π is the familiar income multiplier.

A sample (for example, a time series of annual observations on consumption and income) of size n is assumed to be available. If the Z_t are taken to be nonstochastic, the probability distribution of the sample is determined once we have specified the joint distribution of the n error terms. We shall assume that the errors u_t have independent, identical normal distributions with mean zero and variance σ^2. The likelihood function can then be written in the two alternative forms

$$(5.4a) \qquad f_1(\alpha, \beta, h) \propto (1 - \alpha)^n h^{\frac{1}{2}n} \exp \left\{ -\frac{1}{2} h \sum_t (C_t - \alpha Y_t - \beta)^2 \right\},$$

$$(5.4b) \qquad f_2(\pi, \rho, h) \propto \pi^{-n} h^{\frac{1}{2}n} \exp \left\{ -\frac{h}{2\pi^2} \sum_t (Y_t - \pi Z_t - \rho)^2 \right\},$$

depending on which set of parameters we use. For convenience, we use the precision parameter h (which is the reciprocal of the error variance σ^2) instead of the variance itself.

This multiplier model is precisely the one considered by HAAVELMO (1947) in his classic paper. It is presented here because it is the simplest example of a simultaneous equations system. Indeed, the model is so simple it seems strange to even use the words "simultaneous" and "system" in describing it. There is only one stochastic equation involved and the traditional methods of analysis are easily applied. Yet even in this simple case, the traditional solution is not completely satisfactory. It seems useful then to develop in detail the Bayesian solution and to compare it with the traditional one.

In order to apply the methods of Bayesian decision theory we must first specify the decision problem. What exactly are the acts open to the decision maker and what is his loss function? For purposes of illustration we shall assume that the decision maker is a forecaster whose task is to predict the level of disposable income in year τ given the level of exogenous demand. Further it is assumed that the loss function is quadratic in the prediction error

$$(5.5) \qquad L(\hat{Y}_\tau, Y_\tau) = (\hat{Y}_\tau - Y_\tau)^2$$

where $\hat{Y}_\tau$ is the chosen act. The problem, then, is to find the best forecast given Z_τ and the information from the previous sample.

The traditional solution to the decision problem is to use certain "best" estimates as certainty equivalents for the unknown variables. Thus the forecast is

$$\hat{Y}_\tau = pZ_\tau + r$$

where v_τ is set equal to its mean value zero; p and r are minimum-variance unbiased estimates of π and ρ. These estimates are obtained by least squares applied to (5.3). The Bayesian solution, on the other hand, is to choose the forecast which minimizes

$$(5.6) \qquad \mathscr{E}(\hat{Y}_\tau - Y_\tau)^2 = \hat{Y}_\tau^2 - 2\hat{Y}_\tau\mathscr{E}(Y_\tau) + \text{constant}$$

where the expectation is over the conditional distribution of Y_τ given Z_τ and the previous sample. Taking the derivative of (5.6) with respect to $\hat{Y}_\tau$ and setting it to zero, we find that the Bayesian forecast is simply the conditional mean of Y_τ. Using (5.3) we can write the Bayesian forecast as

$$(5.7) \qquad \hat{Y}_\tau = \mathscr{E}Y_\tau = \bar{\pi}Z_\tau + \bar{\rho}$$

where $\bar{\pi}$ and $\bar{\rho}$ are the mean values of the posterior distribution on π and ρ.

According to (5.7) the Bayesian solution, like the classical solution, uses certainty equivalents for the unknown parameters. The difference between the solutions lies in the particular certainty equivalents chosen. The next task, then, is to derive the posterior density of (π, ρ) and to calculate their mean values.

The posterior analysis is somewhat complicated by the fact that the required posterior distribution concerns the parameters (π, ρ) whereas typically our prior information is expressed in terms of the structural parameters (α, β, h). Indeed, the interesting aspect of simultaneous equation theory—both Bayesian and traditional—is the influence of structural restrictions on the reduced-form distributions. A general Bayesian treatment of this problem appears in chapter 7. In the present example the calculations are elementary. Since the system given in (5.1) and (5.2) contains only one stochastic equation, the transformation between structure and reduced form is simple. Any joint probability density on the structural parameters can easily be transformed to obtain the implied density on the reduced-form parameters.

The Bayesian analysis thus involves two steps: deriving a posterior density from the likelihood function and the prior density, and deriving the distribution of the reduced-form parameters from the initial information on the structural parameters. These two steps can be taken in either order, giving rise to two different ways to proceed. On the one hand, we can use the prior structural density (denoted by D) and the likelihood function $f_1(\alpha, \beta, h)$ to derive the posterior structural density D' and then use the definitions of π and ρ to derive the implied posterior reduced-form density $\bar{D}'$. On the other hand, we can directly use the definitions to derive the reduced-form prior density $\bar{D}$ from the prior structural density D and then use $\bar{D}$ and the likelihood function $f_2(\pi, \rho, h)$ to derive the posterior reduced-form density $\bar{D}'$. These two ways can be expressed diagrammatically as follows:

$$
\begin{array}{ccc}
 & \text{structure} & \text{reduced form} \\
\text{prior} & D(\alpha, \beta, h) & \rightarrow \quad \bar{D}(\pi, \rho) \\
 & \downarrow & \qquad \downarrow \\
\text{posterior} & D'(\alpha, \beta, h) & \rightarrow \quad \bar{D}'(\pi, \rho)
\end{array}
$$

For purposes of illustration, we shall explore both routes in our derivation.

6. THE BAYESIAN SOLUTION

We begin by deriving the posterior density for the structural parameters. The derivation will be done first under the assumption that the parameter σ is known. This is, of course, a very unrealistic assumption and will be dropped later. For the prior on (α, β) we shall take a very simple form. Specifically, it is assumed that the prior information on β is very weak and can be treated as a uniform distribution over the entire real line.[8] Further, we assume that the prior density on α is rectangular over the interval $(0, 1)$. Thus we have the joint prior density on α and β given by

$$
(6.1) \qquad D(\alpha, \beta) \, d\alpha \, d\beta \propto d\alpha \, d\beta
$$

for $0 < \alpha < 1, -\infty < \beta < \infty$.

The joint posterior density can be written as

$$
(6.2) \qquad
\begin{aligned}
D'(\alpha, \beta) &\propto D(\alpha, \beta) f_1(\alpha, \beta, h) \\
&\propto (1 - \alpha)^n h^{\frac{1}{2}n} \exp\{-\tfrac{1}{2}h \sum_t (C_t - \alpha Y_t - \beta)^2\}
\end{aligned}
$$

where h is the reciprocal of σ^2. The marginal posterior density for the parameter α is given by

$$
(6.3) \qquad
\begin{aligned}
D_1'(\alpha) &\propto \int_{-\infty}^{\infty} (1 - \alpha)^n h^{\frac{1}{2}n} \exp\left\{-\tfrac{1}{2}h \sum_t (C_t - \alpha Y_t - \beta)^2\right\} d\beta \\
&\propto (1 - \alpha)^n h^{\frac{1}{2}(n-1)} \exp\left\{-\tfrac{1}{2}h \sum_t (c_t - \alpha y_t)^2\right\} \\
&\propto (1 - \alpha)^n h^{\frac{1}{2}(n-1)} \exp\{-\tfrac{1}{2}h[(\alpha - a)^2 m + ns^2]\}
\end{aligned}
$$

8. This diffuse prior can be thought of as the limit of a sequence of prior densities with ever increasing variances; see DeGroot (1970), pp. 190–201. Stein (1965) discusses some difficulties in using a diffuse "improper" prior distribution.

for $0 < \alpha < 1$. The lower case letters c_t and y_t represent variables measured as deviations from their sample means; a, m, and s^2 are the familiar least-squares statistics

(6.4) $$a = \frac{\Sigma c_t y_t}{\Sigma y_t^2}, \qquad m = \Sigma y_t^2, \qquad s^2 = \frac{1}{n}\Sigma(c_t - ay_t)^2.$$

The posterior density for the marginal propensity to consume is seen from (6.3) to be the product of two curves: (1) a sharply decreasing curve $(1 - \alpha)^n$ representing the Jacobian of the transformation relating u_t and y_t, and (2) a normal density with the least-squares estimate a as mean. These two curves are drawn in figure 6.1. Since the mean of the product will undoubtedly be to the left of the mean of the normal curve, figure 6.1 gives a clear illustration of the upward bias of the ordinary least-squares estimate of the marginal propensity to consume.

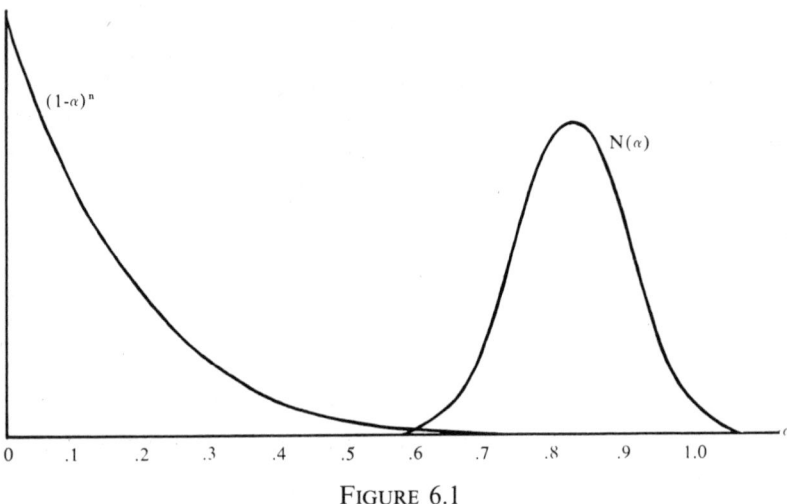

FIGURE 6.1

The Bayesian approach was applied to some actual data to get an idea of the shape of the density given by (6.3). Annual U.S. consumption per capita (1947–64) was used for C_t and disposable income per capita was used for Y_t (all in constant 1964 dollars). The resulting estimates for a and m were found to be 0.862 and 581,700, respectively. Under the assumption that $\sigma = 25$, the posterior distribution looks more or less symmetric with center at 0.775. Both prior density D_1 and posterior density D_1' are drawn in figure 6.2.

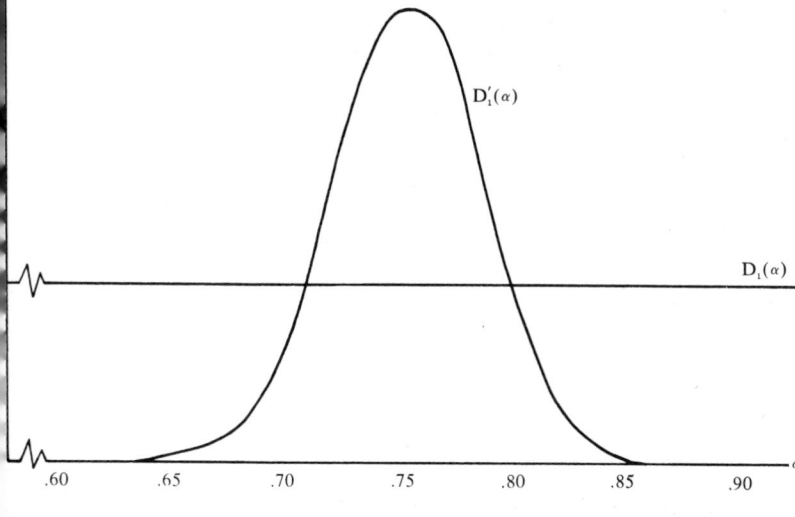

FIGURE 6.2

Now that the density $D'_1(\alpha)$ has been found, it is easy to find the posterior density for the multiplier. Since

$$\alpha = 1 - \frac{1}{\pi},$$

the density for π is given by

(6.5) $$\bar{D}'_1(\pi) = \frac{1}{\pi^2} D'_1\left(1 - \frac{1}{\pi}\right) \qquad (1 < \pi < \infty).$$

This density is drawn in figure 6.3 for the same data as before. It is skewed slightly to the right and has a mean of 4.51. The density for ρ can be found in a similar way; its mean is approximately 1315. Thus, according to the Bayesian theory, the best forecast is given by

$$\hat{Y}_\tau = 1315 + 4.51 Z_\tau.$$

Using ordinary least squares on the reduced-form equation yields the classical solution

$$\hat{Y}_\tau = 1300 + 4.62 Z_\tau.$$

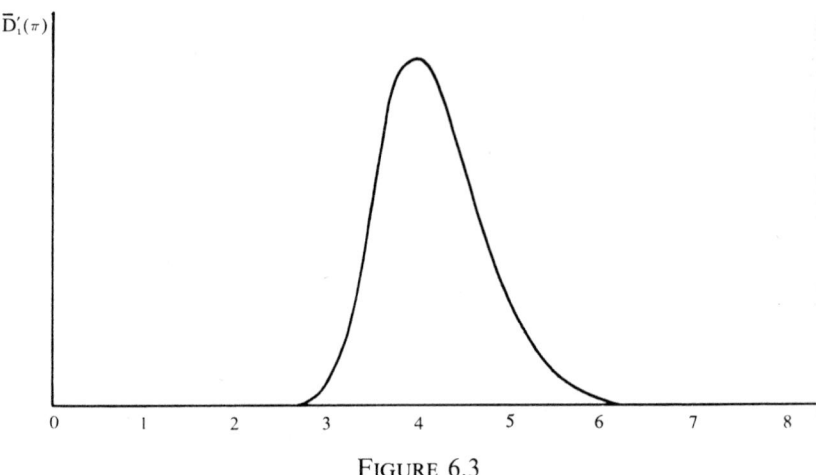

FIGURE 6.3

The Bayesian joint posterior density on (π, ρ) can be found more directly by noting that the prior density (6.1) implies a prior density on (π, ρ) of the form

$$\bar{D}(\pi, \rho) \, d\pi \, d\rho \propto \frac{1}{\pi^3} \, d\pi \, d\rho$$

for $1 < \pi < \infty, \, -\infty < \rho < \infty$. Hence the joint posterior density is

(6.6)
$$\begin{aligned} \bar{D}'(\pi, \rho) &\propto \bar{D}(\pi, \rho) f_2(\pi, \rho, h) \\ &\propto \pi^{-(n+3)} h^{\frac{1}{2}n} \exp\left\{ -\frac{h}{2\pi^2} \sum_t (Y_t - \pi Z_t - \rho)^2 \right\} \end{aligned}$$

and the marginal posterior density for the multiplier is

(6.7) $$\bar{D}'_1(\pi) \propto \pi^{-(n+2)} h^{\frac{1}{2}(n-1)} \exp\left\{ -\frac{h}{2\pi^2} [(\pi - p)^2 \bar{m} + n\bar{s}^2] \right\}$$

for $1 < \pi < \infty$; $p, \bar{m}$, and $\bar{s}^2$ are the reduced-form least-squares estimates analogous to those in (6.4).

THE ANALYSIS WITH UNKNOWN σ

It is now necessary to relax the assumption that σ is known. We shall assume instead that little is known about this parameter and that the density on h, the reciprocal of σ^2, is diffuse. Thus we assume that our joint prior on the structural parameters is given by

$$D(\alpha, \beta, h) \, d\alpha \, d\beta \, dh \propto d\alpha \, d\beta \, dh$$

for $0 < \alpha < 1$, $-\infty < \beta < \infty$, $0 < h < \infty$. Using this prior density we can derive the posterior densities for the parameters and compare them with our previous results. We shall concentrate our attention on the marginal distributions of α and π.

Equation (6.3) is the conditional density on α for a given value of h. By integration we obtain the marginal density

$$D_1''(\alpha) \propto \int_0^\infty (1 - \alpha)^n h^{\frac{1}{2}(n-1)} \exp\{-\tfrac{1}{2}h[(\alpha - a)^2 m + ns^2]\} \, dh$$

(6.8)
$$\propto (1 - \alpha)^n \left[n + (\alpha - a)^2 \frac{m}{s^2} \right]^{-\frac{1}{2}(n+1)} \qquad (0 < \alpha < 1).$$

The posterior density for the marginal propensity to consume is again the product of two curves, but this time the normal density is replaced by a Student density (with n degrees of freedom). Thus, if h is unknown and its prior is diffuse, the least-squares estimate should be used in place of h and the normal density of (6.3) replaced by the Student density. If the prior density on h were not diffuse, the resulting posterior density on α would differ from (6.8). If, however, the prior density on h were of the gamma form and the prior on α remained rectangular, the posterior density on α would remain of the Student form. On the other hand, if the prior distributions on α and h are not of these very special forms, exact algebraic analysis is almost impossible. Then numerical approximation methods are required to perform the necessary integrations.

The marginal density for the multiplier is obtained from (6.7) as follows:

$$\bar{D}_1''(\pi) \propto \int_0^\infty \pi^{-(n+2)} h^{\frac{1}{2}(n-1)} \exp \left\{ -\frac{h}{2\pi^2}[(\pi - p)^2 \bar{m} + n\bar{s}^2] \right\} dh$$

(6.9)
$$\propto \pi^{-1} \left[n + (\pi - p)^2 \frac{\bar{m}}{\bar{s}^2} \right]^{-\frac{1}{2}(n+1)}.$$

Even though (6.7) was more complicated, the density on π (after the uncertainty in h is accounted for) is of the familiar form: a Student density times a Jacobian term. A comparison of (6.7) and (6.9) indicates that knowledge of σ changes substantially the analysis of the reduced form. This, of course, is the expected result given our analysis in chapter 4. Constraints on σ imply constraints on the reduced-form parameters.

The posterior distribution (6.7) should have a smaller variance than the posterior distribution (6.9) since it uses more prior information. Similarly the posterior distribution of α given in (6.3) should have a smaller variance than the one given in (6.8). Our numerical results (summarized in table 6.1) verify these statements. If σ is assumed known and equal to the two-stage least-squares estimate of 25, one finds that the posterior variances of both π and α are lower than is the case where σ is not known.

TABLE 6.1   BAYESIAN ANALYSIS OF HAAVELMO'S MODEL: THE VALUE OF KNOWING SIGMA

	Sigma assumed known to equal 25	*Sigma assumed unknown (Diffuse prior on h)*
Posterior mean of α	0.7749	0.7636
Posterior variance of α	0.00077	0.00370
Posterior mean of π	4.5129	4.4410
Posterior variance of π	0.3343	0.8063

It is of interest to examine how more precise prior information on α affects our posterior distributions. If instead of using a rectangular distribution on α we had used an informative prior distribution centered near 0.75, the posterior variances would fall. This is described in table 6.2 for the case of prior densities of the beta form

$$D(\alpha) \propto \alpha^b(1 - \alpha)^c \qquad (0 < \alpha < 1).$$

TABLE 6.2   BAYESIAN ANALYSIS OF HAAVELMO'S MODEL: INFORMATIVE PRIORS ON ALPHA
(Diffuse prior on h)

Prior density		*Posterior density*			
$\mathscr{E}(\alpha)$	Var(α)	$\mathscr{E}(\alpha)$	Var(α)	$\mathscr{E}(\pi)$	Var(π)
0.50	0.0833	0.7636	0.003701	4.441	0.8063
0.75	0.0208	0.7724	0.002141	4.555	0.6916
0.75	0.0110	0.7723	0.001855	4.536	0.6296
0.75	0.0065	0.7715	0.001607	4.503	0.5595
0.75	0.0045	0.7705	0.001441	4.472	0.5047

The decrease in posterior variance represents the value of a priori structural information. In chapter 7 we shall examine in detail the relationship between prior information and reduced-form precision in the Bayesian context.

The model examined in this section is very simple. Furthermore, the prior information was very weak. More interesting applications of the Bayesian techniques would involve models with a more intricate structure. Unfortunately, little is known about the practical application of Bayesian techniques in more complex situations. An interesting extension of the Haavelmo model is given by CHETTY (1968); a two-equation supply-demand model of the Belgian beef market is analyzed by MORALES (1971). It appears, however, that the application of Bayesian methods to systems of simultaneous equations will be difficult because of the many numerical integrations required. One may hope that approximation methods will be developed to overcome these difficulties. DRÈZE (1968) presents one attempt at simplifying the analysis by developing a Bayesian version of the limited-information maximum-likelihood method of estimating parameters of overidentified structural equations. The method proposed by Drèze allows considerable flexibility in expressing prior probabilities and yet is computationally feasible. Like all limited-information methods, it ignores some of the prior information in order to get simple calculations. This, however, may be a reasonable approach in practice. In any case, some approximations appear to be necessary before Bayesian methods can be used in actual econometric research.

CHAPTER 7

The Value of Bayesian Structural Information

1. INTRODUCTION

In chapter 4 we examined from a classical point of view the general simultaneous equations model

$$By + \Gamma x = u.$$

It was shown that if enough was known about B, Γ, and the error covariance matrix Σ, the reduced-form parameter space was restricted. In such cases an estimator that takes the restrictions into account will have (at least asymptotically) a smaller covariance matrix than the unrestricted estimator. Thus information that takes the form of exact equality constraints on the structural coefficients (e.g., knowing that certain variables do not appear in certain equations) can sometimes increase the efficiency of reduced-form estimation.

But exact knowledge of structural parameters is usually not available. More often we possess only vague information. In such cases the Bayesian approach, which begins with a prior probability distribution over (B, Γ, Σ), seems more convenient than the classical approach, where some parameters are known exactly and others are known not at all. Hence we analyze the following statistical problem: Instead of exact restrictions on the structural parameters, the econometrician possesses a multivariate subjective probability distribution over (B, Γ, Σ). That prior distribution combined with the sample data yields a posterior distribution on both the structural and the reduced-form parameters. We seek the relationship between the posterior variance of the reduced-form parameters and the prior variance of the structural parameters. That is, we wish to measure the value of Bayesian structural information in increasing reduced-form precision.

2. THE GENERAL PROBLEM

In its traditional form, the simultaneous equations model is a special case of the general constrained-parameter model presented at the end of

154

chapter 2. That classical model has the following structure : The likelihood function for the sample Y_n depends on the m-dimensional parameter vector θ and is denoted by $f_n(y, \theta)$. It is known, however, that the elements of θ are derived from a set of more basic "structural" parameters. In particular, each θ_i is a given differentiable function of α, a vector of r structural parameters:

$$(2.1) \qquad\qquad \theta_i = h_i(\alpha) \qquad\qquad (i = 1, \ldots, m).$$

The number of structural parameters in general will be greater than m. However, some additional information is available concerning α. In the classical theory this information is expressed in the assumption that the structural parameters satisfy k independent equations:

$$(2.2) \qquad\qquad \psi_j(\alpha) = 0 \qquad\qquad (j = 1, \ldots, k).$$

The problem is to use the sample data to make inferences about α and θ.

In the framework of classical estimation theory, three general questions may be asked of such a model : (1) Under what conditions is α identifiable and estimable? (2) When and by how much does the knowledge incorporated in h and ψ increase the efficiency of estimating θ? (3) What are efficient estimators of α and θ? In chapter 2 we answered these questions by using the information matrix R_n and the partial derivative matrices H and Ψ. These classical answers were summarized in section 7 of that chapter.

We shall now analyze this problem of constrained estimation from a Bayesian point of view. The likelihood function will be written as $f_n(y|\theta)$ and interpreted as the conditional density of Y_n given θ. The relation (2.1) defining the parameter θ as a function of the structural parameter α remains the same. However, the prior information now takes the form of a probability density on α rather than of exact constraints. That is, the equations (2.2) are replaced by a probability function representing the subjective beliefs of the statistician concerning the probable values of α. We shall assume that the probability distribution is described by the continuous density function $D(\alpha)$ defined over r-dimensional Euclidean space. Furthermore, to facilitate comparison with the classical answers, we shall assume that loss is quadratic in the estimation errors.

Replacing (2.2) by the prior density $D(\alpha)$ represents an important movement to greater realism. The classical theory assumes that some information on α is known exactly so that the parameter space is reduced to a manifold in r-space. It is also assumed that nothing is known about the location of α on the manifold. However, as DRÈZE (1962) has pointed out, this is quite unlikely to occur in practice. Rarely does an economist possess information about which he is absolutely certain. And rarely does he possess absolutely no information about the remaining parameters. Typically the economist has prior information on all the parameters. Some parameters are known more precisely than others, but almost never is it a matter of all or nothing at all.

By allowing the density $D(\alpha)$ to be as concentrated or dispersed as needed to capture the economist's prior knowledge, the Bayesian approach is much more flexible than the classical one. Of course the cost of this greater flexibility may sometimes be high : it is not easy to find a density that captures the economist's vague information, especially when there are many parameters. And, as we discussed in the previous chapter, such a density may not be computationally convenient after it has been specified. Nevertheless, the advantages of the Bayesian approach may often outweigh these difficulties. In any case it is of interest to see how the value of structural information can be evaluated in the Bayesian context.

Again we can ask three questions concerning such a model : (1) Under what conditions is α identified and estimable? (2) How is the precision in estimating θ increased by the use of the structural information? (3) What are efficient estimates of α and θ? However, before proceeding to answer these questions, we must define more precisely what is meant by efficiency and identification in a Bayesian framework.

3. Identification and Precision from the Bayesian Point of View

Suppose we possess a prior probability density $D(\alpha)$ over the structural parameters. Given the relation $\theta = h(\alpha)$, this implies a prior probability function on θ. Combining the prior on θ and the likelihood function $f(y|\theta)$, one can derive by Bayes's formula the posterior distribution of θ (i.e., the conditional distribution of θ given y). The mean of this posterior distribution (assuming it exists) is a function of y and is the Bayesian estimator of θ under quadratic loss. It has the property that it minimizes, for all functions $t(y)$, the expected, or Bayes, risk

$$r^*(t) = \mathscr{E}_{\theta,y}[t(y) - \theta]'Q[t(y) - \theta]$$
$$= \mathscr{E}_{\theta}\mathscr{E}_{y|\theta}[t(y) - \theta]'Q[t(y) - \theta] = \mathscr{E}_{\theta}r(\theta, t)$$

where Q is an arbitrary positive semidefinite matrix. By notational convention $\mathscr{E}_{\theta,y}$ represents the expectation over the joint distribution of θ

and Y_n; $\mathscr{E}_{y|\theta}$ represents the expectation over the conditional distribution of y given θ; and $\mathscr{E}_\theta$ represents the expectation with respect to the marginal (prior) distribution of θ. The risk function $r(\theta, t)$ is simply the classical measure of mean square error.

Suppose the statistician originally possessed the prior distribution D_0 but now possesses the more concentrated distribution D_1. Typically this will mean that D_0 and D_1 have the same expected values, but D_1 has a smaller covariance matrix than D_0. If t_0 and t_1 are the Bayes estimators for D_0 and D_1, respectively, then the gain from having the more precise information about α can be defined as simply the change in mean square error

$$(3.1) \qquad r(\theta, t_0) - r(\theta, t_1).$$

Of course (3.1) is a function of the unknown parameters and can take both positive and negative values depending on the value of θ. Hence in order to get a measure of the gain in estimation efficiency due to increased prior information, we must find some "average" value for (3.1). In the classical case the measure of efficiency gain was evaluated at the true parameter values α^0 and θ^0. This could also be done here. In practice, of course, we would evaluate (3.1) at the best estimate of θ. Before the sample is available, that would be the prior mean.

A second possibility is to take the expectation of (3.1) as a measure of the gain. The problem then arises whether to use the density D_0 or the density D_1 in calculating the expectation. Since the density D_1 presumably describes more precise information, the latter choice is probably preferable. A third possibility is to calculate the Bayes risk for each estimator and measure the gain by the change in Bayes risk. These three possibilities may be stated algebraically as

$$(3.1a) \qquad r(\theta^0, t_0) - r(\theta^0, t_1),$$

$$(3.1b) \qquad \mathscr{E}_1 r(\theta, t_0) - \mathscr{E}_1 r(\theta, t_1),$$

$$(3.1c) \qquad \mathscr{E}_0 r(\theta, t_0) - \mathscr{E}_1 r(\theta, t_1)$$

where $\mathscr{E}_0$ represents the expectation with respect to the density D_0 and $\mathscr{E}_1$ represents the expectation with respect to D_1. The first measure is closest to the classical measure used in the earlier chapters. The last two measures are more in the Bayesian spirit. From a decision-theoretic point of view, (3.1b) would seem to be preferred. However, for our later results it will be more convenient to choose the third measure for gain in efficiency resulting from additional prior information. Since the optimal estimator under quadratic loss is the posterior mean, we have for any Bayes estimator

$$r^* = \mathscr{E}_{\theta,y}[\theta - \mathscr{E}(\theta|y)]'Q[\theta - \mathscr{E}(\theta|y)] = \mathscr{E}_y \operatorname{tr} QV_{\theta|y}$$

where $V_{\theta|y}$ is the covariance matrix of the conditional distribution of θ given y. Thus our measure of the gain from possessing structural information is the difference in expected posterior variance (the expectation being over the marginal distribution of y).

There remains the question of defining identifiability in the case of Bayesian prior information. In classical statistics we say that a model is identifiable if distinct points in the parameter space give rise to distinct probability functions for the sample. Thus the structural parameters of the model described in section 2 are identifiable in the classical sense if, for any two distinct parameter values α_1 and α_2 satisfying (2.2), the likelihood functions $f_n[h(\alpha_1)]$ and $f_n[h(\alpha_2)]$ differ for at least some values of y. If this were not the case, we could never, on the basis of sample evidence, distinguish between α_1 and α_2. In particular we could never find an estimator which was consistent for all admissible values of α.

From the Bayesian point of view, the posterior density function summarizes all of the prior and sample information that is available. If the posterior density for the structural parameter α is highly concentrated around its mean, then we are in an excellent position to distinguish between possible values of α. If, however, this density is highly dispersed, then we are in a poor position. Thus one is tempted to define identification in terms of the degree of concentration of the posterior density. A model would be called unidentified only in the limiting case where the posterior density approaches (in at least one dimension) a degenerate "uniform" density over the entire line. In general this can occur only when both the prior density is "uniform" in some dimension and the model is also unidentified in the classical sense. This follows from the fact that the posterior density is proportional to the product of the prior density and the likelihood function.

This definition of identification is not very satisfactory since it is solely in terms of the posterior density. Thus it is possible, according to our definition, for a parameter to be identifiable even though the data were completely irrelevant. In fact, if the prior density is unimodal and bell-shaped, the model will almost always be identifiable. The problem here is that in the classical case, the concepts of identifiability and estimability are almost equivalent. In our definition we have extended to the Bayesian case the concept of estimability, but have not captured the idea that identification also concerns the way the sample is relevant to the final estimate. Hence we shall use the word "estimable" rather than "identifiable" when referring to a posterior density concentrated around its mean and leave unanswered the question of an appropriate Bayesian definition of identification.[1]

4. A Bayesian Information Inequality

We shall now present some results which relate the precision of reduced-form estimates to the precision of the prior density on the structural parameters. For any twice differentiable multivariate density function $D(\alpha)$ we define the precision matrix F as the matrix having typical element

$$(4.1) \qquad -\int \frac{\partial^2 \log D(\alpha)}{\partial \alpha_i \, \partial \alpha_j} D(\alpha) \, d\alpha.$$

The matrix F measures the concentration of the distribution of α around its mean. If $D(\alpha)$ is multivariate normal, then F is the inverse of the covariance matrix of α. In general, if F is nonsingular, then F^{-1} is a lower bound to the covariance matrix V of α. More precisely, for any density $D(\alpha)$ that is everywhere twice differentiable, $V - F^{-1}$ is positive semi-definite. The inverted matrix equals the covariance matrix if and only if $D(\alpha)$ is normal. This result, which is the multivariate version of an inequality due to Weyl, is proved in the appendix to this chapter.

The precision matrix F is a useful measure of concentration because of the following result, which generalizes a finding of SCHUTZENBERGER (1958):

The expected posterior covariance matrix of any estimator of the structural parameter vector α is at least as large as

$$(4.2) \qquad [\mathscr{E}_\alpha(H'R_nH) + F]^{-1}$$

where H is the matrix of partial derivatives for the function $h(\alpha)$ and R_n is the information matrix for f_n; the expectation is with respect to the prior density on α. If $h(\alpha)$ is linear, a lower bound for the expected posterior covariance matrix of the reduced-form parameter vector θ is given by

$$(4.3) \qquad H[\mathscr{E}_\alpha(H'R_nH) + F]^{-1}H'.$$

These bounds are attained only if the posterior density is normal with variance independent of y.

---

1. For further discussion of the identifiability concept in Bayesian statistics see DRÈZE (1962) and ZELLNER (1965).

The proof of this result is given in the appendix. Here we shall make a few comments about its interpretation. The matrix $H'R_nH$ is the information matrix of α based on $f[h(\alpha)]$. It measures the amount of information concerning α that is available in the sample. In general it will depend on the unknown parameters; hence the first term in (4.2) is the expected sample information. The prior precision matrix F measures the amount of information about α contained in the prior density function $D(\alpha)$. The sum of these two matrices gives an upper bound to the precision in estimating α. It is known that, with a normal likelihood function and a normal prior density, the posterior precision is the sum of prior precision and sample precision.[2] Our result indicates that the normal model gives a bound for other models. The theorem also suggests that if the sum is a singular matrix, then there exists some dimension along which there is zero precision. That is, the posterior density of α is uniform on some sub-space. Hence we can give a partial answer to our first question: The structural parameter α is estimable only if the matrix $[\mathscr{E}_\alpha(H'R_nH) + F]$ is nonsingular. The bound (4.3) is valid even if the matrix is singular. In that case the generalized inverse must be used.

The Schutzenberger inequality does not give a complete answer to our basic question concerning the relationship between the posterior variance of θ and the prior precision of α. In the first place, (4.3) is only a lower bound for the mean posterior variance. In general the variance will be larger—perhaps even much larger. Secondly, (4.3) is valid only if $h(\alpha)$ is linear in α. This is not satisfied in the simultaneous equations model with which we began. It should be no surprise that general exact answers are not possible since the prior distribution of θ is related in a simple way to the prior distribution of α only if h is linear. Thus, exact general results will not be available in the Bayesian framework any more than they are available in the classical framework. The best we can do is to find some approximate answer that will be valid when the sample size is large and the posterior distribution is highly concentrated. Of course, for any specific problem, one can always calculate the expected gain by evaluating the appropriate integrals and obtain an exact answer. This, however, is often a formidable task and in practice we must rely on approximations.

Consider the following modification of our result. Suppose the sample size is large enough that the unconstrained maximum-likelihood estimator of θ is approximately normally distributed. Since this estimator is approximately sufficient for θ, little is lost by replacing the likelihood function

2. See, for example, RAIFFA AND SCHLAIFER (1961), p. 312.

$f_n(\theta)$ by the asymptotic distribution of the maximum-likelihood estimator, at least when n is large enough. Then, if the prior density is nearly normal, the posterior density on α will also be approximately normal. Its precision matrix will be the sum of the prior precision matrix F and the sample information matrix $H'R_nH$. This type of argument,[3] which can be made precise in terms of limiting sequences of prior and posterior densities, leads us to large-sample results similar to those in classical theory. For large n, the expected mean square error matrix of the Bayesian estimator of α is approximately

$$(4.4) \qquad (H'R_nH + F)^{-1}.$$

The expected mean square error matrix of the Bayesian estimator of θ is approximately

$$(4.5) \qquad H(H'R_nH + F)^{-1}H'.$$

In both cases H and R_n are evaluated at the true parameter α^0. Furthermore, the inverse in (4.5) can be replaced by the generalized inverse if the matrix is singular.

To the extent to which these approximations are valid, we can use (4.4) and (4.5) to answer our original questions. The question of the estimability of α depends on the existence of the inverse in (4.4). The question of the value of the structural information depends on the size of (4.5). If there were no structural information at all, the Bayes estimator of θ would approximately equal the maximum-likelihood estimator and its mean square error matrix would be approximately R_n^{-1}. Thus the prior information has value if the matrix

$$(4.6) \qquad R_n^{-1} - H(H'R_nH + F)^+H'$$

is positive semidefinite and nonzero.

Using a little algebra we can derive some simple conditions for estimability and improved reduced-form precision. If the matrix F has rank k, there exists a $k \times r$ matrix P such that $F = P'P$. Then the structural precision matrix can be written as

$$H'R_nH + F = \begin{pmatrix} H' & P' \end{pmatrix}\begin{bmatrix} R_n & 0 \\ 0 & I_k \end{bmatrix}\begin{bmatrix} H \\ P \end{bmatrix} \equiv C'DC$$

---

3. For a heuristic argument similar to the one presented here see LINDLEY (1965), part 2, pp. 128–30. A proof would have to follow along the lines of LE CAM (1953) and is beyond the scope of the present study.

where $C' = (H' \quad P')$ and D is the block diagonal matrix composed of the information matrix and an identity matrix. Since D is nonsingular, $(H'R_nH + F)$ has an inverse if and only if C' has full row rank r. Furthermore, the matrix (4.6) is the northwest submatrix of

$$(4.7) \qquad\qquad\qquad D^{-1} - C(C'DC)^+C'.$$

Since (4.7) is necessarily positive semidefinite, so is (4.6). It can also be verified that either matrix is zero if the other is. But (4.7) will be zero if and only if C has full row rank $m + k$. Since C has the same rank as $(H' \quad F)$, the answers to our original questions may be given as follows:

1) The structural parameter α is estimable if and only if $(H' \quad F)$ has rank r. Thus a necessary condition for α to be estimable is that the rank of F plus the rank of H be at least as great as r. If H has full column rank r, this is assured for any F; if F has full rank r, this is assured for any H. In general, the number of independent Bayesian constraints (measured by the rank of F) plus the number of independent pieces of sample information (measured by the rank of H) must be no less than the number of structural parameters. These results are the same as the classical results if F replaces $\Psi'\Psi$ as a measure of prior information.

2) The matrix $R_n^{-1} - H(H'R_nH + F)^+H'$ is positive semidefinite. It is equal to the zero matrix (and hence the prior information is of no value in increasing reduced-form precision) if and only if the rank of $(H' \quad F)$ equals m plus the rank of F. Since the rank of $(H' \quad F)$ is at most r, the prior information has value as long as the rank of F is greater than $r - m$. Again these results are the same as the classical results if F replaces $\Psi'\Psi$.

3) As we have already stated, the best estimator—in the sense of minimizing Bayes risk under quadratic loss—is the posterior mean.

5. A Limit Result

The previous discussion indicates that the Bayesian and classical measures of the value of information are closely related. In certain cases the classical measure is in fact the limit of the Bayesian measure as the prior information becomes more and more precise.

The classical constraint $\psi(\alpha) = 0$ can be viewed as the limiting case of a prior density on α that is concentrated along the manifold $\psi(\alpha) = 0$. Suppose α is a random variable such that $\psi(\alpha)$ has mean zero and covariance matrix equal to V. Using (4.2) and (4.3) we can calculate a lower bound to the expected covariance matrix of the posterior distribution of α

and at least an approximation to a lower bound to the expected covariance matrix of the posterior distribution of θ. If we consider a sequence of prior densities, each with $\mathscr{E}[\psi(\alpha)] = 0$ but with $\mathrm{Var}[\psi(\alpha)]$ decreasing, we can derive a sequence of lower bounds. It is the limiting value of this sequence that concerns us here.

There is a problem in specifying the sequence of prior densities. We would like to capture the idea of a probability density function that puts most of its mass near the surface $\psi(\alpha) = 0$. But in addition we must specify how that mass is to be distributed along the surface. The classical constraint says that the parameter must satisfy $\psi(\alpha) = 0$ but says nothing further about its value. A possible Bayesian analogue is to assume a prior distribution that spreads the mass uniformly along the surface. The notion of a uniform prior density over an unbounded region is not a happy one. However, since we are interested in the limiting behavior of a sequence of densities, the idea can be made precise by considering a sequence of densities with fixed mean but whose variance (along the surface) grows without bound.

To make things simple, let us proceed with the case where both $\psi(\alpha)$ and $h(\alpha)$ are linear. Thus the classical model is

(5.1)
$$\theta = H\alpha$$
$$0 = \Psi\alpha$$

where H is an $m \times r$ matrix and Ψ is a $k \times r$ matrix. A Bayesian density that is similar in spirit to the exact constraint $\Psi\alpha = 0$ is the multivariate normal density

(5.2)
$$D(\alpha) = \kappa \exp\left(-\frac{a}{2}\alpha'\Psi'\Psi\alpha - \frac{b}{2}\alpha'\alpha \right)$$

with a large and b small. With this density α has mean zero and precision matrix given by

(5.3)
$$F = (a\Psi'\Psi + bI).$$

The concentration ellipsoid for this density is elongated in the direction determined by $\Psi'\Psi$. As a approaches infinity and b approaches zero, the distribution becomes concentrated along the hyperplane $\Psi\alpha = 0$. Thus one way to express the idea that α almost surely satisfies the constraint is to say that α is a random variable with precision matrix (5.3) with large a and small b.

The inequalities (4.2) and (4.3) say that a lower bound for the mean posterior covariance matrix for the Bayesian estimator of α is

$$(H'\bar{R}H + F)^{-1} = (H'\bar{R}H + a\Psi'\Psi + bI)^{-1}$$

and the bound for θ is

$$H(H'\bar{R}H + F)^{-1}H' = H(H'\bar{R}H + a\Psi'\Psi + bI)^{-1}H'$$

where $\bar{R} = \mathscr{E}[R_n]$. Using the identity (4.3) of chapter 1, we find that in the limit as a approaches infinity and b approaches zero

$$\mathscr{E}_y \operatorname{Var}[\alpha|y] \geq \lim_{a \to \infty} (H'\bar{R}H + a\Psi'\Psi)^{-1}$$

$$\geq C - C\Psi'(\Psi C\Psi')^{-1}\Psi C$$

and

$$\mathscr{E}_y \operatorname{Var}[\theta|y] \geq \lim_{a \to \infty} H(H'\bar{R}H + a\Psi'\Psi)^{-1}H'$$

$$\geq H[C - C\Psi'(\Psi C\Psi')^{-1}\Psi C]H'$$

where $C = (H'\bar{R}H + \Psi'\Psi)^{-1}$. These are exactly the classical bounds of chapter 2, section 7, except that R_n is replaced by its expected value. Thus, at least in the linear case, the classical bounds are indeed the limit of the Bayesian bounds when the prior information becomes exact. Using asymptotic approximations, similar results can be obtained for the nonlinear case.

6. SOME QUANTITATIVE RESULTS

The general results of sections 4 and 5 can now be applied to the simultaneous equations model. If X is the $n \times K$ matrix of observations on K predetermined variables and Y is the $n \times G$ matrix of observations on G endogenous variables, then the likelihood functions for the simultaneous equations model can be written in logarithmic form as

$$(6.1) \quad \log f = \kappa - \tfrac{1}{2}n \log \det \Omega - \tfrac{1}{2}\operatorname{tr}[\Omega^{-1}(Y' - \Pi X')(Y - X\Pi')]$$

where κ is a constant. As long as we have no prior information on Σ, it is possible to study the problem of estimating B, Γ, and Π separately from the problem of estimating Σ and Ω.[4] Since we are mostly interested

---

4. The derivation in section 4 of chapter 4 concerning exact constraints carries over to the Bayesian case. If F consists of zeros whenever the element refers to Σ, we can simply ignore the parameters Σ and Ω.

in the former set of parameters, we shall ignore the covariance matrices and define θ to be the vector of Π elements taken by rows; α is then the vector of (B, Γ) elements also taken by rows. The function relating θ to α is

$$(6.2) \qquad \qquad \Pi = -B^{-1}\Gamma,$$

which has Jacobian

$$(6.3) \qquad \qquad H = \left[\frac{\partial \theta_i}{\partial \alpha_j}\right] = [B^{-1} \otimes (\Pi' \quad I_K)].$$

If any element of α is known exactly, the corresponding column of H is deleted. The information matrix for (6.1) is

$$R_n = \left[-\mathscr{E}\frac{\partial^2 \log f}{\partial \theta_i \, \partial \theta_j}\right] = \Omega^{-1} \otimes \mathscr{M}_n$$

where $\mathscr{M}_n = \mathscr{E}(X'X)$. These results were derived in chapter 4.

We are now in a position to determine numerically the value of structural restrictions in increasing reduced-form precision. For this purpose we shall take two econometric models—one artificial and the other based on actual data—and evaluate the matrix (4.5) for alternative prior precision matrices. In this way we can observe how posterior reduced-form precision varies with changing prior structural information.

The first model is the artificial one given in chapter 5 consisting of the two structural equations

$$y_1 + \beta_{12}y_2 + \gamma_{11}x_1 + \gamma_{12}x_2 + \gamma_{13}x_3 = u_1$$
$$\beta_{21}y_1 + y_2 + \gamma_{21}x_1 + \gamma_{22}x_2 + \gamma_{23}x_3 = u_2.$$

The "true" parameter values are again assumed to be as follows:

$$B = \begin{bmatrix} 1 & 1 \\ 2 & 1 \end{bmatrix}, \quad \Gamma = \begin{bmatrix} 0 & 0 & 1 \\ 1 & 1 & 0 \end{bmatrix}, \quad \Sigma = \begin{bmatrix} 1 & 0 \\ 0 & 1 \end{bmatrix}.$$

Using these values and the 3×3 identity matrix for $\mathscr{M}_n$, we can evaluate H and R_n at the true value α^0. We then examine a number of alternative prior distributions. All of them have the following form: the precision matrix F is diagonal with three nonzero elements (corresponding to $\gamma_{11}, \gamma_{12}, \gamma_{23}$) and the rest zero. The three nonzero elements all take the same value denoted by ϕ. Thus we assume that the econometrician knows essentially nothing about $\beta_{12}, \gamma_{13}, \beta_{21}, \gamma_{21}$ and γ_{22} but has a prior distribution on γ_{11}, γ_{12} and γ_{23} which has mean zero,

zero correlations, and equal variances. The normalization constraints $\beta_{11} = \beta_{22} = 1$ are taken as exact.

When the parameter ϕ equals zero, we have no prior information at all and the system is not identified. The matrix $H'R_nH + F$ is singular and no constraints are imposed on the reduced form. Ordinary least squares on the reduced form is the best estimating procedure and yields a covariance matrix that is approximately R_n^{-1}. When the parameter ϕ approaches infinity, the three structural coefficients are known with certainty. We are in the case of exact restrictions and the classical formulas are valid. The system is overidentified and can be estimated with greater precision. The interesting question is to examine the intermediate stages where ϕ is neither zero nor infinite.

This we have done for a number of values of ϕ. As a measure of reduced-form precision we have taken the trace of the mean square error matrix. Thus, using the approximation results of section 5, we calculate

$$\operatorname{tr} H[H'R_nH + F_\phi]^{-1}H'$$

for various values of φ. The results are presented in table 7.1. We observe that the imposition of exact constraints yields a 25 percent reduction in reduced-form variability. Exactly half of this reduction can be attained by relaxing the constraints and assuming they are true on the average but with variance equal to one. Since the magnitude of the coefficients in the model are of the order of unity, a variance of one is quite large. Thus it appears that, when the data are weak, imposing an imprecise Bayesian restriction can be very important in increasing reduced-form precision. This is also seen in our second example, Klein's Model I of the U.S. economy.

Klein's Model I (which we have already discussed in chapter 5) consists of three behavioral structural equations in fifteen variables. With four

TABLE 7.1   REDUCED-FORM PRECISION: ARTIFICIAL MODEL

Structural prior precision φ	Structural prior variance φ^{-1}	Trace of reduced-form posterior covariance matrix
0	∞	21.0
0.5	2.00	19.3
1	1.00	18.5
10	0.10	16.5
25	0.04	16.2
100	0.01	16.1
∞	0	16.0

identities and the normalization constraints, there are potentially thirty unknown structural parameters in B and Γ. Klein, however, imposes eighteen exact restrictions (all of the type that call certain parameters zero) so that only twelve structural parameters need be estimated. A complete Bayesian approach would begin with a multivariate prior density over the thirty structural parameters.[5] This, however, was not done in our calculations. In the first place, the technical problem of working with such large matrices (particularly, the inversion of a 30 × 30 ill-conditioned matrix) makes this impractical. In the second place, many of the exact restrictions are very reasonable and would in a Bayesian analysis receive very high precision. Therefore, we start with Klein's model and relax six of the eighteen restrictions. These six are then replaced with a prior probability distribution. That is, beginning with a model containing eighteen structural parameters, we impose diffuse priors over the original twelve and nondiffuse priors over the added six. Again we assume that the 18 × 18 prior precision matrix is diagonal and that the six nonzero diagonal elements are equal to the common value φ.

In Klein's original model consumption depends on wages, profits, and lagged profits; investment depends on profits, lagged profits, and the capital stock; private wages depend on income, lagged income and time. Thus each equation has, after including a constant term, four unknown parameters. Our model adds lagged income and the capital stock to Klein's consumption function; income and lagged income to his investment equation; and lagged profits and the capital stock to his labor demand equation. These additions seem plausible; it is surely not known with certainty that these variables enter with zero coefficients. Therefore we replace the exact restrictions with the assumption that these variables have coefficients with prior mean zero and prior precision ϕ.

As ϕ approaches infinity, we have Klein's original model. If ϕ equals zero, we have completely ignored six restrictions and have a classical model with eighteen structural parameters to be estimated. Since we ignore six correct restrictions, the reduced form will be estimated less precisely than if we had used them. The intermediate cases, where ϕ is finite but nonzero, are of interest to us here. By varying ϕ we can see how replacing exact restrictions with stochastic ones affects reduced-form precision.

---

5. Indeed, a complete Bayesian approach would also place a prior distribution on Σ. By assuming that the elements of F relating to the parameter Σ are all zero, we are in fact assuming a diffuse prior on these parameters.

The results of our experiment are presented in table 7.2. Again the same three loss functions are used as in chapter 5. We see that the six exact restrictions are very important in reducing the variability of the reduced-form estimates. Ignoring the restrictions entirely causes a fourfold increase in the average variance. By imposing the restrictions in stochastic form much of the loss in precision can be regained. For the model in question, most of the coefficients can be interpreted as marginal propensities. All economists would agree that their magnitudes lie in the range $(-1, +1)$. Thus from an economist's point of view a prior density with unit variance is quite uninformative. It represents almost no information.

TABLE 7.2   REDUCED-FORM PRECISION: KLEIN'S MODEL

Structural prior precision	Structural prior variance	Trace of reduced-form posterior covariance matrix		
φ	φ^{-1}	tr V_π	tr V_π^*	tr $Q_1 V_\pi^*$
0	∞	1.044	0.492	0.291
0.5	2.000	0.715	0.367	0.261
1	1.000	0.707	0.363	0.259
25	0.040	0.578	0.310	0.205
100	0.010	0.471	0.265	0.164
900	0.001	0.329	0.198	0.129
∞	0	0.277	0.129	0.039

Yet such a prior density results in a significant reduction in reduced-form variability. A prior precision that is more descriptive of the degree of uncertainty that economists possess about the parameter would be 100, implying a prior standard deviation of 0·10. This results in two-thirds of the precision gain that would be attained if the coefficients were known with certainty.

The above calculations are based on a series of approximations and do not yield exact Bayesian results. Nevertheless, these examples suggest that prior information that is rather imprecise from an economist's point of view may be very important in increasing reduced-form precision. In a macroeconomic model where collinearity among the predetermined variables is high, every little bit of structural information helps. If imposing exact restrictions is dangerous because they may be false, then imposing stochastic ones is much better than ignoring them. The Bayesian approach to incorporating prior information may be a very attractive alternative to the classical methods currently in use.

Appendix

1. THE GENERALIZED WEYL INEQUALITY*

Let $f(y)$ be the probability density function for the n-dimensional random variable Y. Let S be the region in n-space for which $f(y)$ is strictly positive. We assume that f is everywhere twice differentiable (which implies that f and the partial derivatives f_i are all zero on B, the boundary of S). Then V, the covariance matrix of Y, satisfies the inequality

(A.1)
$$c'Vc \geq c'F^{-1}c$$

where c is any vector of constants and F is the matrix with typical element

$$-\int \frac{\partial^2 \log f}{\partial y_i \, \partial y_j} f(y) \, dy.$$

If F is singular, then (A.1) is still valid if c is in the row space of F and F^{-1} is interpreted as the generalized inverse of F. If c is not in the row space of F, then $c'Vc$ is infinite.

Proof. Using the n-dimensional Stokes theorem (which says that the integral of a differential form over the boundary B of a surface S is equal to the integral of the derivative of the form over the surface), we have

(A.2)
$$\int_S (y_i - \mu_i) \frac{\partial f}{\partial y_j} \, dy = -\delta_{ij} + \int_B (y_i - \mu_i) f(y) \, dy_{[j]}$$
$$= -\delta_{ij}$$

and

(A.3)
$$\int_S \frac{\partial^2 \log f}{\partial y_i \, \partial y_j} f(y) \, dy = -\int_S \frac{\partial \log f}{\partial y_i} \cdot \frac{\partial \log f}{\partial y_j} f(y) \, dy + \int_S \frac{\partial^2 f}{\partial y_i \, \partial y_j} \, dy$$
$$= -\int_S \frac{\partial \log f}{\partial y_i} \frac{\partial \log f}{\partial y_j} f(y) \, dy + \int_B \frac{\partial f}{\partial y_j} \, dy_{[i]}$$
$$= -\int_S \frac{\partial \log f}{\partial y_i} \frac{\partial \log f}{\partial y_j} f(y) \, dy$$

where μ_i is the mean of y_i, δ_{ij} is the Kronecker delta, and $dy_{[i]}$ represents the differential $dy_1 dy_2 \ldots dy_n$ with dy_i deleted. Then for arbitrary vectors c and d, we obtain

* For the one-dimensional version see HARDY, LITTLEWOOD, AND PÓLYA (1952), p. 165.

from (A.2)

(A.4) $$\int_S \sum_i c_i(y_i - \mu_i) f^{\frac{1}{2}} \cdot \sum_j d_j \frac{\partial \log f}{\partial y_j} f^{\frac{1}{2}} \, dy = \sum_i c_i d_i.$$

By the Cauchy-Schwartz inequality, this implies

$$c'Vc \cdot d'Fd \geq (c'd)^2.$$

If c is not in the row space of F, then d may be chosen such that $c'd$ is nonzero and $d'Fd$ is zero. In that case, $c'Vc$ is unbounded. If c is in the row space of F we can exclude the possibility that $d'Fd$ is zero since that will occur only when $c'd = 0$. Hence a lower bound for $c'Vc$ can be obtained by finding

$$\sup_d \frac{(c'd)^2}{d'Fd}$$

subject to the convenient normalization rule $d'Fd = 1$. This results in the value $c'F^+c$ where F^+ is the generalized inverse of F. (That is, F^+ satisfies $FF^+F = F$.) If F is nonsingular, we get (A.1).

The inequality will be an equality only if the two terms in the integral (A.4) are proportional for the maximizing value $d = F^+c$. This requires $\log f$ to be proportional to $(y - \mu)'F(y - \mu)$, which is true only for the normal density.

2. THE GENERALIZED SCHUTZENBERGER INEQUALITY

Let $f[h(\alpha)]$ be the likelihood function in terms of the structural parameters. Then, assuming all of the expectations are finite, the matrix

$$\mathscr{E}_{\alpha,y}[(t - \alpha)(t - \alpha)'] - [\mathscr{E}_\alpha(H'RH) + F]^{-1}$$

is positive semidefinite for any estimator t.

Proof. By Weyl's inequality

$$\mathscr{E}_{\alpha|y}[(t - \alpha)(t - \alpha)'] \geq \mathrm{Var}[\alpha|y] \geq -\left[\mathscr{E}_{\alpha|y} \frac{\partial^2 \log D'}{\partial \alpha_i \, \partial \alpha_j}\right]^{-1}$$

where D' is the posterior density of α given y. (By $A \geq B$ we mean $A - B$ is positive semidefinite.) Hence,

(A.5)
$$\mathscr{E}_{\alpha,y}[(t - \alpha)(t - \alpha)'] \geq -\mathscr{E}_y\left[\mathscr{E}_{\alpha|y} \frac{\partial^2 \log D'}{\partial \alpha_i \, \partial \alpha_j}\right]^{-1}$$
$$\geq -\left[\mathscr{E}_y \mathscr{E}_{\alpha|y} \frac{\partial^2 \log D'}{\partial \alpha_i \, \partial \alpha_j}\right]^{-1}$$

where the last inequality follows from the convexity of the inverse function. By Bayes's formula

$$\log D'(\alpha|y) = \log f[h(\alpha)] + \log D(\alpha) - \log g(y)$$

where D is the prior density on α and g is the marginal density on y. Hence,

$$\mathscr{E}_{y,\alpha} \frac{\partial^2 \log D'}{\partial \alpha_i \, \partial \alpha_j} = \mathscr{E}_{y,\alpha} \frac{\partial^2 \log f}{\partial \alpha_i \, \partial \alpha_j} + \mathscr{E}_{y,\alpha} \frac{\partial^2 \log D}{\partial \alpha_i \, \partial \alpha_j}$$

and

(A.6)
$$\mathscr{E}_y \mathscr{E}_{\alpha|y} \frac{\partial^2 \log D'}{\partial \alpha_i \, \partial \alpha_j} = \mathscr{E}_\alpha \mathscr{E}_{y|\alpha} \frac{\partial^2 \log f}{\partial \alpha_i \, \partial \alpha_j} + \mathscr{E}_\alpha \frac{\partial^2 \log D}{\partial \alpha_i \, \partial \alpha_j}.$$

Combining (A.5) and (A.6) we get

$$\mathscr{E}_{\alpha,y}[(t - \alpha)(t - \alpha)'] \geq -[\mathscr{E}_\alpha(H'RH) + F]^{-1}$$

since

$$\mathscr{E}_{y|\alpha} \frac{\partial^2 \log f}{\partial \alpha_i \, \partial \alpha_j} = \mathscr{E}_{y|\alpha} \sum_p \sum_q \frac{\partial^2 \log f}{\partial \theta_p \, \partial \theta_q} \frac{\partial h_p}{\partial \alpha_i} \frac{\partial h_q}{\partial \alpha_j}.$$

References

Aitchison, J., and S. D. Silvey. 1958. Maximum-likelihood estimation of parameters subject to restraints. *Annals of Mathematical Statistics* 29:813–28.

———. 1960. Maximum-likelihood estimation procedures and associated tests of significance. *Journal of the Royal Statistical Society*, series B, 22:154–71.

Anderson, T. W. 1951. Estimating linear restrictions on regression coefficients for multivariate normal distributions. *Annals of Mathematical Statistics* 22:327–51.

Ando, A., and G. M. Kaufman. 1965. Bayesian analysis of the independent multi-normal process—neither mean nor precision known. *Journal of the American Statistical Association* 60:347–58.

Bancroft, T. A. 1944. On the biases in estimation due to the use of preliminary tests of significance. *Annals of Mathematical Statistics* 15:190–204.

Basmann, R. L. 1963. Remarks concerning the application of exact finite sample distribution functions of GCL estimators in econometric statistical inference. *Journal of the American Statistical Association* 58:943–76.

———. 1965. On the application of the identifiability test statistic and its exact finite sample distribution function in predictive testing of explanatory economic models. Mimeographed paper.

Blackwell, D., and M. A. Girshick. 1954. *Theory of Games and Statistical Decisions.* New York: Wiley.

Chernoff, H. 1956. Large sample theory: parametric case. *Annals of Mathematical Statistics* 27:1–22.

Chetty, V. K. 1968. Bayesian analysis of Haavelmo's models. *Econometrica* 36:582–602.

Chiang, C. L. 1956. On regular best asymptotically normal estimates. *Annals of Mathematical Statistics* 27:336–51.

Chipman, J., and M. M. Rao. 1964. The treatment of linear restrictions in regression analysis. *Econometrica* 32:198–209.

Cramér, H. 1946. *Mathematical Methods of Statistics.* Princeton: Princeton University Press.

DeGroot, M. H. 1970. *Optimal Statistical Decisions.* New York: McGraw-Hill.

Drèze, J. 1962. The Bayesian approach to simultaneous equations estimation. O.N.R. Research Memorandum 67, Northwestern University.

———. 1968. Limited information estimation from a Bayesian viewpoint. CORE Discussion Paper 6816, Louvain.

Dugué, D. 1958. *Traité de Statistique Théorique et Appliquée.* Paris: Masson.

Durbin, J. 1953. A note on regression when there is extraneous information about one of the coefficients. *Journal of the American Statistical Association* 48:799–808.

———. 1960. Estimation of parameters in time-series regression models. *Journal of the Royal Statistical Society*, series B, 22:139–53.

Ferguson, T. S. 1958. A method of generating best asymptotically normal estimates with application to the estimation of bacterial densities. *Annals of Mathematical Statistics* 29:1046–62.

Fisher, F. M. 1966. *The Identification Problem in Econometrics*. New York: McGraw-Hill.

Fisher, W. D. 1962. Estimation in the linear decision model. *International Economic Review* 3:1–29.

Goldberger, A. S. 1964. *Econometric Theory*. New York: Wiley.

Goldberger, A. S.; A. L. Nagar; and H. S. Odeh. 1961. The covariance matrices of reduced-form coefficients and of forecasts for a structural econometric model. *Econometrica* 29:556–73.

Graybill, F. A. 1961. *An Introduction to Linear Statistical Models*, vol. 1. New York: McGraw-Hill.

Haavelmo, T. 1947. Methods of measuring the marginal propensity to consume. *Journal of the American Statistical Association* 42:105–22.

Hammersley, J. M. 1950. On estimating restricted parameters. *Journal of the Royal Statistical Society*, series B, 12:192–240.

Hardy, G. H.; J. E. Littlewood; and G. Pólya. 1952. *Inequalities*. Cambridge: Cambridge University Press.

Judge, G. G., and T. Takayama. 1966. Inequality restrictions in regression analysis. *Journal of the American Statistical Association* 61:166–81.

Kendall, M. G., and A. Stuart. 1967. *The Advanced Theory of Statistics*, vol. 2. London: Griffin.

Klein, L. R. 1950. *Economic Fluctuations in the United States, 1921–1941*. Cowles Commission Monograph 11. New York: Wiley.

———. 1960. The efficiency of estimation in econometric models. In *Essays in Economics and Econometrics*, ed. R. W. Pfouts, pp. 216–32. Chapel Hill: University of North Carolina.

Koopmans, T. C., and W. C. Hood. 1953. The estimation of simultaneous linear economic relationships. In *Studies in Econometric Method*, Cowles Commission Monograph 14, eds. W. C. Hood and T. C. Koopmans, pp. 112–99. New York: Wiley. Reprint Yale University Press, 1970.

Koopmans, T. C.; H. Rubin; and R. B. Leipnik. 1950. Measuring the equation systems of dynamic economics. In *Statistical Inference in Dynamic Economic Models*, Cowles Commission Monograph 10, ed. T. C. Koopmans, pp. 53–237. New York: Wiley.

Le Cam, L. 1953. On some asymptotic properties of maximum likelihood estimates and related Bayes' estimates. *University of California Publications in Statistics* 1:277–330.

Lindley, D. V. 1965. *Introduction to Probability and Statistics from a Bayesian Viewpoint*, part 2. Cambridge: Cambridge University Press.

Lovell, M. C., and E. Prescott. 1970. Multiple regression with inequality constraints: pretesting bias, hypothesis testing, and efficiency. *Journal of the American Statistical Association* 65:913–25.

Malinvaud, E. 1970. *Statistical Methods of Econometrics.* Amsterdam: North-Holland.

Marschak, J. 1953. Economic measurement for policy and prediction. In *Studies in Econometric Method,* Cowles Commission Monograph 14, eds. W. C. Hood and T. C. Koopmans, pp. 1–26. New York: Wiley. Reprint Yale University Press, 1970.

Morales, J.-A. 1971. *Bayesian Full Information Structural Analysis.* Berlin: Springer-Verlag.

Pratt, J. W.; H. Raiffa; and R. Schlaifer. 1964. The foundations of decision under uncertainty: an elementary exposition. *Journal of the American Statistical Association* 59:353–75.

Raiffa, H., and R. Schlaifer. 1961. *Applied Statistical Decision Theory.* Boston: Harvard Business School.

Rao, C. R. 1965. *Linear Statistical Inference and its Applications.* New York: Wiley.

Rothenberg, T. J. 1968. Estimation with inequality restrictions. CORE Discussion Paper 6825, Louvain.

———. 1971. Identification in parametric models. *Econometrica* 39:577–91.

———, and C. T. Leenders. 1964. Efficient estimation of simultaneous equation systems. *Econometrica* 32:57–76.

Savage, L. 1954. *The Foundations of Statistics.* New York: Wiley.

Schutzenberger, M. P. 1958. A propos de l'inégalité de Fréchet-Cramér. *Publications de l'Institut de Statistique de l'Université de Paris* 7 (no. 3/4):3–6.

Silvey, S. D. 1959. The Lagrangian multiplier test. *Annals of Mathematical Statistics* 30:389–407.

Stein, C. 1965. Approximation of improper prior measures by prior probability measures. In *Bernoulli, Bayes, Laplace Anniversary Volume,* ed. J. Neyman and L. LeCam, pp. 217–40. Berlin: Springer-Verlag.

Theil, H. 1961. *Economic Forecasts and Policy.* Amsterdam: North-Holland.

———. 1971. *Principles of Econometrics.* New York: Wiley.

———, and A. S. Goldberger. 1961. On pure and mixed statistical estimation in economics. *International Economic Review* 2:65–78.

Thrall, R. M., and L. Tornheim. 1957. *Vector Spaces and Matrices.* New York: Wiley.

Wald, A. 1950. *Statistical Decision Functions.* New York: Wiley.

Wegge, L. 1965. Identifiability criteria for systems of equations as a whole. *Australian Journal of Statistics* 7:67–77.

Wilks, S. S. 1962. *Mathematical Statistics.* New York: Wiley.

Wolfowitz, J. 1965. Asymptotic efficiency of the maximum-likelihood estimator. *Theory of Probability and Its Applications* 10:247–60.

Zellner, A. 1961. Linear regression with inequality constraints on the coefficients: an application of quadratic programming and linear decision rules. Econometric Institute Report 6109. Rotterdam.

————. 1965. Bayesian inference and simultaneous equation econometric models. Paper presented at the First World Congress of the Econometric Society, Rome.

————. 1971. *Introduction to Bayesian Inference in Econometrics*. New York: Wiley.

————, and H. Theil. 1962. Three-stage least squares: simultaneous estimation of simultaneous equations. *Econometrica* 30:54–78.

Index

Cowles Foundation Monographs

Orders for Monograph 8 should be sent to Principia Press of Trinity University, 715 Stadium Drive, San Antonio, Texas.

Orders for Monograph 3 should be sent to the Cowles Foundation, Box 2125, Yale Station, New Haven, Conn. 06520.

Orders for Monographs 12, 13, 14, 16, 17, 21, 22, 23, and 24 should be sent to Yale University Press, 92A Yale Station, New Haven, Conn. 06520.

Orders for Monographs 15, 19, and 20 should be sent to John Wiley & Sons, Inc., 605 Third Avenue, New York, N.Y. 10016.